STRAIGHT
SHOOTER

STRAIGHT SHOOTER

A MEMOIR OF SECOND CHANCES AND FIRST TAKES

STEPHEN A. SMITH

GALLERY BOOKS / 13A

New York   London   Toronto   Sydney   New Delhi

13A
Gallery Books
An Imprint of Simon & Schuster, Inc.
1230 Avenue of the Americas
New York, NY 10020

First 13A/Gallery Books hardcover edition January 2023

13A is a trademark of Charles Suitt and is used with permission.

GALLERY BOOKS and colophon are registered trademarks of Simon & Schuster, Inc.

For information about special discounts for bulk purchases,
please contact Simon & Schuster Special Sales at 1-866-506-1949 or
business@simonandschuster.com.

The Simon & Schuster Speakers Bureau can bring authors to your live event.
For more information or to book an event, contact the Simon & Schuster Speakers
Bureau at 1-866-248-3049 or visit our website at www.simonspeakers.com.

Interior design by Jaime Putorti

Manufactured in the United States of America

10 9 8 7 6 5 4 3 2

Library of Congress Control Number: 2022919467

ISBN 978-1-9821-8949-5
ISBN 978-1-9821-8951-8 (ebook)

This book would not have been written were it not

for the greatest woman I've ever known: Mommy!

I shed a tear at least once every day. I miss you

so much. But my daughters, Samantha and Nyla,

make it easier. They are the reasons I'm guaranteed

a smile every single day of my life. And of course,

there's always my sister Carmen—my ace. No one

roots for me harder, no one supports me more than

you, sis. You're my rock. I love you to pieces.

We ride together!

CONTENTS

CONTENTS

STRAIGHT SHOOTER

INTRODUCTION

In May 2017, my mother lay in bed inside her house in Queens, New York, dying from colon cancer. She was seventy-six years old.

She'd been through a seven-year battle, rife with operations, chemotherapy, radiation treatments—and diminishing hopes. The cancer had metastasized, spreading to her lungs and, eventually, her brain, and the battle was approaching its end.

During her last months, at least one of my four sisters and I tended to her every day. Yet my mother had only one request as she neared the end: that her husband of fifty-nine years, our father, be at her bedside.

She had never left him, despite the fact that he'd almost never been there for her. My father drank, smoked, womanized, and gambled. He didn't help pay a single bill for the last forty-five years of their marriage.

So even in those final, awful weeks, it didn't surprise any of us that our dad stayed true to his himself: while our mother slowly slid toward the inevitable in an upstairs bedroom inside our childhood home, he remained downstairs, parked in front of the TV, watching baseball games and old Westerns. While she still could, my mother, with assistance from my sisters and me, sometimes made her way down to the living room to be close to him, hoping to steal some of his attention.

Never happened.

His eyes barely left the TV. The only decent thing he did was to stop asking her to get him something from the kitchen.

A month before my mother passed, my sisters—Linda, Arlyne, Abigail, and Carmen—and I sat down with our father at the dining room table to tell him that his behavior was unacceptable. My sisters said, "Look. She's in a very bad spot. You need to pay more attention to her."

My father, a stubborn West Indian, shook his head, looked at them, and replied, "You don't know her like I do. I know my wife; I know your mother better than you do. It's all an act. She's not as sick as you all think."

There was a brief moment of stunned silence. You could hear a pin drop. Then, from my seat at the opposite end of the table, I looked my father straight in the eye and asked, "What the fuck did you just say?"

Then I stood up, grabbed my chair, walked past my sisters, and sat down right in front of him, my face right in front of his. "Mommy's sick," I said, echoing what my sisters had told him. "She's dying. Her days are numbered."

Incredibly, only at that moment did he say: "Okay, I got it now."

"What do you mean?" I asked. "All four of your daughters just said the same thing, and you said you don't believe them."

His response: "They ain't you. They're women!"

My sisters shook their heads in utter disgust. Words couldn't describe how I felt.

My mother died on June 1, 2017, just before midnight. I'd left the house about an hour earlier to go change and clean up at my home in North Jersey. My sister Carmen texted just as I pulled into my driveway. "You need to get back here now. It's Mom," she wrote me. I never left my car, just backed out and made the forty-five-minute return drive to Queens.

"Be strong, Steve," I told myself, imagining what I'd say once I saw her lying there motionless, her eyes closed for the last time, no longer able to smile, laugh, or cry. "I'll be okay." I thought the drive would be plenty of time to get my emotions in check. On his last house call, the doctor had told us she didn't have long left. It was clear she was already transitioning. I thought I had prepared myself for this moment.

But after I parked, before I could even get to the front of the house, I heard cries. I opened the front door and saw my brother-in law Danny, just sitting in the living room in silence, sadness written all over his face. The same could be said for my future brother-in-law Darren, Carmen's boyfriend. My nephew Josh was sobbing.

As I saw this, my legs suddenly got heavy and my heart ached. The eleven steps to the upstairs level of my mother's house felt like a mile.

Carmen, Linda, and our aunt Rita were in the bedroom I grew up in, sobbing, their faces soaked with tears. Arlyne was right next to them, crying. I looked to my right, inside my mother's bedroom, and saw Abigail spooning my mother, hugging her tightly as she sobbed quietly.

Mommy was officially gone. And with her, so went a part of me. I started crying and couldn't stop for a long, long time.

Frankly, everyone was thankful that she'd passed before I got there. They knew that seeing her take her last breath was something I could not endure. "Thank God you weren't there for those final moments," Carmen said. "I don't think you would have ever been the same had you been there at that moment." I was never the same anyway.

My dad, however, was unchanged. His attention that night was riveted on the first game of the NBA Finals, between Cleveland and Golden State. The Warriors held an insurmountable lead when my sisters came downstairs to tell him that it wouldn't be much longer, so he finally dragged himself away from the TV set. He sat beside our mother, patted her, and told her everything was going to be okay. Then he got up, went back downstairs, and, with the game over, watched another Western.

My sisters still haven't forgiven him for that.

Ultimately, my mother's passing freed me to write this book. Folks had asked me for years to write a memoir, but I'd always turned them down for one simple reason: my mother made me promise that I wouldn't do so until after she died. I had told her I would have to write the truth about everything, including my father. She did not want anyone to read about that while she was alive.

So I waited. And waited. And waited. And waited. Until it was time. It's time now.

My story is not always an easy one to tell. If fairy tales are what you're looking for, don't bother skimming through these pages. You won't find them here, especially not in those early years.

But if you stick around, you'll find something far more compelling, and inspirational. You'll see how love, belief, perseverance, self-awareness, family, friendships, and mentorship can take you places you've never been. How they all allowed me to see and experience things I'd never even dreamed of—some things I didn't even know existed—and attain levels of success and happiness I once deemed unimaginable because, for so long, imagination itself was a luxury I couldn't afford.

This is the story of Stephen A. Smith—"Stephen A." these days, no last name necessary. It's the unlikely tale of how I came to be who I am. Love me or hate me—it's always one or the other—my story is one about what my world is like and what I've learned along the way.

This is my truth, based on my experiences, and I believe that everyone—from the impoverished and hopeless to the rich and famous—can learn from the story of how this little scrawny Black kid from a cramped, unheated house in the Hollis neighborhood of Queens went on to become one of the most-watched, sometimes most-reviled, but ultimately one of the highest-paid TV sportscasters at the biggest sports network in America.

It's the actual, often improbable, story of a kid who was left back in the fourth grade because he read at a first-grade level. It's the story of a kid who looked on in shame as his father told his mother, "He's just not that smart. He'll never succeed. Just accept that."

It's about a kid motivated by "friends" in the neighborhood incessantly humiliating him with laughter because he was the only one who got left back. It's about a grown man who still remembers each name, each face, each laugh, to this very day, more than four decades later—despite my success and notoriety.

This book is about a boy who endured peer pressure, cruelty, doubts, and bigotry, as well as temptation from the wrong side of the tracks. Yet somehow that boy came out on the other side, in part because of assistance from the very people on the wrong side of the tracks whom he grew up with, as well as a mother's undying love and devotion, and the numerous folks—white and Black, friends and loved ones—who supported him.

It's the story of the white high school teacher who had me pulled off the basketball team my senior year for the pettiest reasons, knowing it could cost me a basketball scholarship. It's also the story of the Black junior college basketball coach whom I liked even less than the white high school teacher until I grew to appreciate and love that man years later for the lessons he tried to teach me, which I'd been too stubborn to learn. That in itself became its own lesson.

It's the story of the basketball scholarship I eventually got, to Winston-Salem State University, and the father-son relationship I developed with the school's legendary coach, Clarence "Big House" Gaines. And the story of the knee injury that derailed my completely unfounded pro-basketball aspirations, which then led to a professional journalism career—a career that took me from the *Winston-Salem Journal* and the *Greensboro News and Record* in North Carolina to the *New York Daily News* and the *Philadelphia Inquirer*, and then on to TV with CNN/SI (now defunct), Fox Sports, and, finally, to my own show on ESPN.

I've also popped up as "Brick" on *General Hospital* (I'd watched the soap as a kid with my sisters every day after school), as my on-air radio self who gets lit up by Diane (the youngest daughter) on the ABC comedy *Black-ish*, and as a guest host on *Jimmy Kimmel Live!*. (Could my own late-night show be next?)

Along the way, I've made friends and enemies. I've been ignorant and immature and have paid a price for that—my shortcomings were made crystal damn clear with my dismissal from ESPN in 2009, months after I became a new father. What followed was a full year of unemployment and a two-year banishment from television.

Every day from 2009 to 2011, I asked myself: What would I do? Where would I end up? Was it all over for me? Was this my legacy? Would failure be my epitaph?

Over the next decade, I went from being unemployed to receiving the largest contract in the history of sports broadcasting (at the time) for an on-air "talent," as we're known. LL Cool J, who grew up in my neighborhood, once wrote a rap song called "From Hollis to Hollywood." The title perfectly sums up my story.

How did I get there? What tactics did I employ? How did I learn to help myself and others along the way?

It's all here.

This is a book about a life filled with chaos and hardships that turned into a successful life worth living. I explain, and own up to, some mistakes.

As I write this, it's 2022. Not long ago I recovered from a hospital stay due to COVID, the effects of which still linger, both physically and in my outlook on life.

If my story happens to help others to live their best lives as well, even better.

Everyone needs somebody's help. Obstacles don't discriminate. We're all in search of motivational tools to enlighten, educate, and arm us with whatever skills are necessary to march forward and prosper.

The fact that for the last thirty years I've worked in sports, and a vast majority of those years have been spent covering the most driven, competitive, and talented athletes in the world, has given me a more enlightened perspective. This perspective allowed me to expand far beyond the world of sports, from social justice issues to entertainment to politics and beyond.

I've spoken to and interviewed people from Michael Jordan and Magic Johnson to Shaquille O'Neal and Kobe Bryant. From Allen Iverson, Floyd Mayweather, Diana Taurasi, and Sue Bird, to coaches Larry Brown, Pat Riley, and Doc Rivers. From Oprah Winfrey and Gayle King to Jay-Z, record mogul Jimmy Iovine, former Disney CEO Bob Iger, legendary producer and show creator Jerry Bruckheimer, and current Golden State Warriors owner Joe Lacob. From soap opera stars Maurice Benard and Eric Braeden to movie stars Denzel Washington and Jamie Foxx—and many more.

From these people, I've learned how to maneuver through America's treacherous corporate terrain, how to make and sustain friendships, how to persevere through hard times, how to learn from those hard times, then move forward and listen.

Failure was never an option for me: it was succeed or die trying. But how? Watching my mother work sixteen-hour days, six and seven days a week, left me wondering if work was even worth it. She wasn't ever going to prosper—or even have heat in the house or food in the fridge. She did it solely to survive. Watching her energy and hard work being snatched from her by a husband who barely lifted a finger to help her—or any of us—left me asking myself, "Is this really living?" The answer was simple: "Hell no!" There had to be a better way.

Don't get it twisted: I never blamed my mother for our circumstances. I revered her for adapting and overcoming all the obstacles we faced. Still, I knew I didn't want the same life, the same hardships. I wanted to travel a different path—both *because* of her and *for* her.

But there's also the flip side: I wanted to make sure I was nothing like my father. Because of him, I've never taken more than three drinks in a week in my life. I've never smoked or done drugs, including marijuana—what I refer to on my shows as "the weeeeeeed." And I've never married, partly because I'm usually on the road for well over half the year, but mainly because I've never wanted to dishonor my marital vows, as he did so flagrantly.

I do have two beautiful daughters, Samantha and Nyla, and they are my world. I toil, struggle, scratch, and claw, all so they can live a life of comfort—so they never have to experience the struggles I experienced too early in life. My mommy drove that home for me when I was just sixteen: "Promise me you'll be responsible. Promise me you'll take care of your family. Promise me you'll never be like your father!"

There was only one answer to a plea like that from a woman like her: "I promise, Mommy! I swear! I promise!"

I've kept that promise, though there have been challenges and slip-ups along the way. But on my worst day, I could never be as bad as my father.

This book is the culmination of all I've learned, from others and from my own experiences. Make no mistake: this is *a ride* you're about to take. That's assuming, of course, that you're about winning the game of life, and that you're about doing whatever it takes to keep standing upright—no matter how many times you get knocked down.

Finally, my story can be told, with Mommy's blessing.

CHAPTER 1

MY DAD WAS NO HERO!

I was born in the Bronx before it began burning, in the fall of 1967, the youngest of six kids. Arriving four years after the next-oldest sibling, my sisters and brother always joked that I was "the mistake." My mother would have none of it.

"You shut up!" she'd mock-scold them in her sternest West Indian accent. "He was the only one who was *on purpose!*"

I was about a year old when we moved from our apartment in a dilapidated building on Hoe Avenue to a narrow, aluminum-sided single-family house with a leaky roof and postage-stamp yard on 203rd Street in Hollis, Queens, a mostly Black, working-class neighborhood lined with other narrow single-family houses. Fronted by chain-link fences or scraggly hedges, most of the homes had a neat but needs-work-I-can't-afford look. Hollis didn't resemble the overcrowded projects in the Bronx, but it had many of the same problems.

Folks in that part of Queens made livings as bus drivers, train conductors, nurses, paralegals. Others sold drugs or stole to buy drugs. No doctors or lawyers—there wasn't none of that in my neighborhood. Manhattan's skyline glowed in the distance but still took more than an hour to reach by the Q-2 bus and then the F or E train, most locals' main mode of transportation. Manhattan to us was a place where people went to work and then rushed back home. You had to have actual money to live there; at the time, you didn't need much of that to live in Hollis. Planes from nearby JFK International Airport roared overhead, drowning out our hollering while we played football in the streets.

When I got a little older, those planes also drowned out the rappers and break dancers who suddenly sprouted up in parks and on street corners all over the place. They arrived along with the crack epidemic, hoping to emulate the success of Run-DMC, the neighborhood group turned hip-hop pioneers.

Run-DMC started out in local spots like Hollis Park, Jamaica Park, and Ozone Park, rapping for the DJs who competed there. They quickly put my 'hood (birthplace of such dignitaries as jazz trumpeter Roy Eldridge, New York Governor Mario Cuomo, and civil rights activist Rev. Al Sharpton) on every hip-hop fan's map. Their songs were the soundtrack to our lives: "It's Like That" (released when I was sixteen), "Hollis Crew," "Sucker M.C.'s," "My Adidas," and the novelty hit "Christmas in Hollis" ("It's Christmas time in Hollis Queens / Mom's cooking chicken and collard greens"). To this day, they're still cued up in whatever car I drive—you don't come from Hollis and not have Run-DMC in your library.

They were just dudes who were around. My brother, Basil, was tight with the group's DJ, Jam Master Jay, who grew up right across the street, half a block up. I saw Joey "Run" Simmons all the time when he dated a drop-dead-gorgeous girl on our block named Tonya, and I would also see his brother Russell Simmons, who founded Def Jam Records. LL Cool J grew up just a few blocks from them, at his grandmother's house, on Farmer's Boulevard.

But even in the toughest times, Hollis clung to its urban village roots. Some sections were more tense and dangerous than others. Mothers in the neighborhood—like Mrs. Miller across the street, and

Mrs. McKnight (my friend Mark McKnight's mother, known as Mommy Alice) two houses up from mine—kept an eye on everything from what seemed like permanent perches in their front windows and front steps. If you misbehaved, your parents heard about it. These women weren't assigned those roles; it wasn't part of some "neighborhood watch" program. They just cared about the community and made sure everybody did the right thing. As kids, we hated it. Looking back, I appreciate how lucky we were to have these ladies looking out for us.

I had aunts and uncles scattered around the boroughs like branches of some Caribbean social club. They all came from nothing and moved here from the U.S. Virgin Islands in search of something else—in search of more. My parents, Ashley and Janet, did the same. They met as teenagers at the church in St. Thomas that my mother attended every Sunday. My father was one of the guys who stood outside throwing rocks at the pretty girls when they came out. Apparently, back then that's how you showed your love.

Damn if it didn't work: they got married in 1958, shortly after my mother became pregnant with my oldest sister, Linda. My mother was seventeen, my dad nineteen. They moved to New York in the early 1960s in search of the better life their relatives had sought before them, some with more success than others. Then they had the rest of us: Basil, Arlyne, Abigail, Carmen, and me.

My father eventually found work managing a ServiStar Hardware store on 135th Street in Harlem, next door to the women's-clothing shop owned by my uncle Frankie called the Choice Is Yours. My mother stayed home to raise us kids until my dad checked out, when I was about six (he didn't leave, my mom didn't run him off, he just checked out; we'll get to it in a minute). After that, in the early seventies, my mother went to school to become a nurse, ultimately rising, by the mid-1980s, to assistant head nurse at Queens General Hospital, down the street from St. John's University. She'd also moonlight eight-hour shifts at a nursing home at the end of our block.

Other than sharing Caribbean roots, my parents were opposites. Six feet tall, about two hundred and five pounds, with big hands and rich brown skin, my father was outgoing, the life of the party, a sharp dresser (or so he thought) who wore three-piece suits and shiny shoes and loved to sing and dance to calypso around the house and at family gatherings. He'd been a great athlete, a basketball and baseball player whom the Brooklyn Dodgers and New York Yankees, he bragged, once expressed interest in signing when he lived in St. Thomas. He practically glowed. He was the kind of man other kids with overworked, bone-tired parents looked at and said, "Wow, what a great dad you have!"

My mother was pretty, and always pleasant, but also introverted and private. She hated for others to know her business. Her best friend her whole life was her sister, my aunt Rita, who only ever left St. Thomas to come visit my mother. Mommy was about five feet eight inches tall and light-skinned, coming from mixed parents (white mother, Black father). I mostly remember her bustling around the house wearing the plain white blouse and white pants of her nurse's uniform—she worked all the damn time. She was only loud inside our house, where we six kids, and especially me, had her screaming in her lilting singsong the whole day long.

"Stephen, take out the garbage!"
"Stephen, wash the dishes!"
"Stephen, clean your room!"
Like that.

Our little house in Hollis could get jam-packed. There was only one working bathroom in the Smith residence, and it often didn't work. Same with the shower and sinks. Lots of times hot water wasn't available, or the heat was turned off, because of an unpaid utility bill. The bedrooms were tiny—a touch bigger than a jail cell—but we still doubled and tripled up in bunk beds when we went to sleep. My sister Linda slept in the unfinished attic.

Yet none of that stopped my mom from playing the role of Mother

Teresa. She allowed numerous relatives from both sides of the family to crash at our house, sometimes for months, when they hit hard times. As many as a dozen people crammed into the place for weeks on end.

We didn't have much. My four sisters had to share clothing, most of which my mother got from Goodwill. I had three outfits at a time for all of my childhood and into my teens. Breakfast was almost always cereal, with our own version of 2 percent milk: whole milk mixed with tap water, to make it last longer.

The cereal often came out of the box piping hot. In normal homes, the cereal box is put away in a cabinet or on top of the fridge, in clear sight and easy reach of everybody.

Not in my family. Cereals like Honeycomb, Sugar Pops, and Cap'n Crunch were an extravagance, tantamount to a night out on the town ordering filet mignon with a glass of red wine. As a result, we six kids were constantly hiding it from each other.

My preferred hiding spot: behind the dining room radiator. If I didn't stash it there, it wouldn't last twenty-four hours before everybody devoured it and I'd have to wait at least a week or two for my mother to buy another box.

If that behavior sounds like crabs in a bucket, well, hell, it was. We were always hungry. Sometimes we approached what felt like starvation. So no matter how much we loved one another, love was not always part of the equation when our stomachs moaned and our heads ached because of a lack of food. Overall, we were definitely about family— mess with one of us and you messed with all of us. But when it came to food, it was everybody for him- or herself.

If a fly found its way into one of our bowls, we spooned it out and kept on eating. We didn't run from mice or rats when they were in the vicinity of our meals—they ran from us! At one point, we did a stint on government cheese and bread and were damn grateful for it.

Later on in my life, when I'd moved out and moved on, making a decent living, folks would ask incredulously, as I poured sugar onto almost everything I ate, "How'd you get so addicted to that stuff?" My answer was simple: growing up, we usually had bread but rarely had meat. So for lunch or dinner we'd literally take sugar and spread it over the bread to make *sugar sandwiches*.

My sisters and brother and I suffered. We struggled. The old line "I didn't even know we were poor" didn't apply to us. We always knew we were poor. And it was debilitating as hell.

But our pain didn't emanate solely from the conditions we endured. What made it even more injurious, more scarring, was the reality that things did not have to be that way. Our circumstances were by choice.

My father's choice.

Other fathers in my neighborhood came home once their workday was over. Not mine. Four or five nights a week, my dad just departed from the hardware store and didn't come home for days. He'd leave on a Wednesday, come back home on Sunday. Sometimes he'd change it up and leave on a Thursday instead, but I never, ever saw him on a Friday or Saturday night. I knew something was up, but I was still too young to know what. I'd ask my mother, "Where's Dad?" She never had an answer—until the night she showed me by finally showing herself.

That's when my world shattered and changed forever.

I was about ten. My mother grabbed my hand that day and said simply, "Come with me." We turned at the corner at the end of our street and walked another half block. She didn't say a word until we stopped in front of the house belonging to my uncle Freddie, my father's older brother.

Once there, Mommy told me to knock on the door and ask for my father. I thought that was strange but did as I was told. I rapped on the door with my little ten-year-old fist and called out to my father's brother, "Is my dad here?"

Nothing happened for a long minute, but I could hear the muffled sound of somebody moving around inside. Suddenly my dad cracked open the door. He stood there and stared at me. He hadn't seen my mother, who was hiding off to the left of me. After glaring at me for another minute, he asked, "What are you doing here? What the hell do you want?" All hell broke loose. My mother burst out, bulldozed past my surprised father into the house, and aimed straight for the woman I would later learn was his mistress.

But suddenly my mother froze in her tracks: the mistress was holding a baby in her arms. Seeing my mother coming at her, the other woman lifted the baby in front of her, using the infant as a shield.

When my mother paused for a split second to make sense of what she was seeing, my father grabbed her, lifted her off her feet—he didn't hit her, he never struck my mother, that was the one thing he ever did right, he knew his children would kill him—and pulled her away. He then snatched me with his free hand and, with one swift movement, tossed us both back outside.

Once we were out there, my dad slammed the door shut and locked it. The sounds rang in my ears like gunshots. My mother, who I'd never seen look so broken, raced back to the door and, with stunned neighbors watching from their yards, pounded on it with her worn-out fists and screamed his middle name, which she always called him—"Basil! Basil!"—all to no avail. He never came back out.

I was devastated. It was the first time I had an inkling of why he didn't come home so many nights and of the reason why my mother wouldn't tell me why. Even as a ten-year-old, I could deduce there was another woman in the picture and that nothing about it was right.

Our neighbor Doris saw my mother and me walking around the corner to my uncle Freddie's house, and she told Carmen and Arlyne to get over there, so they came over—and we all headed back home together. During the short walk, which seemed to take forever, my sisters focused their anger and disgust on our father's infidelity.

But I couldn't shake a whole different thought: my father had put me and my mother out of the house instead of the other woman. He could have sat us down, told us to wait, taken her home. Something. Anything. Instead, he put us out like yesterday's trash and locked the door.

Until that night, my father was my hero, not because he'd done much that was particularly heroic, but just because he was my dad. I'd always looked at him a certain way, as someone larger than life, someone I'd someday want to be like. He was that dad everyone else told me I was so lucky to have.

Not anymore. From that day forward, my image of him changed. I realized that we—my mother, my four sisters, my brother, and I—were not as important to him as his other family.

And we never would be.

That was the hardest part to accept back then, and it's the hardest part to accept now. My family was not poor because we lacked the funds to live better—my father had a steady job and my mother worked like hell. We were poor because my dad had another family on the side, just ten minutes away, at a house he shared with his mistress. That's where he spent all his money, when he wasn't gambling.

My dad fed his mistress and *her three* kids, not us. He paid *their* mortgage, not ours. He put food in *their* refrigerator, put clothes on *their* backs. He even paid for *her* kids to go to summer camp. He never had anything to offer my mother when it came to *us*.

While we sat around, our stomachs aching and our heads throbbing, he was elsewhere. When it was freezing cold and we had no heat in the house, he was nowhere to be found.

I remember vividly, when I was eight, one of my sisters hovering around the kitchen, visibly fuming. My mother was rummaging through paperwork and working the phone feverishly, sounding more desperate than I'd ever heard her.

Turns out we were on the verge of being evicted, because my father had stolen the house-insurance money out of my mother's dresser drawer and gambled it away playing spades. It was explained to me that failure to pay the insurance bill could lead to foreclosure.

Somehow, my mother handled the matter by the end of that workday, fending off the insurance company until a later date. That evening, once things finally calmed down, my father came waltzing through the front door, drunk, singing and dancing, as usual. When my mother confronted him, he just laughed.

"Relax!" he said cheerfully. "You handled it. I knew you would."

He was right. From 1972 until she retired, Mommy paid all the bills. Most of the financial relief she ever received came from me. My father never paid a bill again, right up until he died, in August 2018.

He never apologized for it, either. Never displayed the slightest remorse or regret.

Never.

CHAPTER 2

"THE BOY JUST AIN'T SMART"

From the time I was six, I thought I was stupid. Although I talked well—and *a lot*—and articulated my thoughts fluidly enough that some folks swore one day I'd become a lawyer or a public speaker, it was all a façade. I couldn't comprehend what I was reading, a deficit that my oratory skills only served to hide.

It got worse each year, stunting my ability and willingness to grow intellectually. Before long, I was in the second grade but reading at a first-grade level. Then I was in the third grade—still at a first-grade reading level.

I got decent grades anyway, mostly As and Bs. I gave presentations in front of the class based on recall of whatever the teacher had taught us. I could ask and answer provocative questions. For much of the time inside the classroom, squirming at my desk with all those other squirming kids at PS 134, I don't remember feeling like there was anything wrong. Then, at the end of each school year, we'd take a reading comprehension test to determine whether or not we should be promoted to the next grade. I was helpless on those tests.

That's when I felt the profound shame of thinking I just wasn't smart. When I was left back the first time, in third grade, a stint in summer school was enough to get me moved up in September. But my reading deficiency continued through the fourth grade, and when I bombed the comprehension test at the end of that school year, I was left back yet again, this time for the whole next year.

Had I not been so determined to get myself together and rid myself of the shame I felt, I truly believe I eventually would have wound up dead or in jail, like many of my childhood friends wound up, because without an education, the streets of Hollis were eager to claim me. I was lost. I was the only one I knew in the neighborhood left back, and the kids on my block—smart-ass New York City kids—were merciless. Donald, Mark, Willie, Billy, and Tony—practically everyone in Hollis within shouting distance of 203rd Street was laughing at me at earsplitting volume.

"Boy, you got left back *again! Ha ha!*"

Everybody laughed except Poolie, my closest friend. He lived right across the street. Big and tough and eager to show that he was both, Poolie took care of anybody who messed with me. He always had my back, always took my side in any argument, and never backed down from anyone.

After I was left back that second time, however, even Poolie felt helpless to do anything. I mean, it's not like the other kids were *wrong*—hell, Poolie was never left back.

"*Daaaamn,*" was all he could come up with to comfort me.

Forty years later, I still remember all those kids' names and faces and the things they said. But they were just kids. They didn't know any better. I knew that even then and didn't hold it against them, as much as it hurt—as much as it still hurts.

Instead, I held it against myself. I believed I deserved their abuse and absorbed accountability for it. But I also was convinced I'd get better. I knew that if I could stomach the embarrassment of that setback and still march forward, I could withstand anything.

But there was something else that caused me to let them off the hook, a bigger chip that was dropped on my shoulder: their laughter and taunts weren't anything compared to the shame delivered by my father. I'd get over that, too, but I would never let it go.

The day I learned I'd be repeating the fourth grade, I sat on the steps of our back porch and cried. I was hiding from the world, too ashamed to show my face to anybody. But between sobs and sniffles, I overheard my parents talking through an open kitchen window. My mother had just told my father that I'd gotten left back for the second consecutive June. Her voice sounded worried, empathetic, in search of a solution.

My dad's voice was the opposite: matter-of-fact, resigned, dismissive.

"Give it up, Janet," he told her, like he was talking about a sink he'd never be able to fix. "The boy just ain't smart. He's not going anywhere. Accept it."

My mother must have heard one of my sobs and peeked out the window. She cringed when she realized I'd overheard every word that my dad had said about me. She was so hurt by that knowledge that she looked as if she were in more pain than I was—something I wouldn't have thought possible. That made everything even worse.

And my dad?

He did what he always did: retreated to the living room, sank into his chair, and read the paper or watched TV.

He'd be gone in a day or two anyway.

My mother became so consumed by the fiasco of my hearing my father's cutthroat dismissal that it distracted her, for at least a little bit, from his other shenanigans. She did whatever she could to cater to my emotional needs. She knew I was a wreck.

For instance, a few days afterward, she shocked me by taking me to a movie theater to see *Grease*, starring John Travolta and Olivia Newton-John. I remember that day so vividly because it was the only time that either of my parents ever took me to a movie theater. I knew we couldn't afford it.

When I asked my mom, "What are you doing? You never go to the movies yourself, so why would you take me?" she said, "Because I love you and I want you to know that, always." And she left it at that.

The fact is, the words my father had muttered about me did hurt like hell. They really did wound me deeply. Yet somehow I knew almost instinctively that blurting out those blunt, unthinking words was the best thing my father ever did for me. From the moment I heard him insult me, my determination kicked in.

My dad had counted me out. Not only that, he'd implored my own mother to give up on me too. Thank God she refused. His doubts were my fault, I thought. It became my responsibility to change his thinking.

I didn't go about it alone, of course. I wasn't that damn smart. My sister Linda, working that summer before she went off to college at Stony Brook, on Long Island, leaped into action. As the oldest child, with my mother now working sixteen-hour days, Linda ran the household and saw this problem as hers to fix. The second she heard about my struggles, she started helping me with my reading comprehension. Tiver, the brilliant older brother of my buddy Ronnie, who lived around the corner in a house I hung out at all the time, also took it upon himself to tutor me, which I never told Linda about. So I was getting massive help from two people who genuinely cared about me.

As bright as both of them were, they were flying blind, at least at the start. My problem wasn't labeled dyslexia yet. Back then it rarely was. At school they simply called it a reading deficiency. But ultimately, as the weeks and months passed by, my sister and my friend's brother were the ones who discovered that dyslexia was the cause of my problems. They tutored me day after day until, slowly but surely, I started to comprehend what I was reading.

To this day I have no idea how they did it. I just sat there and did what they told me to do. I do remember that my sister was big on repetition and made me do things over and over until they became automatic — like I was shooting jumpers in the park. And as I became more comfortable reading and writing, I gained more and more confidence. I became both smarter and more analytical in everything I did. One thing fed the other.

I never got left back again.

Just how far I'd come was underscored for me at a parent-teacher night a few years later, in seventh grade, at P.S. 192. I dutifully stood at my mother's side, trying not to fidget as she talked with my social studies teacher, Mr. Caravan. Tall and thin, and extremely robotic and deliberate when he spoke, Mr. Caravan made a point of coming up to my mother after his general presentation to speak with her personally.

"Please allow me to tell you this, Mrs. Smith," he began inside the no-frills classroom. "Your son is not a dummy."

My ears perked up; my attention shifted from whatever was distracting me in the hallway or on the ceiling or outside the window and settled directly on Mr. Caravan. I never knew his first name; I don't think any of us kids even thought teachers had first names.

"Sometimes he believes he's a dummy, because he never fails to acknowledge that he got held back twice in elementary school," Mr. Caravan went on. "It sticks with him. He never lets it go."

My mother nodded. I don't think she was sure where this was going. Neither was I.

"But here is what I've noticed about him," Mr. Caravan continued. "He gets extremely bored very easily. So, if there's something he is not interested in, he drifts. He pays little to no attention and misses things. But when he's interested in a subject, he's as sharp as they come. Find out what he's interested in and have him do that. You'll have a star on your hands."

As he spoke, I tried my damnedest not to get antsy, not to look around, not to break away and find something else to mess with. I wouldn't have believed what Mr. Caravan said if I hadn't heard it with my own ears. I still had minimal confidence, because I believed so little in myself.

But his words were one small sign: change was under way.

✳   ✳   ✳

When Mr. Caravan said those words to my mother—words so different from what my father had muttered just a few years earlier—they lit up all kinds of thoughts and dreams in my head. I suddenly fantasized about being a lawyer, a profession I knew about mostly through watching TV murder mysteries and dramas like *Matlock* and *Perry Mason*. I pondered becoming a politician, because I loved watching presidential debates. As a young teenager, I watched *World News Tonight* with Peter Jennings and *Nightline* with Ted Koppel. They defined credibility and substance, new concepts I'd learned about since my reading breakthrough, and traits I knew I would need if I was ever going to be taken seriously at whatever I chose to do.

Yet what I gravitated to most was sports. While I grew up practically in the geographic center of America's sporting universe—two Major League Baseball teams, two NFL football teams, two NBA basketball teams, and two NHL hockey teams all played their home games within about twenty-five miles of my front door—I only experienced it from watching the games on TV. I had never watched a game in person.

That shaped my hunger. It was one more thing back then that I saw but never got to touch, because we simply did not have the means.

The only live sporting event I attended before I turned fifteen, when my uncle Freddie finally took me and my brother to a Yankees game, was the horse races at nearby Belmont Park.

The track was three miles away, closer when we took our shortcuts. Me and my buddies would hop a fence at the park when security wasn't looking, then bet a dollar whenever we had a little money. Back then, the tellers at the betting windows barely looked up when we plunked down loose bills and called out a horse's name in our squeaky, prepubescent voices. To them, our money was as good as the next sucker's—the more the merrier!

But my regular seat for any sporting event remained in front of the tube. I watched sports all the time. I'd even take breaks from playing touch football on the rock-solid concrete of 203rd Street to check in on the Yankees with my dad. He'd celebrate a strikeout from pitchers Ron Guidry or Goose Gossage, a home run from Reggie Jackson or Don Mattingly. I'd witness him yelling at the TV screen, applauding a demonstrative diatribe by manager Billy Martin or owner George Steinbrenner.

Other times, I watched games with my sister Linda, who always knew her sports. It was a joy watching with someone who was an even bigger fan than my father or me. Neither the NBA's Knicks nor the New York Giants of the NFL had a bigger fan than Linda Laverne Smith. She knew the names of every single player. Screaming at the TV one minute, throwing something at it the next, Linda became so volatile when she got frustrated watching either one of them that we'd all just leave the room and let her watch the games by herself.

Conversely, no one was happier when the Giants won Super Bowls in 1986 and 1990, led by Phil Simms and Jeff Hostetler, respectively. In fact, I had actually forgotten that the Giants won Super Bowls in each of the last four decades (1986, 1990, 2007, and 2011) until Linda reminded me.

"What other team has done that shit?" she asked rhetorically. "Uh-huh. Try this answer: No Goddamn body!"

Most of the times, though, I'd watch games by myself. But there was a purpose to it. While my father, my sisters, and others watched the games for the sheer enjoyment, I appreciated the commentary just as much as the action on the court or field.

Although I was only five years old, I vividly remember Howard Cosell's call of "Down goes Frazier! Down goes Frazier!" when former heavyweight boxing champion Joe Frazier got smashed by George Foreman in two rounds on January 22, 1973; there isn't a year that goes by when I don't watch the replay of that fight, along with the call from Cosell. Plus, my father laughed for the next forty-five years over Foreman knocking Frazier upside the back of his head, labeling it the funniest knockout in boxing history.

I sat in awe of Bryant Gumbel, marveling at his hosting ability. From NBC Sports to the *Today* show on NBC, to *The Early Show* on CBS every weekday morning, his ability to transition from sports to news was seamless. I viewed Gumbel as royalty, knowing that he was the standard-setter. And I admired the hell out of him for being a Black man, capable of putting himself in that position, swearing to myself that I'd never truly arrive in the broadcast business unless I received his stamp of approval one day.

I heard the language of broadcasters; from Cosell to Gumbel, to Brent Musburger, Jimmy the Greek, Bob Costas, and, of course, the late, great Ed Bradley of *60 Minutes*. I absorbed the things they brought to the table—their interviewing skills, poignant delivery, and overall respect they commanded—just as I absorbed the run-on rhymes of rappers in the park.

From very early on, I just knew how to talk. I didn't try to emulate anybody, didn't try to create a distinctive voice. It all just got slapped together and came out in the form of a sharp tongue and a talent for rapid-fire, informed responses. I always had something to say and always had a comeback for everybody—everybody, that is, except my mom. When she talked, it was the beginning and the end of the conversation.

Maybe I absorbed some of that, too.

What I saw on TV seeped onto the playground. I played football in the street and baseball in a local police athletic league, but my real love was basketball. My brother, Basil, played on the neighborhood's outdoor courts. So, when I was nine years old, not long before he moved out, I followed suit.

I tried to emulate what I watched, or what I saw others on the playground trying to emulate: Dr. J, then Magic Johnson and Larry Bird.

Filthy fakes, no-look passes, bombs from the outside—the must-see TV in our living rooms filtered down to the court at P.S. 192, on 204th Street and Hollis Avenue, a block and a half from my house.

I went there every chance I got, to the exclusion of nearly everything else. Many times I felt as if that was the only escape from what ailed me, mentally and emotionally. I went there to get away from doing homework, to get away from my sisters' telling me what to do, to get away from Mommy throwing chores at me, to get away from my father getting away from us. At night, I loved the solitude I often felt even as I stood in the middle of the country's biggest, baddest city the incessant rounds of honking car horns and ear-piercing police sirens were replaced by the squeak of my sneakers and the jazzy beat of my dribble.

The more I practiced, the better I got, until I was one of the best players in the neighborhood. We played three-on-three or one-on-one. When nobody was around, which was usually early evening, I shot by myself for hours—stepping back and shooting, sliding and shooting, head-faking and shooting. Or just shooting and then shooting again. I launched a minimum of two hundred jumpers every evening. The ball and the net were barely visible in the alternating flicker of the green, red, and yellow glow that emanated from a stoplight across the street. It was the park's lone illumination. The late Kobe Bryant told me on many occasions: "When you're in the gym alone you can do anything you want." I was already developing that belief those evenings on that playground.

Early evening was also when the local drug dealers began to filter into the park. For me, they were saviors. They thought I had potential as a basketball player, and knew I wasn't built for the streets—my one altercation, getting busted and held for two hours for jumping a subway turnstile at Forest Hills station when I didn't have the fare, scared me straight and made me vow to never run afoul of the law again—so they not only left me alone but provided protection from anyone else who tried to mess with me. They only had one rule: I could shoot until the sun went down; then it was time for them to take over the playground and handle their business.

"Time for you to get home, lil' man," they'd tell me, and without another word I'd dribble down the sidewalk—*bam! bam! bam!*—all the way back.

If I walked into the house on a night when my father was home, I'd invariably sit and watch whatever game he was watching. As complicated and confusing as our relationship could be, he was still my dad—flawed, bullying, infuriating, but still my dad. To a kid that age, that was enough. He was *it*. It's not like a friend you fall out with and replace with another friend. It's your damn dad. He's the person you have to answer to whether you like it or not—whether he believes in you or not. And if he doesn't believe in you? You *make* him believe in you.

I would amount to something, damn it!

My dad had an insatiable appetite for sports, especially baseball. He was a die-hard Yankees fan who literally forbade us to watch the Mets before we turned eighteen—even though they were less than fifteen minutes away, at Shea Stadium in Queens. He'd sit there watching the Yankees day and night, no matter how late it was. He religiously read the *New York Post* and the New York *Daily News*. He loved the opinion pages, constantly gauging the credibility of the columnists, a determination he made by putting their opinions up against his own.

As I got older, I joined in. I mastered sports because I loved the subject matter, just as Mr. Caravan had predicted. The more I read, the more I felt compelled to read, elevating my knowledge and adding substance to whatever came out of my mouth.

As I'd hoped, my father took notice.

"What the hell is going on with this boy?" he asked my mother once, after my thirteen-year-old self decided to debate him about wanting the Yankees' then third baseman, Craig Nettles, traded. "You listening to him? He actually sounds like he has some damn smarts after all."

I liberally stole sports opinions from him, the only thing I've ever taken from him in my life. He'd critique how managers handled pitchers, and then how they all failed in comparison to former Yankees' manager Billy Martin, the brilliant, feisty, hard-drinking throwback who was his all-time favorite. He'd lament when pitchers were left in too long or taken out too hastily. How they'd throw sliders when they should've thrown fastballs and fastballs when they should've thrown sliders. He'd constantly complain about hitters swinging at bad pitches, or trotting to first base instead of sprinting all out, or foolishly attempting to steal when a power hitter was at the plate. But nothing upset him more than a third-base coach waving a runner around the bag only to have him be thrown out at home.

"That man is an *ee-dee-ot*, me son," he'd blurt in his harshest West Indian–ese. "Fire his damn ass right now!"

My dad loved irascible Yankees owner George Steinbrenner precisely because of that: George had my dad's impatience and fired anybody for the slightest reason.

Yet while my dad taught me about baseball and how to analyze the game, he indirectly taught me, without ever knowing it, things that I would use to my advantage throughout my career—things I use to this day.

He taught me that listening to what someone else wants could be a quick way to turn a foe into a friend. He taught me to develop a passion for what I do and never to be apologetic about it. And most of all—and this was absolutely not his intent—he taught me to recognize and appreciate the benefits of criticism, instead of folding to it.

Knowing that my father once considered me a lost cause and said as much to my mother, I could have avoided him and given up. He really was a damn bastard at times. But instead, I embraced the challenge of simply being around him, inhaling and dissecting what he said about me, and then figuring out ways to make those unforgettable words he once said to my mother as meaningless to me as possible. I'd have many tough editors and producers at newspapers and in TV during the years that followed, but never anyone as brutal as he was.

It took months of sitting in front of him, absorbing his looks of discontent and disappointment, but the longer I looked, the easier it got. Eventually, I began to challenge his opinions instead of challenging the very legitimacy of his having an opinion at all. The result: as I approached my sixteenth birthday, my father wanted to talk to me *more*, not less, and I wanted to *listen* more so that I could respond. I was putting myself in the lion's den that was him, to help me sharpen myself and everything that I wanted to be. I was gathering intel about sports and life, even if he didn't know that that's what I was getting out of it.

Absorbing my father's criticism and being able to take it constructively made me feel better about myself, which made me better at everything I did. It made me grow and feel more confident in verbalizing what I had studied and learned, which was incredibly important, because now the possibility of a college education was no longer merely a fantasy. This self-imposed learning I had undertaken with my father was allowing me to dream about one day being anything or anyone I might want to be, envisioning possibilities for myself I had never envisioned before. I became open to any and all possibilities, excluding one: becoming like him.

Yep! We finally reached a point where he would test me by asking what I had seen as we were watching a game—the equivalent of those reading-comprehension tests that once determined whether I could move on to the next grade. But I wasn't fazed. I was a teenager now. I knew how to read now. And I had a passion for what I was learning, because it was sports. So, to me, my father was no longer intimidating at all, no matter how intimidating he tried to be.

I would watch the games intently, study the highlights, pinpoint what mattered most to him. Eventually, my father went from trusting my evaluations and soliciting my opinion to simply conceding that I knew more than he did about certain sports-related particulars. He made this concession because I actually watched more games than he did. He had come not only to depend on me but to respect me.

That's as good as I ever got from him. Over the years that followed, right up until he passed away in 2018, my dad never called me once to ask about college, to check up on my career, nor to inquire about my personal life, even after my daughters were born.

Sports was the whole of our conversational relationship. If we didn't talk sports, we didn't talk at all.

And that appeared to be okay with him.

Before my sixteenth birthday, it was perfectly okay with me too.

CHAPTER 3

A LIAR TO MY MOMMA

My newfound confidence came at a price.

    I now had potential, and my father knew it. Yet instead of being happy about this—and supporting, guiding, and nourishing me—he merely became more confrontational and territorial.

My maturing into the man I hoped to be was not his priority. It was a challenge. In his eyes, I needed to understand that our house was "His House" and things were to be done "His Way"—despite the obvious fact that he was rarely home, didn't pay any bills, and didn't seem to care what the hell was going on. I was constantly threatened with getting my "ass whipped" for so much as looking at him the wrong way. He repeatedly told me to "shut up, no one wants to hear what you have to say." Everything—and I mean *everything*—was contingent on his mood. Nothing mattered more than what he deemed convenient or within his control.

Problems with the electricity? He was the only one allowed to "hire" the electrician. Plumbing issues? He knew the plumber, not you. Carpentry, automotive, yard work, etc.—if anything entailed payment to an outside source, he was the one who provided the source, my mother was simply designated as the one who had to do the paying, which disgusted us to no end.

Inexplicably, my mother was a total pushover with my father. All of us trusted her with all of our hearts regarding anything or anyone except with matters pertaining to our father. He was her weakness; the only person on earth who had a chance of convincing her that something was in the best interest of her kids when it actually served only his.

My mother was far from a pushover with me. Her shorthand for what she expected out of her youngest child: "Don't be a knucklehead." So, when I was in junior high school and stupidly told her that I was wavering about going to college, my mother didn't mess around at all by dismissing it as me just running my mouth. She took it very seriously, declaring that I wouldn't embarrass her by becoming "some unemployed bum" and enrolled me in Thomas A. Edison Career & Technical Education High School, just across Grand Central Parkway from the hospital where she worked.

"You'll learn a trade," she declared. "You'll do whatever it takes to make sure you have a job. Period. You're not about to run the streets or end up unemployed. Over my dead body."

And so it went. Thomas A. Edison was the first school I couldn't walk to. Although it was only a few miles away, it took me more than an hour to get there every weekday, with bus transfers and the inevitable transit delays. I looked out the bus windows wide-eyed at the big, shaded yards that fronted the Tudor and Mediterranean homes of the first neighborhood we passed outside of Hollis, Jamaica Estates. That was the childhood home of another dude who, like Jam Master Jay and LL Cool J and the rest, found fame far beyond Queens; Donald J. Trump.

I would receive a call from Trump years later, in 2014, when he wanted to talk about his wish to buy the Buffalo Bills football team. I told him that most of the NFL owners would likely stand in his way. They weren't about to let him into that good ol' boys club.

His reply, verbatim: "If these motherfuckers get in my way, I'll tell you how I'll get back at them: I'm going to run for president!"

That's what he said, and, sure enough, that's what he did. As much as I despised how he behaved during his presidency, I'll give him credit for that.

Speaking of Trump, let me pause for a second to say this about our 45th president:

I loathed his presidency for reasons that might not be obvious. I don't like to judge an administration's overall significance on a moment-to-moment basis. That's best viewed through the prism of history. Partially as a result, I'm neither a Democrat nor a Republican, but a registered Independent.

I'll be damned if I trust either side. As far as I'm concerned, too many lobbyists influence our politics, the positions taken by politicians and, ultimately, because the politicians are acting on behalf of powerful interests rather than acting and speaking as independent representatives answerable to the public, their very ability to conduct themselves with traditional decorum is affected. As a result, there's no compromise, very little gets accomplished for the American people, and this country grows more and more divided every time there's an election. And the cycle continues, and the situation only gets worse.

I'll let history be the judge of presidents in the grand sweep of things, but morality and statesmanship are day-to-day issues that I track closely. Is a president looking out for the best interests of the country or for himself? Do you present yourself publicly as president of all the people, or only of those who voted for you?

By that standard, Trump was an utter disgrace.

He maligned war hero John McCain for "getting caught" in Vietnam, even as McCain was dying; and then he maligned him again after his death. He fanned the proverbial flames of existing racial tensions and exacerbated the situation with his petulant undiplomatic style. He then went somewhere beyond petty upon the death of Georgia representative John Lewis, a true civil rights hero, when he simply dismissed him because "he didn't have nice things to say about me."

He exacerbated tensions with the Asian community with his repeated referrals to the COVID-19 pandemic as the "China flu" or the "kung flu," knowing full well the increased hostility it would ignite toward their community and the danger it could place them in. Then he downplayed the pandemic because he thought it might affect his reelection. And he repeatedly declared that "the election was rigged" without regard to the damage his assertions would cause, evidenced by the insurrection at the U.S. Capitol on January 6, 2021.

In my opinion, more than eighty-one million Americans did not vote for Biden. They voted against Trump. They were either fearful of a civil war engulfing the country, or they were just embarrassed as hell by a commander in chief conducting himself like such a petulant child.

To summarize the obvious, Trump's willingness to throw away any chance at reelection came down to his ego, above all else. To allow his emotions and self-interest to usurp what he personally believed to be in the best interest of the country—himself—even when so many citizens believed in his policies and thought he was the right man for the job, is both unconscionable and unforgivable.

Supposedly, Trump believed he was the best that America had to offer for the presidency, correct? So why let such petty, egotistical matters—like encouraging mask-wearing or admitting that you'd been vaccinated—get in the way of what you believed was best for the country? Especially knowing that he and others felt his reelection was a lock, based on how the country's economy was viewed as doing before the world was engulfed by COVID-19?

But I digress.

Back to my school days.

※　　　※　　　※

Since I was a fool, telling my mother that my dreams of becoming a law-yer had evaporated and that I had no intention of going to law school one day, I started high school majoring in "electrical installation." My assignments ranged from changing light bulbs to installing outlets and other electrical equipment. It excited my mother, because there was always something in the house that needed to be fixed, and she was more than happy to let me experiment on small jobs. It spared her having to pay an electrician.

My father was having none of it. His childhood buddy was the "ultimate handyman" (his words). So Real (pronounced "re-EL") had become our electrician, carpenter, plumber, and anything else my dad needed him to be.

The rest of us were dubious. His "handyman" once claimed to have fixed the pipes in the basement of my sister Carmen's house; turned out his "fix" was sticking tube socks in a hole in the pipe to stop the leaking. He rarely finished any work we called him to do. Instead, he'd drink and watch baseball games with my dad, sometimes for days at a time, even before starting work on whatever my mother had been coaxed into hiring him to do.

Nothing was done on time. Two-hour jobs turned into two-week projects. But my father continued to insist on using his friend, and that he be paid by my mother.

The reason eventually became clear: my sisters and I later learned that my father took half of the money for himself—yet another way he robbed us to pay for his other family and his own vices.

As my high school years slid by, my father and I grew further apart. The hell with watching games with him. As my concern for my mother grew, I started to invite confrontation with him rather than avoid it. I saw how his selfishness and bullying was wearing her down. Working sixteen-hour days with zero financial help will do that.

All I saw was a man who didn't want to work, who leaned on my mother to do his job, and who didn't possess a speck of shame about it. I lost any last strand of respect I had for him. I no longer was the bullied kid desperate for his approval. I was through with caring about what he felt about me and focused on how I felt about him.

I stopped saying "hello" unless he did so first. I barely watched games with him anymore, choosing to head to the park or over to my friend Ronnie Robertson's house. Conversations that he'd instigate were met with short, terse responses. Jokes and laughter no longer existed.

Dad noticed.

He didn't like it.

I didn't give a shit.

I fantasized throughout high school about making the varsity basketball team at Thomas Edison but didn't try out until my junior year. I was just a five-foot, nine-inch, 130-pound street baller trying to survive. I was always hungry, I never had good clothes, my mom was struggling like hell. The only thing that took my mind off it all was playing basketball in the park. That was my escape—from home, from my shitty self-esteem, even from the fellas on my block who had real home lives that only made me long for one of my own. I was messily evolving, overcompensating for my absentee father. Couple that with the usual teenage-boy fluctuations in mood due to raging hormones and a 'hood that threw up a challenge seemingly on every block, and you got yourself a damn mess.

Me.

But then I'd go up against older dudes on P.S. 192's court who started saying, "That cat can really play!" At a time when I still didn't think all that highly of myself, I'd found a place where other people thought highly of me. It got to the point where even the drug dealers started to bet on me. That was real pressure—the last thing you wanted to do was make them lose. I honestly don't think they would have done anything to harm me—I mean, I knew most of them—but I didn't have the luxury of knowing that at the time. Looking back, I realize that that pressure built character.

Yet when I finally tried out for the high school team my junior year, I didn't make the cut. I lacked skills that kids who'd played organized basketball developed—the kind of defending and play-making techniques good coaching hones. I just didn't have the money (or the talent) for those travel and AAU programs, like the Gauchos or Riverside. They were reserved for the young phenoms I know about, from Rod Strickland, Dwayne "Pearl" Washington, Mark Jackson, and Kenny Smith, then on to Kenny Anderson and Lloyd "Sweet Pea" Daniels (who, by the way, was better than all of them). I wasn't in that category.

And scrawny and undersized as I was, I wasn't going to out-muscle anybody, either. But my jumper was deadly enough that some players still viewed me as a threat.

One of Thomas Edison's best players made sure I didn't get the chance to showcase any of my assets. It was personal for him—dude didn't like me as much as I didn't like him. It had been like that for years. I don't even remember what our beef was: he thought I had an attitude, I thought he had an attitude, and while our disdain was apparent whenever we passed each other in the halls, it never went further than that. I chalk it up to teenage-boy bullshit: you make somebody else feel miserable to make yourself feel better. Simple as that.

But at the tryout, he had the upper hand, and he used it. He convinced other teammates to freeze me out so I wouldn't get the ball, and double-team me whenever I did so that I'd never get a shot. It worked to perfection. The coach, Harvey Stoller, didn't know me from Adam and couldn't have cared less about whatever teen drama might be playing out. All he focused on was who could play. To him, I was invisible. End of story.

I got cut after the first day of tryouts.

I was heartbroken. But I also learned a valuable lesson: before getting lost in the shuffle, toot your own horn. It was up to me to make sure the coach knew who I was so that he'd pay attention to what I was doing and what was being done to me. By the time the next season rolled around—and after hundreds more hours spent on playground courts—I made sure Coach Stoller would know whether I could play or not. I wasn't going to get lost in the shuffle this time.

With tryouts imminent, I visited the coach at his office and told him what had happened the previous year. Then I asked him simply to look for me on the court during tryouts: if I wasn't good enough, fine, but I wanted the chance to prove otherwise. I added that I also wanted his star player—the one who froze me out the last time—to be on the court when I was. I wanted that more than anything. I needed the coach to see I was legit. My purpose was to accentuate the point that I was worthy of being on the Thomas Edison varsity—which is exactly what I did. The other guy was bigger and better, a kid who could use his body to great effect against somebody like me, and who had a savvy, all-around game. But when he went against me one on one this time, I just let it fly, hitting shot after shot after shot. More and more students kept filtering into the gym when they heard what was going on, eager to watch the show.

This time, Coach noticed.

I made the team.

My first thought afterward:

"What a beautiful year this will be!"

I had school. I had basketball. My mother appeared to be in better spirits because she became more focused on herself and less focused on whatever my dad was doing.

It started off promisingly enough. I was having an up-and-down season on the court—sometimes starting and playing, sometimes making mistakes that limited my playing time, sometimes not playing at all. But I felt like I was progressing, picking up techniques and game-awareness that my years on the playground hadn't fully provided. In one tournament held in Manhattan, inside the gym of the Fashion Institute of Technology, a mostly art-and-design school that also fielded a ranked junior college basketball team, I poured in twenty-seven points. I was finally establishing some honest cred.

But my hopes of a beautiful year evaporated just a couple months into the season: I received a failing grade on a botched assignment in electrical installation. That made me ineligible to play basketball for two months, which was essentially the rest of the season.

I went ballistic, decrying the unfairness so emphatically that the tensions reached the school principal. My beef: Mr. B. was arbitrary and petty and messing with lives. If you showed up a minute late for class, he'd deduct five points one day, tens points another—or, depending on who was late, no points at all. If you didn't pronounce the word "answer" as "An-SWER"—another ten points off your final grade. If you questioned any of this, if you looked at him wrong—more points! After signing a paper, points were deducted because I didn't attach my middle initial to the rest of my name. He didn't just do it to me, he did it to everybody, just to mess with our heads. The principal finally suggested that my parents meet with Mr. B. in person to resolve the matter.

Only my mother showed up at the first meeting. Hearing Mr. B.'s explanation—one I deemed totally bogus—my mother became so flabbergasted that she told him, "Mr. B., I'm going to send his father up here to talk with you, because I'm at a loss. I hear what you're saying, but here's the problem. My son is right here, swearing to your face that you're lying, and my son never lies to me."

Now, understand, Janet Smith knew I had a mouth on me. But she also knew I respected authority, never disrespected my elders, and never got in trouble. And what she said was absolutely true: I had never, ever lied to her up to that point. So she left it to my dad to come to my rescue. Unfortunately.

Within seconds of my dad's arrival at Mr. B.'s classroom the next afternoon, it became clear that that wasn't going to happen. The very first words out of his mouth:

"So, what did Stephen do now?"

Mr. B. smiled appreciatively. I knew I was toast. For the next thirty minutes, he spewed his interpretation of what had gone on between him and me. Whenever I interjected, my father blurted, "Shut up!" and then added, to Mr. B., "This is how I know he's not telling the truth about you."

It went on like that seemingly forever. They got so chummy I finally couldn't help myself and during one pause broke in, "What are you guys going to do next? Go out and grab a drink together?"

Bottom line: the failing grade stood, and I remained ineligible.

I felt betrayed by my father—again—and said that to my mother the second we got home. As we talked, we all made our way into my parents' bedroom, where I looked at my dad with total disgust and asked, "How could you do that to me?"

His answer: "Get the fuck out of here right now before I beat your ass."

My father had it all over me in terms of size, and his temper was fiercer as well. He was someone you feared more than respected. But on this day I neither feared nor respected him. I turned and walked to the door, something reminiscent of a scene from the movie *A Few Good Men*, in which Lance Cpl. Harold Dawson shows his disdain and lack of respect for Tom Cruise's commanding-officer character by putting his hands in his pocket after Cruise asks, "Whatever happened to saluting an officer when leaving the room?" Instead of leaving and closing my parents' bedroom door, I closed us all inside. I then turned back around and stood defiantly in front of my father's face.

At that point, Ashley Basil Smith was not my father, and I was not his son. He was nothing to me, just as I felt I had been nothing to him all these years. He immediately jumped up to pummel me, but my mother leaped between us and screamed for me to leave the room while she continued to block my father.

He was furious. He shouted that he was going to beat my damn ass the second he saw me again. My shouted response, before storming out of the room and then out of the house: "That would be the first fatherly thing you've done in my life."

After fuming for a few hours, I returned home. My mother had a suitcase packed for me at the door. She wasn't throwing me out; she was sending me to be with my brother, Basil, a traveling salesman, who was working in Waco, Texas, for a two-month period at the time. When my mother called him after I left to explain what had gone on, my brother told her he'd take me in for a few days until everyone calmed down.

Basil and I weren't all that close growing up. He was nine years older—and when I was eight he left to join the air force, literally the day after graduating from high school. He knew the dynamics of our house. So, while I was down in Texas with him, our bond grew closer and closer. My brother simply reminded me, again and again, of the importance of keeping my cool, of waiting things out until the chance came for me to get the hell out of there. Nothing would ever be resolved before that. He told me not to sweat what I couldn't control, and our father was definitely the thing that none of us would ever get a handle on.

I finally settled down and reset, and after a few days returned to New York.

What I encountered after stepping off the plane at LaGuardia was one of the worst experiences of my life.

While I was walking to the baggage claim, a little boy, maybe five or six years old, suddenly ran up to me and jumped into my arms. My dad, assigned to pick me up since he was the only family member with a car, stood right behind him.

Stunned and confused, I asked him, "Who's this?"

My dad's beaming response: "Your little brother!"

It was as if all the usual commotion at the airport suddenly ground to a halt. I knew my father had another family, of course, but I never knew he'd actually fathered another son. I'd heard some noise in the neighborhood about him having another kid, but I thought it was nothing more than his taking care of someone else's kid—which he also did—not one of his own. Then the infant in his mistress's arms that fateful day at my uncle Freddie's flashed through my mind.

My slack-jawed response:

Nothing.

It was a rare moment in my life when I had no words.

I was speechless. I picked up my bag and walked to the car. I was totally confused on how to come across to this kid, whom I not only didn't know but until just minutes earlier didn't even know existed. I didn't want to act out. He was still my brother and just an innocent kid. None of this was his fault. He was as much a victim of my dad's thoughtless narcissism as the rest of us.

Then it got worse. After tossing my bag in the trunk, I saw my dad motion toward me to sit in the back. His mistress was already sitting in the passenger seat up front.

I barely opened my mouth during the twenty-minute ride to Hollis. Neither did anyone else in the car, at least that I remember. The thoughts roiling in my head made me nauseous. "What if Mommy sees us? I know she'll lose it. God forbid she thinks I'm okay with this! Or worse: What if she thinks I had something to do with it!"

My worries, at least temporarily, were for nothing. Instead of driving to the middle of the block, where our house was, my father dropped me off on the corner, about fifty yards away. Before speeding off, he called out, "Make sure you tell your mother I was alone when I picked you up."

I couldn't focus on his cowardice right then. I was fixated instead on the pain my mother would feel if I told her what had happened. She would be apoplectic, over both my father's deceit and the nerve he had introducing me to his mistress and the son he had with her.

So when I walked through the front door and she asked where my father was, I did what I'd never done in my life.

I lied to her.

"Did he come pick you up by himself?"

"Yes."

Lying to my mother in that moment remains one of the worst feelings I've ever experienced.

I went to school the next day. When I came home, my mother was seated on the edge of her bed, crying. She was never home at that hour, she was always at work, and when I saw her like that I assumed something tragic had occurred in the family and ran to comfort her. The tragedy was worse than I thought.

"Why did you lie to me?" she asked.

I gulped. I stuttered. Then I lied again.

"What are you talking about?"

Her tone was flat and frightening.

"Why didn't you tell me your father picked you up at the airport last night with his mistress and their son?"

I couldn't even look at my mother. I just put my head down and said, "I'm sorry. I didn't want to hurt you, but I didn't know what to do. I don't know how any of it happened."

My mother proceeded to tell me that my father had called his sisters back in St. Thomas—his voice cracking, sounding like he was fighting back tears, according to my aunts—to brag about how his sons had just met each other. He went on about what a wonderful occasion it was and how we had made plans to see each other again.

Not true. The lies he told forced me to give my mother a blow-by-blow account of what had actually taken place. She vowed to handle the matter herself the second he came back home. I told her not to bother.

"I'll handle this," I said. "It's time for me to step up."

It was long overdue. Now nearly eighteen, I realized in that moment I had spent far too much time being a boy instead of a man. I'd also spent too much energy on being all I could be for me, and not enough time being what I needed to be for my mother, including keeping her from having to provide so much for me. If ever there was a time when she needed me to be the man of the house, this was it.

My anger swelled. It was one thing for my father to do whatever he wanted, but it was something else entirely for him to do so many things to belittle and hurt my mother. She didn't deserve that strain on her heart. No woman does. It was time for change.

I was in my bedroom the night he finally came home. I heard the creak of his footsteps on the stairs as he headed to the bedroom where my mother slept. I went in right behind him, told him to come to my room and asked my mother to wait downstairs. To say you could cut the tension with a knife was not a cliché on this night.

I repeated for him what my mother told me, about how he called his family in St. Thomas to brag about my meeting my half brother. He denied nothing. In fact, he seemed to bask in the glow of it all, adding that he'd do it again and that he had no regrets—as if he was even capable of regret.

"What about Mommy?" I asked him.

"She's wrong," he said. "She shouldn't want you to avoid your own brother. And if you feel the same way she does, you're wrong too."

We locked eyes. I was through with him—not just now but forever.

"Let's get one thing straight: nobody comes before Mommy. Ever," I began. "Not your mistress. Not your other son. And definitely not you. I feel bad for that kid, because he's done absolutely nothing wrong, but anyone who goes up against Mommy in my eyes is going to lose.

Especially you. I will not add more pain to what you've already caused her. So, there will be no more meetings with me and your other family. We clear?"

Nothing could ever be clear to him that didn't put him first, so his response was hardly surprising.

"To hell with you. That is your little brother. Your mother has no business keeping you from him. She's wrong for doing that, and you're wrong for accepting it."

That was the real beginning of the end. There were no more conversations after that night. There were barely *hi*'s or *bye*'s. Birthdays, Thanksgiving, Christmas—didn't matter. The most generous way to describe our relationship from that point on was "cordial."

Barely!

I never saw my half brother again. Years later, I heard he passed away. I still don't know any of the details. Clearly, it had been a sad situation but a necessary one at the time, because my father's actions put me and my siblings in the position of having to choose between a mother we adored and a half brother we didn't know.

My dad did show up for my high school graduation. We took pictures together and feigned affection for each other publicly, but that was it.

CHAPTER 4

"YOU GOT GAME"

My arrival at Winston-Salem State University, where the direction of my life would be forever altered, was a flat-out fluke.

I didn't land at WSSU the usual way. Without any interest in fashion or technology, I spent my first year after high school at the Fashion Institute of Technology, a massive building in the heart of New York's fashion district. It was the only school to offer me financial aid. It was basically a partial basketball scholarship to play at the junior college level ("JuCo"), a result of my twenty-seven-point tournament performance inside the school's gym shortly before I became ineligible to play at Thomas Edison.

From the outside, FIT, as the school is known, seemed like a total mismatch for me. Most of the students looked like white arty types. Famous alumni include fashion VIP's Calvin Klein, Michael Kors, and Nina Garcia. The fellas on the basketball team were the opposite of that: poor city-school players who needed to boost their grades or their games or both. Virtually all of us were Black.

The only kid I knew on the team was the guard in high school who'd shut me out during my junior year tryouts.

But JuCo ball is a great leveler: we were all there to get someplace else.

Our coach was Marvin Rippy, a national JuCo coach of the year whose past teams had been ranked as high as fifth in the country. Rippy was also Black and roamed the sideline in a white shirt, tie, and cardigan sweater. When he sat down during games, which was rare, it was on a chair somebody borrowed from the cafeteria.

Rippy was a staunch disciplinarian who'd run you to death if you messed up, as befit his teams' pressing, fast-break style. The year I was there the team finished 35–4 and was at one point ranked fifteenth in the nation.

Despite the Tigers' success, hardly anybody else at FIT cared. We were lucky to draw a couple dozen fans for home games in our subbasement gym, located around the corner from a dance studio. The school finally dropped the program in 2010.

Later, FIT's place on my résumé prompted coaches and professors to tease me with questions like, "What'd you major in? Sewing?" The school was more than that: I majored in advertising and communications. Though I had no intention of going into advertising, I wanted a major with credits that would transfer to another school once I moved on from FIT.

And I was determined to move on.

I still had a lot of growing up to do, on and off the court. With less than a full year of high school basketball experience, I was clearly seen by Coach Rippy as a project—a street baller who could really shoot but had a lot more to learn. Frustratingly, I mostly learned from a seat on the bench.

Off the court, I didn't have a minute to spare, cultivating an endless capacity for work. I took the maximum eighteen credit hours a semester. Why? Anyone who grew up poor knows the answer: when you're relying on financial aid, you take as many hours as possible because you don't know how long your education will be paid for. I also found a full-time job to offset the cost of books and expenses, as well as any extracurricular activities I might pursue, that my aid didn't cover.

My mother had made it clear she wasn't supporting another do-nothing man in the house.

My job at a Barnes & Noble bookstore in midtown Manhattan started every weekday morning at 8:30. Like many other Hollis commuters, that meant the following routine: wake up at 6 a.m., shower, dress, then hustle up the block to catch the Q2 bus on Hollis Avenue. Twenty-five minutes later I'd jump off at Hillside Avenue and 179th Street to catch the F or E train for another forty-five minute ride to midtown near Rockefeller Center. From there, I walked a couple blocks to the job.

Except for a half hour lunch break, I was on my feet until 4 p.m., helping one customer after another. I then raced across town to FIT—from 48th Street and Fifth Avenue to 28th Street and Eighth Avenue—to make the team's 4:30 p.m. practice. After nearly two hours in the gym, it was another sprint to make my classes each weeknight from 6:30 to 9:20 p.m. After class, I retraced my morning route back to Hollis, walking through my mother's front door around 11:30 p.m.

Whatever homework or studying I couldn't fit in during lunch break or on weekends, I did then. I'd eventually fall asleep, wake back up at six, and do the same damn thing all over again.

Then came the "meeting" that changed my world forever.

Ronnie Robertson, one of my dearest friends as a kid, lived two blocks away, on 201st St. and 111th Avenue. His entire family was like a second family to me. His brothers, Tiver and Curtis, along with his sister, Pamela, treated me like their little brother. Although we've lost touch over the years, I'll love them for life.

Pamela's boyfriend at the time was a dude named Harold "Funny" Kit. Funny hooped it up big time in the 1970s, including playing college ball for a coaching legend whom everyone in the basketball universe knew simply as "Big House."

Clarence Edward "Big House" Gaines began coaching at Winston-Salem State in 1946. In 1967, Winston-Salem won the Division II national championship, becoming the first member of the historically Black colleges and universities (HBCUs) to achieve that feat. Players he coached included Cleo Hill, the first African American from an HBCU drafted in the NBA's first round; and Earl "the Pearl" Monroe, a former Knicks star and an NBA Hall of Famer.

Coach Gaines led the Rams to twenty-win seasons eighteen times and was inducted into the Basketball Hall of Fame in 1982, as I was still launching jumpers on that unlighted court at P.S. 192.

I didn't know what was in the cards when Funny took me to a court one clear but cold February day in 1988 at Jamaica Park, a few blocks from my mother's house. He wanted to play me one on one and said if he liked what he saw, he'd put me up against more formidable competition.

He was scouting me, of course, at Pamela's urging, but I wouldn't know that until later. I just saw it as another chance to play some ball. I had recently left the team at FIT. I wasn't playing much and Coach Rippy's quick hook whenever I made a mistake activated the insecurities I still carried just beneath my confident-seeming surface.

Competition—going up against bigger and better players—never scared me. But coaches sure as hell did. I was the kind of athlete who constantly looked over at the coach whenever I made a mistake on the court, fearful that he'd yank me.

I was too used to street ball. I'd go up against all-star talent in summer league play, average twenty-five points a game, but because those rosters were so short, I never worried about getting pulled after a bad play. School ball was different. Mess up there and coaches subbed you out in a heartbeat.

Looking back, I was mentally weak.

Coach Rippy was trying to toughen me up. But I was too impatient, or too worried about my own ego, to learn the lessons he was trying to teach me. I'd give anything to have had the mind-set then that I have today. It's one of the reasons I'd later have so much admiration for NBA great Allen Iverson.

A.I. was a little dude who didn't fear anything, especially coaches. He understood that players operated best when they didn't worry about mistakes, and he combined the best aspects of street ball's creativity and the more disciplined game played in college and the pros.

That was brought home for me during a playoff game I covered in 1999 for the *Philadelphia Inquirer.* The game matched Iverson's 76ers against the Orlando Magic. Philly's top draft pick that year was a streaky point guard named Larry Hughes.

Hughes had a fine rookie season and was having a terrific playoff series when at some point he messed up. Sixers' coach Larry Brown immediately called a time-out for the sole purpose of yelling at, and then yanking, Hughes.

A.I. sized up the situation the moment the ref's whistle blew to halt play. He literally sprinted across the floor before Brown could lay into the young rookie, covered both of Hughes's ears, and ushered him to the bench. A.I. then went back to Brown and told him to leave Hughes alone, that he was doing fine and didn't need Brown messing with his head and confidence.

Brown calmed down; so did Hughes. The Sixers went on to win the opening playoff series in four games. The fearlessness that A.I. showed was something I simply didn't have, and I admired the hell out of it.

What I thought would be a quick hour at the park with Funny turned into an intense all-day workout: shooting drills, ball-handling drills, passing and defensive drills. He paid special attention to my footwork. Funny also knew a few of the fellas who balled at the park and had them waiting for me. Big, physical dudes who weren't afraid to throw an elbow or anything else—a couple of them were neighborhood dope dealers—they knocked me around pretty good to see what I could take.

They could also hoop.

It was all part of Funny's plan.

"You're not embarrassing my ass," he told me at one point. "I'm not doing a damn thing for you until I can verify what you've got."

Apparently, I showed him enough. As darkness fell over the court, we called it a day and Funny gave me his assessment:

"You can ball. Tell your momma you're going away next weekend. I'm taking you south for a tryout at my alma mater."

I knew nothing about Winston-Salem State. In fact, I knew nothing about HBCUs, had no historical reference for them. Growing up on the East Coast, it was all Big East basketball and whatever else I saw on TV. I'd never seen, or even heard of, an HBCU program in my life.

Yet, desperate to get away from where I'd grown up and put myself in a position for a better life, all I needed to know was that Winston-Salem State was a four-year school with a program that offered full scholarships and a bachelor's degree. I'd figure out the rest when I got there.

As promised, Funny picked me up early the next Saturday morning and we started the long drive south. We sped down I-95, through Delaware and past Baltimore, D.C., and Richmond, before picking up I-85 and snaking down through North Carolina.

We passed a whole different world from New York City: wooded hills and red barns and cows who didn't give a damn about who was driving by them. We only pulled off the road to gas up or get something to eat at a rest stop.

The car radio blared R&B and hip-hop the whole way down as Funny went on about Coach Gaines and all he had accomplished over the decades. He talked about the great players he'd coached, and the challenges he'd overcome growing up and coaching in the Jim Crow South, which included much of the same rural terrain we were speeding through.

He also emphasized Coach Gaines's intolerance for bullshit and elaborated on his no-nonsense approach. Coach would jump clean up his ass if Funny wasted his time bringing some nobody from Hollis, Queens, down to his school if he couldn't ball.

"Coach will let me know within five minutes whether or not it was worth it," Funny explained. "If he thinks you can't play, he'll tell me right to my face that I wasted his time. To you, he'll just say, 'Nice meeting you, boy.' So, if there was ever a time in your life you need to be ready, it's now. Fuck pressure."

To prepare me for that challenge, Funny went on about my mental game and improving my confidence—areas that had taken a hit not only during my time at FIT but throughout my entire childhood.

"You got a game," he told me. "But you got a lot of demons in your head."

Ten hours later, the highway deposited us in Winston-Salem. We found an InnKeeper motel and rested up for the practice I'd attend on Sunday afternoon.

The next day we drove onto the redbrick campus at the edge of downtown and headed straight to the 3,200-seat C. E. Gaines Center, named after the man himself. The team's practice facility was in the Whitaker Gymnasium, the Rams' run-down former home, right next to it.

The team was already scrimmaging when we arrived. Coach eyed the action from the bottom row of the empty bleachers. At age sixty-four, he was still as big as a damn house. He came as advertised: six feet five inches, two hundred eighty pounds. When I approached, he never got up but simply looked me up and down, turned to Funny, and snapped: "This is the little motherfucker you've been bragging about?"

Funny laughed, though not too hard.

"Yeah, Coach," he said, then looked at me with something between hope and pity before he added, "I did my part, bro. You're on your own now."

Like Funny said, Coach Gaines made sure his time was not wasted. He meant what he said and said what he meant. He had zero tolerance for fools, and he had even less tolerance for fools he deemed lazy.

That I was a street baller who'd played less than a season in high school and rode the bench at a JuCo better known for fashion than basketball, made the likelihood of my ever meeting, let alone playing for, a man of Coach Gaines's stature seem all but impossible.

I'd barely had time to stretch or warm up when, a couple minutes later, Coach blew his whistle to halt play and insert me into the scrimmage. He teamed me up with a couple starters, including his senior point guard, Charlie Spell.

Charlie quickly showed the generous character he'd developed after four years under Coach Gaines. When Coach made it clear I was supposed to be a shooter, Charlie made sure I knew how certain plays were run so that I got the ball and could showcase whatever I brought to the table. Charlie had the ability to make everybody around him better, even an unknown, undersized New York City kid like me.

Less than five minutes in, however, Coach Gaines's whistle stopped play cold. Watching me run around and pass the ball every time it was thrown to me, he'd seen enough. He summoned me to his bleacher seat and, in front of the entire team, asked, "Ain't you supposed to be a shooter?"

"Uh, y-yes, sir," I stuttered, nervous as hell.

Coach wasn't interested in my answer. Only in his solution.

"Then shoot the fucking ball, man!"

His words echoed through the empty gym. Everybody roared with laughter. They knew I was simply overcompensating for nerves. Before I stepped back onto the court, Charlie wrapped his arms around my shoulders, looked me in the eye and said simply, "Relax, bro. You're here for a reason. Just do what you came here to do."

That did it. Over the next hour or so in that old gym, everything vanished from my mind except basketball. Suddenly, I was no longer Stephen Smith. For the next hour, I looked like someone whom the basketball world would come to know as Steph Curry.

I couldn't miss: from the wing, the corner, the key; from fifteen feet, twenty feet, twenty-five feet. It didn't matter. Whatever I put up went in. I never shot like that before or since. During one stretch, someone counted seventeen straight made three pointers. Throughout that after noon, I don't remember the ball even touching the rim.

When Coach Gaines's whistle ended the practice, players left the floor shaking their heads. Charlie put his arms around me again and told me it was one of the greatest shooting performances he'd ever seen, scrimmage or no scrimmage.

Another player, Toby, walked up to me and said with confidence: "Welcome to Winston-Salem State, bro."

As I walked out of the gym with Funny, Coach Gaines was waiting outside his office. He waved me over and asked a few questions about my academic aspirations, what I wanted to be after college, and, most important, was I ready to go to work.

When he finished interrogating me, all Coach said was, "See you in August, son."

I'd gotten a full scholarship.

Finally!

CHAPTER 5

"GODDAMNIT, THAT BOY WANTS TO BE SOMEBODY!"

My arrival at Winston-Salem State was inauspicious, to say the least.

I did not take a flight to Winston-Salem. There was no car service waiting for me, either. Most poignantly, there was no one accompanying me. I was all alone.

My mother, busy with a double-shift workday, simply kissed me goodbye, reminded me to make her proud, and ultimately warned, "don't embarrass me," before sending me off with $100 in my pocket.

My sisters all hugged me and wished me luck before saying goodbye, with Linda, the avid sports fan, serving as the only exuberant one, imploring me, "Go handle your business, bro."

My father just said, "See ya, Stephen. Good luck down there," and went back to watching an old Western. I was officially a young man now. And if I didn't have anyone figuratively holding my hand before, no one officially was holding it now. A few pairs of jeans, some shirts, sneakers, and one pair of shoes were all I had as company.

I was on my own.

The Greyhound bus took sixteen hours to get from Port Authority on 42nd Street in New York City down to Winston-Salem State. A cab got me from the bus station to campus. When I arrived, Coach Gaines was on the steps of Brown Hall on campus, ready to register me in.

Life at an HBCU was a revelation. I was surrounded by Blackness— proud Blackness. It was different than growing up in a Black neighborhood in New York City. Hollis, Queens, felt like a community that had been thrown together there simply because we all were in the same economic boat—a very, very leaky economic boat. At Winston-Salem, there were Black kids who were well off, Black kids who weren't, and everything else in between. Yet it felt like all of us were there to handle our business, aspiring to get a college degree.

That played out in front of us every day. Black men and women were in leadership roles everywhere. Most of the professors were Black. Most of the administrators were Black. The school's chancellor was Black. They all extended their hands to uplift the students they oversaw.

The fact that they looked like us made it especially meaningful. They weren't just doing their jobs, they were investing in us. In return, they expected us to pay them back with a commitment to excellence, along with our involvement in matters that affected our community.

Coach Gaines embodied everything I wanted to be: intelligent, accomplished, a forceful activist (yet one who knew when to engage in diplomacy). He'd taken on causes his whole career: integrating basketball, pushing for the hiring of Black coaches, giving HBCUs a higher profile.

Born May 21, 1923, on the banks of the Ohio River in Paducah, Kentucky, Coach Gaines grew up surrounded by coal mining country. Despite his smarts, talent, drive, and size, his only college options were the three HBCUs that accepted him: Lincoln of Pennsylvania; Howard, which he attended for two years; and Morgan State, in Baltimore, where he transferred to play football and earn a BS in chemistry. The experience of being treated as a second-class citizen despite his first-class brains and character should have left him scarred and bitter. Yet, somehow, it never did. At least not noticeably.

"You march on and move forward, son," Coach Gaines would tell me repeatedly. "Either that or let it get the best of you, then don't do shit in life. Your choice."

Those weren't the only words Coach said that would resonate with me. While most players practiced and then fled the gym to go about their business, I practically lived in Coach Gaines's office. I could be found there almost every weekday, not to beg for playing time, but because I was fascinated by what I might learn.

Example: one day, out of the blue, in walked a tall, thin, balding Black man in his seventies who represented practically the whole history of basketball. John McLendon, retired by then, had once mentored Coach Gaines. His own mentor was none other than the actual man who'd invented hoops: James Naismith.

While coaching eight teams to a national Black college championship, and three more to NAIA (National Association of Intercollegiate Athletics) titles, McLendon himself invented or helped develop some of the most important components of the modern game: the fast break, the full-court zone press, and the four-corners offense. He'd basically taken the game his own mentor created, then helped reinvent the whole damn thing.

Being a fly on that office wall during the back-and-forth between McLendon and Gaines was like sitting in on a doctorate-level class in basketball and life.

They talked. I listened.

Walking through the door on another random day: Earl "the Pearl" Monroe, the greatest player in Winston-Salem history and an inventor and perfecter of so many moves (like the spin) as a playground legend in Philadelphia that he was dubbed "Black Jesus."

Winston-Salem eventually retired Monroe's number ten. His

exploits in college became another example of sport's impact outside the lines. So many locals wanted to watch him play during the team's 1967 national championship run that games were moved off campus, from the cramped confines of Whitaker Gymnasium, where I'd auditioned months earlier, to the much bigger Winston-Salem Memorial Coliseum. In a town where sit-ins were necessary to forcibly desegregate lunch counters just a few years earlier, Blacks and whites sat together in awe of Monroe's talents.

On days when no one visited his office, Coach Gaines provided his own history lessons for me, talking about the challenges he faced, how hard it was for his generation compared to mine.

"Tough times make tough people," he'd say. "Compared to us, you young fuckers got it easy as hell. That's why y'all are so damn soft. If not physically, definitely mentally."

Those words resonated with me.

Despite the numerous times he'd chide me about the chronic tendinitis I had in both knees, Coach always supported me. He admitted on several occasions that it damn sure wasn't because of my production on the basketball court. It was because he thought I had a shot at achieving big things in life that would ultimately benefit the university, the Black community, and society as a whole.

We talked about everything—politics, societal issues, basketball— and I became comfortable enough with "Big House" to say whatever was on my mind. He didn't always care for the mouth I had on me, but he knew I was keen on gathering facts, unafraid to be a contrarian, and fearless in confronting the "establishment" if I truly believed it was wrong. He knew I wouldn't take on battles without the ammo I needed to put up a fight.

Coach Gaines viewed me as a rebel. But more important, he stressed that if I was going to be a rebel, I should at least have the decency to be a rebel with a cause. He insisted that I stand for something, and that I not be like typical folks he deemed as doing things just to benefit themselves.

He thought I could someday have influence on the lives of other Black people, and he wanted me to understand what that responsibility meant and what it would require.

He wanted me to embrace it.

I didn't know it as I sat in his office those many days, but my future takes—on *SportsCenter*, *First Take*, CNN, ABC, Fox News, et al.— were being honed.

I had brought that recurring limp from chronic tendinitis in both of my knees with me to Winston-Salem State in 1988, courtesy of playing every day since I was a kid on the hard, unforgiving streets of New York City. Coach Gaines would watch me hobbling around like someone three times my age, then growl with a straight, annoying face: "I'm from Kentucky, son. Do you know what we did to horses we saw hobbling around in Kentucky? We'd shoot 'em!"

Coach knew I could still ball, even on jacked-up knees; in my mind, I was damn sure there weren't twelve people on any campus who could ball better or who were more deserving of being on a roster than me—even if I mostly rode the bench and watched other Rams get more playing time. Coach Gaines subscribed to the Iron Man theory of substitution and rarely played more than six men during a game.

My time would come, so long as my knees got healthy. I was convinced of that.

Yet all the swagger in the world didn't matter in the end. What mattered was that the ache and stiffness in my knees didn't allow me to practice and play continuously. I couldn't always do what I needed to on the court, even if I still thought I was better on suspect wheels than most other players were on healthy ones.

Coach Gaines knew I was never going to be a star player, but he didn't care. "Wanna know why that boy's still around?" my teammate and one of my best friends, Marc Turner, told me he asked one day, following a practice I had missed inside the Whitaker Gymnasium. "Goddamnit, that boy wants to be somebody." He expected his faith in me to be validated long after I stopped shooting and the ball stopped bouncing.

Ambition was important to Coach Gaines, but ambition with purpose, direction, and focus meant everything to him. While almost every college coach swears he prioritizes turning young boys and girls into accomplished men and women, Coach Gaines embodied that uplift, in his own gruff manner.

It was the HBCU way.

Make no mistake about it, Big House wanted you on his team because you could play. Period. But he didn't want to talk with you if playing ball was all you were about. He'd endured too much, made too many sacrifices. He had seen too many lives ruined or lost to tolerate folks wasting their blessings or chances.

History had taught him the value of time and opportunity. For those willing to waste their opportunities, he had neither the time nor the patience.

I knew he loved me, even if it came through in his signature curmudgeonly way.

That is, until I broke his heart.

My knee exploded three months into the season.

It happened during a scrimmage on a cold, bleak Sunday night inside the Gaines Center in February 1989. I took a pass in stride while sprinting up court on a fast break and charged toward the hoop. As I rose to finish at the rim, I heard a loud pop that echoed in that otherwise-empty gym like somebody had jumped on some Bubble Wrap.

Pain shot up my body with every step, but I stayed on the court, hustling back on defense, then trying to sprint the other way in transition. I finally stopped and asked to come out. I hobbled over to Coach

Gaines and, for the first time since I'd heard it pop, looked down at my knee. Swollen to three times its normal size, it looked more like a balloon ready to burst. I didn't need a doctor to know something was drastically wrong.

The worst was confirmed once I arrived at the Wake Forest University Medical Center: cracked right patella—busted kneecap. The doctor called my mother, and, after the two of them talked for several minutes, he handed me the phone.

There was a brief moment of silence on the other end. Then the same mother who'd worked tirelessly through all her ups and downs, who never had time to go anywhere because she never took a day off from work, said simply, "I'm on my way down there."

I knew it had to be bad.

I underwent reconstructive surgery once the swelling subsided, four days later. Extensive rehabilitation would be a minimum of eight months, and doctors couldn't guarantee if I'd ever walk straight again, let alone play basketball.

For all intents and purposes, my basketball "career"—half a season as a high school sub, half a season as a JuCo sub, half a season as a Division II college sub, along with two memorable tryouts and all the incalculable hours on New York's asphalt courts—was now kaput. The cold reality of that left me devastated.

Following the surgery, another dose of cold reality hit me square in the face: my mother's insurance wouldn't cover my medical expenses in North Carolina. If I wanted to rehab my knee under a doctor's supervision, I would have to leave Winston-Salem and return to New York.

I was not interested in hearing any of that. Being at Winston-Salem State, away from New York, at an HBCU where I was surrounded by my own was absolute heaven. I had also fallen in love with a hazel-eyed beauty from the Tar Heel state named Michelle, whose looks paled in comparison to her personality. She was one of the sweetest girls in the world. She humbled me—no easy task. She was never unkind: if I did something that wronged her, she didn't hesitate to let me know, but she expressed it not with anger but by showing me that she'd been hurt. It was impossible to stay mad at her. She loved me to pieces, and I loved her back. So, my mentality was that it would be a cold day in hell before I left school to head back home. Whatever it took, I was staying, even if I had to rehab my damn self. I put off leaving for as long as I could.

I hobbled around campus the rest of that semester and stayed through the summer, working two jobs: camp counselor at a Salvation Army Boys & Girls Club, in Winston-Salem, every weekday from 7:30 a.m. to 4 p.m., then a night shift loading and unloading eighteen-wheelers for Roadway trucking, in nearby Kernersville.

I tried rehabbing the knee on my own, but it never got much better, and I wasn't able to resume playing basketball. Evidently, sporadic visits to the weight room, in between summer work and that fall semester's classes, weren't enough to strengthen it. I couldn't deal with the pain any longer. I hated the idea of leaving college, Michelle, and the teammates I lived with in Brown Hall (Marc Turner, Kevin "Skeet" Edwards, Boris Battle, Gary "Spank" Stephens, Monte "Money" Ross, and Phil "Playboy Smooth" Hayes)—our on-court camaraderie had morphed into a brotherhood. The thought of returning to the streets and combustion of New York, just because my mother's medical insurance wouldn't cover me in North Carolina, left me feeling depressed and resentful as hell.

I was convinced I'd lose everything I'd worked so hard for. I didn't know if I'd ever be healthy enough to keep my basketball scholarship. I was worried about losing the sweetest girl I'd ever met. I didn't even know if I'd ever come back to college.

When I broke the news to Coach Gaines in his office that December that I was leaving, the look of disappointment on his face bordered on shame. It sounded like I was simply quitting—on him, the team, the school. It ran counter to everything he stood for.

"Just go, boy," he said, shaking his head. "Just go!"

I'm reminded of that moment every time I watch the scene from the movie *Lean on Me*, when Morgan Freeman, as tough-love principal Joe Clark, is told by a student that he's leaving school because "it's just not cut out for me."

Clark's response: "You'll be dead in a year, son. You hear what I'm saying? You'll be dead in a year."

That mood and the look on Freeman's face reflects the essence of the moment when I told Coach Gaines goodbye: the disappointment, the shame, and the belief that I was headed down a dead end was palpable.

Even now, all these years later, I still can't shake that feeling.

The only other person I said goodbye to was Michelle. That wasn't much easier.

"This is so unfair," she said, crying uncontrollably. "I can't believe you're doing this!" I kissed her goodbye and headed back home to New York.

I couldn't take any more goodbyes. Depressed and inconsolable, I split with hardly a word to anybody else.

For eight months, my life was dominated by excruciating rehab three times a week, including electrical-stimulus machines and squats and running. After all that, I still wasn't much closer to ever getting back on the court. My mother gave it to me straight, no chaser.

"Well, so much for basketball," she told me. "Now you see what can happen to you in a single moment. So, what do you plan to do with the rest of your life?"

The only thing I aspired to at that moment was to not live at home. Before my injury, I'd been locked in on basketball and what I might parlay it into, perhaps even a stint playing overseas. Clearly, I was dreaming. Clearly, I had some figuring out to do, otherwise I'd never get my mother off my back.

I was majoring in mass communications because I could talk and write, but I never really thought about it much beyond that. But with my mother waiting impatiently for me to answer, and my sister Linda standing to the side, I just blurted out, "I'm going to be a broadcast journalist."

The only thing I knew about being a broadcast journalist was that I idolized two people above everyone else: Bryant Gumbel and Howard Cosell. There were others I respected and liked—Ted Koppel, Bob Costas, Ed Bradley—but Gumbel and Cosell stood out. Gumbel was easy for me to idolize. He covered sports. He anchored and delivered hard news on NBC's *Today* show before he went on to win Emmys on HBO's deep-dive feature and investigative show, *Real Sports*. Simply put: he was a Black man who could do it all.

"If you're going to do TV, he's who you should want to be like," Linda interjected. "You're a Black man. Reading a prompter and having a smile on your face ain't the kind of career that's going to take you places. You'd better bring something else to the table. Knowing how to write and report will take you far, whether you're in front of the camera or not."

Gumbel's existence confirmed for me that I didn't have to be a white man to succeed at broadcasting.

But Cosell was my ultimate inspiration. He was an icon. His distinctive voice on ABC's *Wide World of Sports* helped make boxing popular again in the U.S., his undaunted outspokenness a perfect complement for the outsize brashness of Muhammad Ali.

Cosell also defined the modern-day color commentator with his tell-it-like-it-is role as part of a wildly popular three-man crew, with Frank Gifford and "Dandy" Don Meredith, on *Monday Night Football*, from its 1970 inception to 1983. Cosell never played college or pro sports. Yet there he was, entrenched as the preeminent voice in the world of sports. No one was more recognizable, more magnetic, or more captivating in front of the camera.

Given his inherent shortcomings—nasally pipes, face for radio—Cosell's success cemented my belief that even a kid from Hollis, Queens, could be a major player in sports broadcasting. I didn't have to play professionally to pull it off.

Though my mother had questions, she co-signed at once when she heard me fantasizing right in front of her about what I could become. But before I could take any steps in the direction of my newly stated dream, I first had to learn one more lesson.

A month before the 1989 fall semester began, I traveled down to Winston-Salem to tell Coach Gaines I planned to return to school. If I wasn't a changed man, I was definitely a more focused one. But he didn't look happy to see me. When I asked if I could earn back my scholarship, he scowled and barked, "Not before you see Mr. Hindsman."

Theodore Hindsman was head of the university's financial aid department. Unlike Coach Gaines, Mr. Hindsman displayed a perpetual smile no matter what the circumstance—good news, bad news, no news. In the year I had come to know him, I never saw Hindsman display a frown even once. It actually drove me kind of nuts.

Yet when Hindsman saw me walk into the financial aid office this time, that's exactly what he did: frown. He didn't say a word, either, not even hello.

"Hey, Mr. Hindsman," I said, smiling, oblivious as to why he would be perturbed at seeing me. "Coach Gaines sent me to see you."

"What could you possibly want from me," Hindsman replied, almost rudely brushing me off. "We have nothing to talk about."

I'd never seen Mr. Hindsman interact like that with anyone. It alarmed me so much that I turned around and then waited six hours for him in the parking lot in the back of the Financial Aid Building until he left his office at the end of the day. I had to get to the bottom of it.

Standing next to his car, I insisted he tell me why he'd treated me that way. He answered with his own question.

"Why did you leave school without coming over to my office to explain yourself and say goodbye?"

Before I could answer, Mr. Hindsman exploded on me. He went on to tell me that although I'd lost my basketball scholarship because of my knee injury, my grades were good enough for him to award me an academic scholarship. He said he had called to give me the news, but I never answered my phone, and that only then was he aware of the quitter I was. (Back in New York, I didn't return anybody's calls—I'd been too depressed.) Because I never called him back, Mr. Hindsman explained, he had been forced to give the scholarship to another deserving student. I'll never forget what he said to me next, right there in the deserted parking lot.

"For more than a year you got to know me and a whole bunch of professors. You convinced us, no matter how much you loved basketball, you were interested in being more than a ballplayer. Then the second you had basketball taken away from you, you quit.

"You quit on this school. You quit on Coach Gaines. You quit on the professors who believed in you. You quit on me. And you did something I never thought you'd do: you quit on yourself. I'm ashamed of you. I'm disappointed. You're not the Stephen Smith I knew, that's for sure."

It was the first time I cried since childhood.

Tears streamed down my face. It hurt more to hear those words from Mr. Hindsman than it had hurt when I sat on my back porch in Hollis years earlier and overheard my father tell my mother I was a "lost cause."

My father didn't believe in me. But Mr. Hindsman did. So did Coach Gaines. So did my professors, all of whom cared about me, were demanding of me, let me know they expected big things from me and wouldn't let me take any gifts I had for granted. They all saw something in me and let me know it. They held me to a higher standard.

I didn't really have a clue what it was they expected me to be. I still wasn't very confident. I just knew I was a workaholic and hoped that my hard work would pay off.

The day Mr. Hindsman ripped into me is the only time in my life I've found myself begging for forgiveness. Hearing the disappointment in his voice, knowing I'd let so many people down by giving up, truly shamed me. I'd been short-sighted and selfish, thinking of nobody but myself. And I knew that Mr. Hindsman had every right to say what he said. He spoke on behalf of everyone who felt they knew better about me, who expected more.

In his searing, heartfelt diatribe, Mr. Hindsman had defined for me the true meaning of accountability. I had some making up to do, big time—to him, Professor Marilyn Roseboro, Professor Larry Little, Dr. Brookshaw, and Dr. Sadler, to name just a few. It wasn't enough for Mr. Hindsman to hear me apologize. He needed me to show my remorse to him, to Coach Gaines, and to all of my professors by acting and behaving in a way that let them know I was an ambitious young man aiming to make a difference. Not one who would flee the moment times got rough.

I had to prove I wasn't just talking the talk, that I had honestly portrayed who the hell I was.

Mr. Hindsman informed me that the first step on the way to earning back his trust would be working for a man named Robert DeVaughn, who headed the telecommunications department at WSSU. In doing so, I would keep my basketball scholarship—despite the fact that I could hardly play, due to my knees—but it would be wrapped up into a work-study program, meaning I'd now have to earn my scholarship money; I wasn't getting it for free anymore.

I was determined to get back in Mr. Hindsman's good graces, but I thought that would mean working for *him*, not someone I'd never met, and I couldn't help myself from telling him how I felt.

"Come on, Mr. Hindsman," I said. "I know you're trying to punish me. I get it and I accept it. But help a brother out, man. I don't know this Mr. DeVaughn. He's probably boring as hell. For all I know he's not going to teach me anything. He's just going to run me ragged with menial tasks, or he's going to have me falling asleep on the job. Please don't do this to me."

Mr. Hindsman flashed his huge smile and said: "Boy! Turn around."

I did as he asked, and found a short, pudgy guy, cigarette in hand, standing there with a smirk on his face.

"Mr. Stephen A. Smith," said Mr. Hindsman, "meet Robert DeVaughn—your new boss!"

He'd heard every word I said.

All I could say was, "Awwwwww, damn!"

When I wasn't studying, attempting to play basketball on my still-ailing knees, or working with Mr. DeVaughn, I devoted much of my time to writing for the *News Argus*, the student newspaper, mostly covering sports, under the byline Stephen A. Smith. Using my full name, middle initial included (which stands for Anthony, by the way), was a tribute to my mother, who gave me that name and always believed in me no matter what anyone said. I also covered Pop Warner football for the local Black-owned weekly, and hosted a late-night R&B show called *Tender Moments* on the school's radio station.

My on-court and off-court worlds soon collided and forced me to make a choice. Like the journalists I admired most, I chose to tell it like it is. Perfect example: Coach Gaines was in declining health. What worried us players most was how forgetful he'd become. He sometimes arrived at games wearing an eye patch; unbeknownst to most people, he'd suffered a couple of minor strokes.

I worried that one day he was just going to collapse on the sidelines, but he was a formidable legend and nobody seemed willing to confront him about his condition. The team knew it. We assumed his family and some administrative officials knew it. The fan base knew it. But I was the one who told Coach Gaines about my worries directly, during one of our sessions inside his office. I suggested that he needed to retire.

His response to me was pure Big House:

"Fuck off."

But I didn't let up. I told him I was dead serious and that if he continued to look unhealthy, I was going to write a column in the school paper saying he needed to step down.

He couldn't care less.

"Boy, I don't give a shit what you do," he said.

So I wrote the column.

And the shit hit the fan—with everybody but Coach Gaines.

My teammates later said they just prayed for me, knowing the blowback I'd get for the column. Assistant coaches, ever loyal to their legendary boss, wanted me tossed off the team. Hell, the damn chancellor of the school wanted me expelled (years later he claimed he had no recollection of the story).

Only Coach Gaines came to my rescue.

"The boy told me to my face he wanted me to retire, and he told me why," he explained to folks at the time. "He's an aspiring journalist who prides himself on calling it as he sees it. I didn't agree, because I didn't have to. But I have no problem with him doing what he did, because he looked me in the face and told me beforehand. That's how you're supposed to handle things in life, if you can. So just leave him alone."

For those wondering where I got the validation for my no-nonsense approach: Look no further.

Thus was Stephen A., Mr. Straight Shooter, born.

*   *   *

My first career break came when John Gates, a respected editorial-page editor at the *Winston-Salem Journal*, who taught a course in critical and persuasive writing, liked an essay I wrote for his class. He thought I was a natural sportswriter. A week later, he asked if I wanted to get lunch. To my surprise, when the next week arrived, he took me directly into the office of Terry Oberle, the sports editor of the *Winston-Salem Journal*.

Oberle talked with me for about five minutes, including about the column I wrote calling for Coach Gaines's retirement. He asked about my ambitions and my availability. Then Oberle asked me one last question:

"Can you start tonight?"

Five minutes earlier, I was writing for the student paper and relying on my mother and sister Arlyne to send me twenty bucks a week so I could buy the basic food groups I lived on: tuna fish, cereal, and milk. Beginning that night, I was a sports department clerk at the *Winston-Salem Journal*, making four hundred dollars a week!

It felt like I'd been handed fifty thousand dollars.

At the time, there was one Black reporter on staff—and then me as the new clerk. But Oberle's belief in me fueled my ambition, and the other writers and editors, all white, were just as supportive. That included Steve Mann, a die-hard conservative who didn't let a day go by without grumbling so I could hear: "Mike Tyson is a piece of shit." He knew it would rile me: Tyson, in his prime, was my favorite fighter.

After a week of mastering various clerical duties, including setting agate—the small-print stuff that's used to fill newspapers—I was assigned to write a feature about the Wake Forest men's soccer team, then ranked third in the nation. I'd never covered soccer in my life; in fact, the only time I'd ever watched the sport was during the 1980 Olympics, when Pele was an international superstar. That's it.

When I explained that to Oberle, he said what any boss worth his salt usually says:

"Figure it out."

I drove over to Wake Forest that afternoon and met the coach, Walt Chyzowych. A Ukrainian-born former coach of the U.S. national team, Coach Chyzowych didn't look like he suffered fools lightly. So I cut the bullshit and got straight to the matter at hand:

"I don't know a damn thing about soccer but I'm an aspiring sports writer, I've been assigned to write a feature on you guys, and it will go a really long way if I do this well. Can you please help me?"

Coach Chyzowych looked me straight in my eyes, paused for a few uncomfortable seconds, then asked: "When is this article due?" When I told him I had a week, he grabbed his whistle and blew, summoning his entire team over to the sidelines where we stood.

"Guys, this is Stephen A. Smith," said Coach Chyzowych. "He's the new guy on staff for the *Winston-Salem Journal*. He's been assigned to write an article on our program, and he's got a week to get it done. So for the next five days, you guys are to grant him whatever time he needs to talk to you, about anything he wants to talk about. He is to have complete access. We are going to help him. Understood?"

As a novice reporter, I could not have been luckier. Chyzowych and the players answered every question I had and explained anything I didn't understand. In five days, they gave me a crash course about soccer.

Early the next week, the paper ran a two-page pull-out feature on the program with my byline. It was prime newspaper real estate for any reporter. For a damn clerk, it was gold.

The next day Oberle called me back into his office.

"Congratulations," he said. "You're the new beat writer for Wake Forest soccer."

While still going to school, I filed at least four to five stories a week. I learned the sport, I learned the players, and I learned to report hard enough to stand behind whatever I wrote. Coach Chyzowych only encouraged that stance. Brutal honesty made him a successful coach, so he expected no less from whoever covered him and his players. The only times he called me out were when he thought I wasn't being candid or upfront enough in my stories.

"Do your job," he told me a few weeks after I started, when he thought an article was too soft or light on his players. "If you see things a certain way, call it. We see you at practice. You always come into the locker rooms. You talk with the guys. You asked what happened and you're always fair. That's all you owe an athlete, coach, or anyone you cover.

"So call it like it is," he repeated to make sure I got his point. "You're not in the business to be liked. You're in the business to be respected. Honesty, integrity, and fairness is what gets you respect. Not being liked."

Validation number two.

I completed my academic credits at Winston-Salem State in December 1991, then interned during the 1992 spring semester at the *Atlanta Journal-Constitution,* where I was afforded the chance to cover Atlanta Braves games, write about college football and pro basketball, and gain additional experience working in a newsroom. It enhanced my résumé, because I was accumulating published clips that actually appeared in a reputable newspaper while I was still a student, further showing editors how much I really wanted to be in this business.

That May, I marched across the stage in the graduation ceremony, accepting my bachelor of arts degree in mass communications. As the first in my family to receive a college degree, I was ecstatic. Both of my parents were in attendance, along with my sister Arlyne, and my college sweetheart, Michelle. (She graduated the following year.)

They all looked happy and proud, and I got the sense they all recognized how hard I'd worked to get here. But they sent me another message too.

"The hard work starts now, Steve," Arlyne told me. "You're officially an adult."

I knew what she meant, and to be honest, I was petrified. I no longer had school to hide behind. I had to get out there and earn a living now.

CHAPTER 6

"YOU'RE GONNA BE THE
BIGGEST STAR IN SPORTS MEDIA!"

After graduating, I landed a job at the High Point, North Carolina, bureau of the Greensboro *News & Record*, and lived in nearby Archdale. Officially, I was an editorial assistant, not a reporter, earning $15,300 a year, but though I wasn't earning much money, I was gaining valuable experience that I expected would pay dividends down the road. I was making contacts and cultivating relationships within the industry.

Things were good. I was over the whole basketball thing; I had recovered from the disappointment of knowing that my dreams of hooping were in the past. My passion for sports would be fulfilled through journalism.

Between 8:30 a.m. and 6 p.m. each weekday, my job included listing school-lunch menus, calendar items, and local birth listings. But several nights per week, from 7 p.m. to nearly midnight, I covered high school sports. I was not paid extra, just compensated with gas money for the miles I logged, which I piled up in droves. Pick any small town between Greensboro and Charlotte and I was there.

The sports culture in that area was huge. People cared, and teams were loaded with athletes who were going places. It wasn't quite *Friday*

Night Lights, but it sure as hell tried to be. For me, it was a chance to get bylines for the portfolio I'd need when it was time for me to move on. My initial goal then was simple: Show my commitment to being a newspaper journalist. Focus on the job. Master the craft.

There was no Twitter, Facebook, or Instagram. You didn't acquire a voice using 280 characters to accumulate millions of followers. Before social media, there were steps you had to climb before reaching a place where you could editorialize and give your opinion.

The task for me felt especially daunting, given how few Black journalists populated newspaper sports departments and how even fewer reached the level of featured columnist. But I was up for the challenge. I knew the route most aspiring columnists had to take: staff reporter, beat writer, then maybe features writer or investigative reporter, and then, only after years of those jobs, would I ultimately aim for a spot as a general sports columnist. A lofty goal, no doubt, especially back in the 1990s.

So I kept my head down and worked my ass off. While happy with the progress I was making with my career, I was bored as hell in High Point. The only thing it was known for was being the furniture capital of the world—and I could not afford any furniture. I was a city kid out of his element. I had no real money and couldn't even afford the highway tolls I'd have to pay to drive back to visit New York.

At that point, working as an editorial assistant at a print newspaper, thinking about broadcast journalism was only a distraction.

Except to my brother, Basil.

Nobody stoked my ambition more than my big brother. Whatever our relationship lacked when we were younger, because of our age difference and the general chaos in our house, it was more than made up for during my high school years, and especially after that visit to Texas. My brother became the father that my father never was. He also became my most reliable friend, closest confidant, and biggest booster.

When he had left our house, he had limited confidence and abundant self-doubt. But when he visited home a few years later, he was a new man. At six feet fall, maybe 180 pounds, with a medium-sized Afro and a perpetual smile, Basil became Mr. Positivity—in fact, he was a fan of Dale Carnegie—Mr. "How to Win Friends and Influence People"—and had become a salesman extraordinaire.

He was also hell-bent on making sure his little brother distanced himself from our father and the neighborhood and found a way to get rid of the questions and doubts plaguing him.

Even from a thousand miles away, he was there for me at every critical juncture. He was there when I got left back in school and doubted myself. When I wondered if I'd ever be good enough to earn a basketball scholarship. When I questioned if I'd ever be smart enough to get a college degree and make something of myself. When I worried if I'd ever be man enough to earn my father's respect.

During every one of those moments, Basil was there to provide a nugget of uplift. He never believed failure was anyone's destiny and he fixated on making sure I never let doubt dominate my thoughts. That's what he provided during every conversation, every phone call, every visit.

In August after my graduation, he was staying in Georgetown, Maryland, on one of his sales trips, and I drove up to see him. When I griped about how much I hated living in High Point, Basil brushed aside my complaints and insisted that I'd only just begun.

"Newspapers aren't your last stop," he said. "You'll be on TV. You'll be at ESPN. You're gonna be the biggest star in sports media. You're gonna be a household name. When you speak, people everywhere are gonna listen. You'll be the modern-day Howard Cosell. Just wait, you'll see."

It was pure Basil.

Two months passed. On October 11, 1992, my phone rang at 11:00 a.m. as it did every Sunday during that football season. Linda and Basil called every Sunday during the NFL season so we could make our picks of that week's games. We threw in five bucks a week and at the end of the season someone would collect the winner-take-all pot.

I loved those three-way calls. Linda, a die-hard Giants fan; me, a die-hard Steelers fan (courtesy of the Immaculate Reception in 1972, which I witnessed the first time I ever watched football); and Basil, who just wanted to win the damn pool. He was about the dollars, not fandom. We trash-talked the way sports fans trash talk: as a way to bond. If the Steelers lost that week, Linda rode me unmercifully. If the Giants lost, I returned the favor.

These calls would go on for at least an hour. Between picks, we caught up with whatever else each of us had been up to that week, and what was going on with the rest of the family and our mutual friends. Basil was a roving salesman, selling magazines door-to-door with at least a dozen others who traveled together in a minibus across the country, stopping in a city for a month at a time, then moving on to a new town and a fresh set of doors to knock on. That October he was in Texas. Greensboro was about a nine-hour drive to New York for me, and I felt a million miles away from everything there, so the calls with Linda, where she'd catch us up on all the news of the neighborhood, gave both me and Basil a taste of home.

So, when the phone rang as it typically did on Sundays, I snatched it quickly with my sheet full of picks already in hand, ready to fire away. This time, however, only Linda was on the other end of the line. Her voice was subdued, solemn.

"What up, Sis? You ready to get your butt kicked this week with these picks?"

"Nah, bro, I'm not calling about our picks," she said. "Basil's in the hospital in El Paso. He was in a bad car accident last night. He's not breathing on his own. They're trying to save him now. We just found out minutes ago."

My heart dropped. I couldn't speak. I was paralyzed. All I could hear were her words "he's not breathing on his own."

When we hung up, I dropped to my knees and prayed: "God, please save my brother. Please don't take him away from me." *Basil will survive*; that's what I kept saying to myself.

Then I washed dishes, vacuumed the apartment—anything to distract me from thinking the worst. The whole time I kept reminding myself of what Basil told me over and over through the years: "Keep thinking the worst and that's exactly what's going to come your way. Don't make me tell you that shit again!"

I tried, with every fiber of my being, to think positive, but I was scared shitless.

Everything just felt wrong. I felt it. I knew it. And my attempts to make Basil's words preeminent in my thoughts were to no avail. I couldn't stop imagining the worst. Forty-five minutes later, the phone in my apartment rang again. The moment I picked it up, I heard screams in the background. It wasn't difficult to decipher that it was Linda on the line and my sisters Arlyne, Abigail, and Carmen in the background. They've been my sisters all my life. I know them.

"He's gone, bro," Linda said, her voice cracking as I heard my other sisters wailing. "They couldn't save him. He died five minutes ago."

My mother took the phone to talk to me herself. She was more spiritual than ever at that stage of her life. A devout Episcopalian, everything was simply God's plan in her eyes. That's why she stayed with my father, despite everything he'd done to her.

Nothing was cruel. Nothing was unfair. Nothing qualified as a cause to be miserable.

"God has made his decision," I remember her saying that morning. "Everything is all right. Basil's in a better place."

I hung the phone right up on my mother. I didn't even say goodbye, because I did not want to hear those words in that moment. My brother was gone. I hated God's plan. And I expressed as much with my tears, after I collapsed on my couch and cried.

And cried. And cried.

My big brother, my best friend, my most trusted confidant, was gone. In the days that followed, I learned what happened:

Basil was in one of those stretch minivans that fit about fifteen people. He'd driven most of the day through Texas and decided to let someone else take the wheel so he could get some sleep. The new driver briefly took his eye off the highway while playing with the radio.

Somebody cut in front of him. The driver looked up and swerved sharply to avoid the other vehicle. The van flipped and rolled over numerous times.

My brother didn't have his seat belt on because he was lying down, asleep. Of the fifteen people in the van, Basil—my brother—was the only one killed.

And a part of me died, too.

With the family still broke, still struggling, I had to scrape up enough money to get to New York later that week for the funeral. When I arrived at our house in Hollis, neighbors and friends sat on their front stoops, despondent and silent. My sisters were inconsolable. My mother was her stoic self. My father, meanwhile, walked around crying and repeating, "It should've been me who died."

We all shook our heads: none of us believed he was the least bit sincere.

I gave a eulogy at the service held inside a packed funeral home on Linden Boulevard, a few blocks from our house. I talked about Basil's laugh, his jokes, his incessant positive attitude. The mood lightened for a minute when I told the story from when I was eight, when all of us kids were playing Family Feud in the house, with Basil acting as a stand-in for the famed-host, Richard Dawson. When he asked us, "Name a beverage," I jumped up first and screamed, "Steak!"

Basil laughed about that story anytime anyone brought it up, until the day he died.

I then reminded everyone about how much Basil was loved and cherished and how he had earned every bit of those sentiments. I talked about the lives he touched along the way, pointing to some friends from Basil's days in the air force, who'd traveled from Germany, Japan, and the Middle East to attend his funeral. And, of course, childhood buddies — hard-core dudes from Hollis — who had to be held up by loved ones due to how despondent they were over Basil's passing.

Basil left behind two daughters, Shanelle and Candace, which was heartbreaking. Candace, his younger daughter, who was about three, went up to Basil's coffin at the funeral and said, "Why is everyone looking sad? Daddy is just sleeping!" Everyone who heard it immediately started bawling.

After we buried him at a cemetery in Yonkers, New York, I walked around in a miserable, zombie-like state, at some point passing by the park at P.S. 192. A handful of people from the neighborhood, drug dealers and hard-core criminals whom Basil knew from childhood but hadn't been at the service were waiting, knowing that I'd eventually drop by.

"We couldn't have our last image of him in a casket," Kenny Bang, Poolie's big brother and a dear friend of the family's who was not one of the criminals I alluded to, said on behalf of the people who didn't attend. "That's the only reason we weren't there."

A few months later, I was back in New York and I ran into Jam Master Jay on the street. He'd been performing out of the country with Run-DMC when Basil was killed. He couldn't believe Basil was dead.

Neither could I.

I drove back to North Carolina a few days after the funeral. I never thought about suicide, but I sure as hell didn't like my life much at that point. I didn't give a damn if I lived or died. I was empty, still in mourning, still disbelieving.

That's where my head was when I got inside my black '85 Mercury Topaz late one night after work and started driving down Main Street, the commercial center of High Point. I was headed toward Archdale, where I lived, when out of the blue I was seized by an overwhelming sense of hopelessness.

"Fuck it," I told myself, then floored the gas pedal. The speedometer quickly reached ninety, almost three times the street's speed limit.

If I crashed, got hurt, died—so be it. That was my attitude as I flew through red light after red light in the heart of High Point. The street was mostly empty at that hour, but I easily could have killed myself or, worse, somebody else. My behavior could not have been more selfish, more self-centered, more irresponsible. Never once did I think about the damage I could have caused to others.

I just didn't give a damn. About anything.

Almost out of town, I finally came to my senses and slowed down. I'd pushed it and gotten away with it. Divine intervention? I don't know, but that was enough. I lived to see another day.

Yet here's the thing: that "fuck it" mentality carried over into the next morning. Rather than pushing me to risk my life again, however, it suddenly sharpened my vision of what I wanted to do next.

Instead of saying "fuck it" because my brother was gone, I recalled my brother's penchant for pushing the envelope and just going for things he truly wanted instead of being slowed or stopped by worries of failure.

"No barriers! No limits! They're all a figment of your imagination," Basil constantly said.

That was Basil's belief, and he wouldn't tolerate anyone around him who thought otherwise.

For me, less than two years out of college, it meant going for the career I truly aspired to instead of accepting this crawl-before-you-walk mentality to get where I wanted to be in sports journalism.

Instead of settling for working at the High Point bureau of the Greensboro *News & Record*, with aspirations of one day landing a full-time reporter's job and then moving on to one of the newspapers with larger circulations like the *Charlotte Observer* or the *Atlanta Journal-Constitution* on a full-time basis, I decided to head for the media capital of the world.

My home.

New York.

The New York *Daily News*, the *New York Post*, the *New York Times*, New York *Newsday*—they were all among the largest papers in the country at the time. All I needed was the balls—and the hustle and the writing clips—to get there.

Basil's death transformed me. Once the reality of it truly hit home in the days after his burial, it went from being a source of despair to one of inspiration.

I went to sleep and woke up thinking about the words he had said: "You're going to be a household name." Those words would push me during the years that followed whenever I felt too tired, too frustrated, too apprehensive, too apathetic, or even just too pleasantly distracted.

Those words kept me laser-focused, no matter the barriers my life or corporate America would throw up. My big brother had believed in me, and I wasn't going to let him down. That was my mission. To ensure I completed it, I made a solemn vow: I would not visit Basil's gravesite again until I fulfilled the proclamation he'd made the last time we saw each other, back in Georgetown: that one day I'd end up at ESPN. So it was up to me to make it happen.

That was in 1992. I had some tall steps to climb between then and the day I would finally get to revisit his gravesite, eleven years later—by then having become both a general sports columnist and an NBA analyst/insider for ESPN. But as I began thinking about what I had to do next, figuring out how to get back to New York, I could almost hear Basil whispering to me, "That's what the hell I'm talking about, bro. Go for it!"

So I did.

Fuck it!

* * *

My first step: I called the sports editor at the *Daily News*. I told him I wanted to be a sportswriter and that I wanted to come back home to New York to do it. I then asked if I could send him the clips I'd accumulated while interning in Atlanta and Winston-Salem, along with the high school football stuff I was writing while moonlighting in Greensboro.

The editor, Kevin Whitmer, was a young, enthusiastic, on-the-rise dude himself, so when he told me to send him anything I had, that's exactly what I did—nonstop. Two months later, in December 1992, I came back to New York for Christmas and called Whitmer again, requesting a face-to-face meeting. I told him all I wanted was two minutes of his time; I just wanted him to be able to attach a face to my name so he could at least differentiate me from everybody else clamoring to work there. He obliged.

I took the familiar route from my mother's house to his office: the Q-2 bus to 179th Street and Hillside Avenue, followed by the F train to Rockefeller Center, then walked eight blocks to the Daily News building, then located at 42nd Street near Third Avenue. I could feel the juice of a big-city paper the minute I stepped into the Daily News lobby.

I showed up at Whitmer's office with my résumé and more clips in hand. Whitmer was big and bedraggled, with glasses and a curly white man's Afro. He was a damn good editor who didn't mind taking chances on people. He sized you up not just by your skill, but your hunger and want-it attitude. He was my kind of guy.

I wanted to be his and every executive's kind of guy. First order of business was keeping my word. If I said a couple of minutes, I made sure I wasn't going to take more than a couple of minutes of their time. That little nugget would prove that I was a man of my word and, more important, that I valued their time just as much as they did. That way, they would continue to answer my calls and accept my requests for meetings in the future, because they knew they could trust that I would do what I said I would do.

I thanked him for reading and critiquing my stories the last couple months and assured him that more were on the way. There wasn't much else for me to say. I already felt like I was imposing on a really busy guy, so I got up to leave. Whitmer stopped me before I reached the door.

"I don't have a job for you, as you know," he said. "But I may have some freelance opportunities. You interested?"

I couldn't say yes fast enough. The Greensboro *News & Record* and I were both ready to part ways. The bosses there knew I was bored and unhappy. One of them actually caught me saying as much about a month earlier, when I accidentally included him on an email I meant to send only to a coworker. So the decision was very easy.

When I got back to Greensboro the next week, I packed up my tiny apartment, loaded what little I had into my '85 Topaz, and got the hell out of town.

My first assignment for the *Daily News* was a feature on Nate "Tiny" Archibald, a retired Hall of Fame basketball player and native of the South Bronx.

As a six-foot one-inch guard, Tiny Archibald's storied career included an NBA championship with the Boston Celtics while playing alongside Larry Bird. He'd retired from basketball in 1984, got a night-school master's degree from Fordham University, and was now teaching at a city school in Harlem.

Archibald was known to be a private man, with little interest in talking to the media—a fact that Whitmer knew when he threw me the story. So, I just showed up at the school where he taught at the end of the day, met Archibald in the schoolyard while he was watching kids after the final bell, and shot straight with him the same way I had with the Wake Forest soccer coach back in college. I told him I was a freelancer aspiring to become a full-time sportswriter and that an interview would go a long way toward helping me to achieve that goal.

Archibald grew up in a two-bedroom apartment in a Bronx housing project, the oldest of seven kids. He clearly appreciated my hustle, our similar background (impoverished; many siblings), and agreed to talk. The story, about one of the greatest players in NBA history now wanting to help kids instead of cashing in, was a hit at the paper and translated into a dozen more assignments over the next three months. The *Daily News* was offering $1,000 to $1,500 per article as a freelancer.

I still kept my eyes open for other opportunities. I applied for a three-year paid internship shared by the *Los Angeles Times* and New York *Newsday*, called the Metpro Internship program. With more than three thousand applicants for twenty-four slots, I didn't think I stood a chance, especially when many of those applicants came from prestigious journalism schools like Northwestern, Columbia, and the University of Southern California.

But in April 1993, I got selected for the internship—likely due to my on-the-job experience and having more than 250 published clips from four different newspapers.

I immediately went to Whitmer to tell him of the offer, figuring I was gone. But Whitmer, right on the spot, devised a plan that would alter my life. He told me the high school sports department at the *Daily News*, shut down at the time because of labor and financial problems at the paper, was reopening in August 1993 and that he could hire me as a full-time sportswriter then.

My eyes widened. But there was a catch: between April and August, Whitmer explained, I'd have to earn my chops covering crime.

I wasn't smiling at all. I was nervous as hell. Although I knew I had to take the job, I'd never covered crime. I was a novice, I knew it, and was damn near in panic mode. Luckily for me, I had a Basil-like presence in my life: my cousin Derrick Dawson.

Although we were always tight, despite Derrick being far away, being born and raised in St. Thomas, VI, our bond had grown since Basil's passing. "My Cuz," as I affectionately call him, took it upon himself to become my closest confidant and one of my biggest cheerleaders.

Derrick wouldn't allow doubts to seep into my head. He reminded me of what I was capable of and demanded that I never wilt beneath any challenges that came in my direction.

"Steve, you're the shit, Cuz! What's up with all the damn doubts, man?" he would say. "Stop putting that bullshit in your head. If anyone was made for this, it's you. Basil was absolutely right."

So I jumped at it.

I accepted the job. I moved to Jamaica Estates in Queens. I roomed with one of my best friends to this day, my childhood buddy Kardell Brooks—and my relationship with my Cuz only blossomed.

I didn't know how well I'd do, but I had Derrick cheering me on. This helped immensely, but it was still daunting as hell.

When you aspire to cover dunks and three-pointers, touchdowns and sacks, transitioning to stabbings, shootings, and dead bodies isn't easy. My days and nights were filled with writing stories about fatal car crashes, home invasions, and murders.

The nightmare of that world was brought home to me most vividly two months into the beat. That June, New York State troopers pulled over a 1984 Mazda pickup truck without a license plate on the Southern State Parkway, about ten minutes from my sister Carmen's house. They noticed something stashed under a tarpaulin in the trunk: a decaying corpse.

The dude behind the wheel turned out to be Joel Rifkin, the notorious serial killer believed to have murdered at least seventeen women. He dismembered most of them. A golfer stumbled across the head of one victim on the seventh hole of a golf course in New Jersey.

When it leaked after the arrest that it was possible there were other victims buried in a wooded area near JFK International Airport, editors dispatched me to the scene in case more bodies popped up. I wound up at the homes of other victims to get comments from their families.

I respect the hell out of reporters who regularly cover this beat. Knocking on doors to ask for comments from someone who has just found out that his or her child was murdered isn't for the squeamish. Twice that day I had doors slammed in my face. One parent who talked to me wailed and asked incoherent questions while all I could do is say how sincerely sorry I was and try to slide in a question of my own to get a quote.

It was all part of acquiring the tools of the trade. You learn quickly how to ask the tough questions under the most trying circumstances. It wasn't what I pictured myself doing for a living, but it did make me appreciate all the more how much I liked covering sports. Regardless of sport's high-stakes nature, at the end of the day we're supposed to primarily talk about games and the athletes who play those games.

There's euphoria and misery in sports—but not death.

There's blood, sweat, and tears—but not death.

There are winners and losers—but not death.

There are athletes and coaches who take big losses hard, who suffer career-ending injuries or defeats. But none of that comes close to matching the unbearable pain on the face of that mother in Queens, standing in her doorway as she talked to me about her murdered daughter.

The lessons from those months on the murder-and-mayhem beat paid off four months later, once I transferred to the high school sports desk.

Covering prep hoops in New York City was a dream come true. The talent—topped by future NBA star Stephon Marbury—was unrivaled. But no one played a bigger role in my own future than a kid named Karlton Hines.

In 1993 he was a young guy with unlimited potential whose life took a hard left turn and was snuffed out way too soon—in broad daylight, on a busy street corner, by a bullet to the back of his head. It was one of those rare stories when sports and death intersect.

His name, again, was Karlton Hines.

Hines had been a six-foot-five power forward lauded by all who'd seen him play. He had averaged twenty-four points per game as a high school sophomore in East Harlem. He also played on the city's best AAU team, the Gauchos, that included three future NBA first-round picks (Kenny Anderson, Jamal Mashburn, and Eric Mobley) and one future second-round pick (Conrad McRae). Powerhouse college programs like Syracuse wanted him badly, with coaches making regular recruiting trips to his apartment in the Bronx's notorious Melrose Houses housing projects, just a couple miles from where I spent the first year of my life.

But after transferring to a prep school in Maine known for its hoops, then quitting and being ruled ineligible to play again back in New York (he used a fake address when he enrolled), Hines was on the streets, leaving the basketball world behind him. Then five years after playing his last high school game, he was gunned down in broad daylight (2:30 p.m.) on Boston Road, in the Bronx.

According to an eyewitness, Hines was shot in the back of the head. The shooter then fired at the fleeing witness, hitting him in the back of the leg, then walked back over to Hines and shot him several more times to finish him off.

Just like that, Hines went from basketball legend to another cautionary tale about New York.

I jumped on it. The Hines story played to two of my coverage strengths: basketball and the streets. I knew the actors in both those worlds.

My first calls were to a couple of "street agents"—guys whom players use to contact college coaches for the best opportunities, and on whom AAU and college coaches relied to funnel money from their programs to the players. They immediately put me in touch with Hines's family. I took the rest from there.

I found the eyewitness who had been shot trying to flee the scene and interviewed him from his hospital bed. ("His body dropped before I could touch him," he said of his friend.) He put me in touch with other friends, who talked about what a good living Hines made dealing drugs in the South Bronx. I talked with Hines's high school coaches, who'd heard about his drug dealing even back then. I talked with Syracuse coach Jim Boeheim, who called Hines an "NBA-caliber player." I went to the projects where he grew up and talked with his mother, his brothers, his wife.

His mother didn't believe Karlton would ever have dealt drugs, but police records painted a different picture. Then I learned the most tragic detail of all: Hines's father had been stabbed to death on the same street corner, just months before Hines was born.

Before his death, Hines was thinking about making a comeback. He'd started working out with the Gauchos and talked about playing again in a professional summer league.

But he was said to be in the streets way too deep. What resonated with me was the brazenness and swiftness of it; in that world, if somebody wants you dead bad enough, they can get you. There are stone-cold killers who have no qualms—zero—about taking your life if you rub them the wrong way. I'd seen it play out in my own neighborhood growing up. I had friends who got caught up in the drug game. They were shot and killed, became addicts, or ended up in jail.

Those appeared to be the only three options in the drug game.

The *Daily News* splashed my story, headlined "Street Struck," across two pages in the End Zone of the sports section, including a funeral photo of his flower-draped casket that I was given by the family.

The story began:

Broad daylight, a pool of blood, a few witnesses and a dead body.

Karlton Hines, a former New York City basketball phenom, was standing in front of an auto body shop in the Bronx about 2:30 p.m. on April 18. He had $5,000 in his pocket.

Nothing was taken except his life.

Hines was 23 and on the streets. Five years ago, many in the basketball community thought he'd be blooming in the NBA by now, not the victim of a vicious homicide, which police say is possibly drug-related.

The story ended with heartbreaking quotes from Hines's two little daughters.

"My daddy's in heaven," said Kyerrah, 3.

"But heaven doesn't come down," said Kyesha, 5.

Then she began to cry.

My career was never the same.

From that point on, editors viewed me as someone from the streets with street connections, who could get stories few others could get anywhere near. I also knew the world that was often connected to those same streets: the players and coaches, as well as the handlers, runners, and street agents, who accompanied them.

My brother had reminded me of that all the time.

"I don't give a shit how high you climb," Basil would tell me. "Don't ever forget where you came from. I'm not telling you to be some ignoramous who doesn't know how to act. But always know who you are, who your people are. Don't ever forget us. Because no matter how we can be with each other as people, we're all we got in the end. Remember that shit!"

There was something else I would always remember from that time. I was hired at the *Daily News* during a period of financial strife at the paper. There were strikes. There were sales.

There were layoffs and shutdowns.

Yet as young and ignorant as I was about the business side of things, I also became enlightened about how pivotal business was to what we did in the newsroom. Somebody had to cut the check. As much as we liked to talk about the journalism, the real-world translation was that if you didn't have an impact, you were expendable. To start off in this business under those circumstances taught me a lesson they don't teach in journalism school:

Be impactful. That's the difference between an employee and a talent.

That lesson propelled me: it was never enough for me just to do a job well—everything I did had to have an impact. I wanted to become someone whom nobody else could be like. And who wouldn't be forgotten.

I wanted to do stories that would damn well guarantee that I would never be expendable.

CHAPTER 7

I'VE GOT PLANS FOR YOU

In October 1994, a little more than a year after I'd hustled my way onto the *Daily News* sports desk, the *Philadelphia Inquirer* hired me away, largely because of the Hines story and others like it. That meant I'd have to leave the confines of Jamaica Estates for Voorhees, South Jersey, about twenty miles outside of Philadelphia. Philadelphia, a blue-collar town if there ever was one, was a place I knew I'd enjoy working in. Living there was another matter. I opted for a modern apartment in Voorhees, along with a suburban lifestyle. It gave me a sense of peace I knew I'd never have in a city. Plus, it was an easy decision because one of my dearest friends in the world—Tonya Fox—lived in the same town and had found the perfect place for me. It would turn out to be a habit of hers: over the next several years she always would be the one to find places for me to live. She's one of the few people on the planet I trust without question.

The *Inquirer* assigned me to cover Saint Joseph's University sports but moved me to their number one college beat—Temple University basketball and football—after just two weeks on the job.

That was considered an upgrade largely because of the reputation of one man: basketball coach John Chaney.

Raised in Philly and an HBCU grad (Bethune-Cookman), Chaney was tough as damn nails. He was also outrageously good copy. The year before I got there, after a rough loss to the University of Massachusetts, Chaney made headlines when he interrupted opposing coach John Calipari in the middle of a post-game press conference with an out-of-control rant, calling Calipari a "son of a bitch," charging the podium, and having to be pulled from the room by security and some of his own players.

That was an extreme example of the kind of fire that burned inside Chaney, and what allowed him to push Temple's basketball program to national prominence and land him in the Hall of Fame.

I knew Chaney. He loved me, in his way, but not nearly as much as I loved him. We had a similar relationship to the one I had had with Coach Gaines. At least once a week during the basketball season, Chaney would call me into his office to cuss me out about something I'd written. I also looked forward to his lectures to me about life and what I should be aiming for in order to be all I could be. As with Coach Gaines, berating you and holding you accountable—even if it was delivered with a string of obscenities—was how he showed his love. If either of those men had no use for you, they didn't waste their time talking to you. And they stopped talking if they decided you were someone who didn't listen.

So I listened. I learned. I called it as I saw it.

And I raced up the *Inquirer* ladder.

From 1994 to 2003, I went from the college beat to the NBA beat, from the NBA beat to NBA columnist, and from there to the slot I'd coveted since I was an editorial assistant in Greensboro covering high school football games for nothing but gas money:

General sports columnist.

According to the National Association of Black Journalists (NABJ), back in 2003 when I was named a general sports columnist, I was the twenty-first African American in American history to be appointed to such a prestigious position. I had had help along the way. When I arrived at the *Inquirer* as a young Black journalist, I was lucky to have two powerful mentors: Acel Moore and Mike Bruton.

Acel started at the paper as a copy boy in 1962, eventually won a Pulitzer Prize for local investigative reporting, and cofounded the NABJ. Bruton came to the paper in 1983 and covered everything from the NFL to the NBA to the Olympics, and, with his experience in both the press box and the newsroom, became a father figure to me. Both were staunch guardians of my career. Having navigated the roughest racial terrain and tolerated more than I'd ever have to, they never hesitated to espouse words of wisdom or protect me from bureaucratic bullshit. Anytime I felt shortchanged on assignments, promotions, or raises, they'd speak up. If you fucked with me, you had to deal with those dudes. I simply would not be where I am in my career without them both.

(I'd be remiss if I neglected to mention former deputy sports editor Rob King, who's now at ESPN, along with editors Phil Dixon and Robert Rosenthal and Butch Ward. These editors in charge of the paper during my years at the *Philadelphia Inquirer* did everything to help me.)

Because of them, I was able to simply do my job. Through the years, I had become connected with everyone in the basketball universe at every level—high school, college, pro. I had the cell phone numbers of scouts, executives, AAU coaches, street runners, players—you name it. Figuratively speaking, I knew where all the bodies were buried, and who was doing the burying. Getting the news first mattered to me, but an even bigger priority was finding out the "why" and the "what" behind every story. Those questions consumed me.

Why was a player traded? Why was a coach or general manager fired? What was the dirt behind it all?

The only way you learn what's really going on in sports is the same way you find out what's happening on the streets: through relationships. It's not like with politics, where paper trails and policies and legislation provide evidence of positions and facts, even when the subjects of your stories won't talk. In sports, your information was worth shit, for the most part, unless you had actual subjects providing the intel. Directly or indirectly.

Nowhere did those relationships come more into play than during the six years I covered the 76ers, 1997 to 2003. No beat was crazier, and nothing had a bigger impact on my future. Not only was I on the road at least two hundred days a year with one of the league's most high-profile teams, I also had to cover their star, Allen Iverson, who marched to the beat of his own drum, and was a full-time beat unto himself.

With the 76ers, I continued to build my reputation as someone who had access to information that others did not. It's what often separated me from the pack. Wherever the story was, I'd go, often staying up all hours of the night. Being connected to the same street element that a lot of the players were connected to helped make me an unorthodox journalist. Friends, hangers-on, bartenders, family—they all knew me. Places most white journalists wouldn't go into—I didn't hesitate. No matter what time of day or night.

If Iverson was at a casino, I knew about it. If he was at a club until three in the morning, I knew about it. If he or some other teammates were in a fight, I knew about it. There was always some rumor floating around about Iverson. He was the kind of player who hung out until late with a posse of dudes, who was sometimes then late to practice, but who always showed up for games and averaged twenty-five points while being the smallest guy on the court. He was an absolute warrior.

I didn't print everything I saw or knew. My personal philosophy: a player's personal life was his business—as long as it didn't show up in a police blotter or in court. If it did, then it was my job to report it. If I saw a player walk out of a hotel room with somebody other than his wife, that was none of my business. If I knew he was smoking weed, that was his business. If he then played like shit the next game, I'd have a line in a story the next day like "I don't know what he was doing last night, but . . ."

I'm still that way. I have no interest in divulging someone's personal business. But do something stupid or illegal that puts you in the police blotters and, to me, that was your ass. Play like you're supposed to play, I have nothing to say. Play like shit, you are not going to want to see what I have to say.

I was also plugged into the people in management who knew what was really going on. Sometimes my reporting even affected the moves they made.

In 1999, I learned that the Sixers were about to make a blockbuster trade with the Toronto Raptors. The deal basically boiled down to 76ers' guard Larry Hughes for Toronto's star-to-be Tracy McGrady. The way McGrady's career would soon take off (he'd become a seven-time All-Star and two-time scoring champion), his pairing with Iverson could have made the Sixers a dynamic contender for years. I sought out Philly general manager Billy King for a comment. King and I couldn't stand each other at the time. He undoubtedly felt I was arrogant and bombastic; I felt he was arrogant and two-faced, especially when it came to me. (I was wrong—he is neither—and we are great friends now.) He asked me if I could hold the story, because it might threaten the trade.

I said I'd consider it if he asked me nicely. He laughed it off, thinking I was joking. But I was dead serious, strictly because of the way I felt he treated me. When he realized I was serious, he still refused. So I said: "Fuck it, I'm writing it." The next day, the story got published in the *Philadelphia Inquirer* and was also picked up on a wire service, meaning that it could be found just about anywhere. Raptors' fans saw it and raised holy hell about it, and Toronto nixed the deal the next day.

✳   ✳   ✳

Something else happened in 1999 that made me feel a lot less powerful.

The night was April 22. Just minutes earlier I had departed from the Palace of Auburn Hills following a 76ers vs. Pistons game, heading to the Romulus Marriott Hotel near the Detroit airport, about a fifty-five-minute drive. Two of my white colleagues from other papers who were covering the game were riding with me through Troy, Michigan, when I was pulled over.

Initially, two cops approached my rental car. Knowing I wasn't speeding, I'd asked the cops what I had done. They responded by simply telling me to get out of the car. Upon exiting my rental, six additional cops from three other cop cars surrounded me—leaving me to feel as though I were some killer just apprehended after a manhunt.

It wasn't long before I was informed that I had been driving with a suspended license. It turned out that there was an outstanding fifteen-dollar late fee I hadn't known about from a previous speeding ticket.

The cops handcuffed me behind my back right in front of my colleagues, told them where I'd be held, shoved me into the back of the police vehicle, and drove off, taking me to the local police precinct, where they held me for three and a half hours.

I was furious beyond comprehension.

As I uttered what racist bastards they were under my breath and plotted to sue the hell out of them the second I was released from jail, the only thing that assuaged me in that moment was a dear friend of mine named Audrey Irvine. She was an editor at CNN, and the one person I was smart enough to call once they tossed me behind bars.

Audrey was relentless, calling the officers every five minutes. She was particularly irritated when they informed her that bail was $250 and that, with $241 in my pocket, I was exactly nine dollars short. They wouldn't release me for hours.

Eventually, they were left no choice, because Audrey would not let up. The officer literally said, "You win! I can't take that woman's mouth another second."

I said absolutely nothing, which is what I do when I'm furious.

It wasn't until the next day that I took the liberty of informing my family of what had happened. Predictably, everyone was aghast, lamenting the typical state of affairs where a young Black man and the police are concerned.

"At least you're still alive," my sisters sighed.

Everyone responded that way, actually.

Except Mommy!

"So what did YOU do?" she asked, matter-of-factly, much to my annoyance. I responded: "Absolutely nothing, Mommy!"

"Well, why did they say they pulled you over?"

"They said I was driving with a suspended license, Ma," I responded. "But how would they know that when I was driving a rent-a-car and not speeding or committing any violations?"

Mommy wouldn't let up.

"Was your license suspended?"

"Yes, Mom. I paid the fine, but they say it arrived late, so I owed fifteen dollars. See what I'm saying?"

Mommy's response: "Yes, I do see. I see that your license was suspended because you had a previous violation that got it suspended in the first place. So had you not gotten a ticket before, you would've had nothing to pay that arrived late, and you never would have been in the system for a suspended license. That's what I see!"

I just sucked my teeth and said, "Ma, just put Linda on the phone."

In that moment, I was only slightly more pissed off at the police officers than at my mother. Right up until Linda spoke, that is:

"Why'd you even bother telling Mommy," she said. "You know she's going to look at you—and make you look at yourself—before she even thinks about anybody else. When are you gonna learn?"

I had to laugh at that. She was right.

"Own what you say and do," my mom always said. "Stand on it, even if the fallout is something that is not in your favor."

*　　*　　*

TV never left my radar. While writing for the *Inquirer*, I started talking about basketball on a local Comcast station in Philly. The viewership was tiny and I didn't get paid, but they gave me clips of my appearances so I could create a portfolio.

In 1998, I flew to Atlanta to audition for a weekly NBA show at the now-defunct CNN/SI, a relatively new twenty-four-hour sports network that combined the resources of CNN and *Sports Illustrated*. After the audition, they hired me on the spot.

Two years later, Fox Sports Net developed *The Best Damn Sports Show Period*. They offered me a job as daily cohost. The show, filmed in Los Angeles, had an irreverent take on just about everything, with Chris Rose as the main host and featuring comedian Tom Arnold, Roseanne Barr's ex.

I loved those guys. And coming from the streets of New York City, working for Fox Sports at its L.A. headquarters at the corner of Pico Boulevard and the Avenue of the Stars—with the palm trees, the year-round sunshine, and, yes, the beautiful women of Southern California—I would be as close to heaven as I'd ever been in my life.

But I had a future to think about. At that time, my television aspirations were to become an NBA insider and overall basketball aficionado. That meant knowing the players, the coaches, the executives, the agents— all the goings on within the circle of the National Basketball Association. I decided that working alongside a comedian could hurt my ability to be taken seriously, particularly when I was called upon to address serious issues. So, despite being offered a three-year, $1.3-million deal (I was making $200,000 a year at the time), I respectfully declined. I did sign on as a contributor, at one-third the full-time salary they offered. A friend, former NBA player John Salley, ultimately took the job.

I never regretted the decision. I worked at Fox as a contributor from

2000 to 2003. But my mission wasn't to land at Fox. It was to land at the "Worldwide Leader in Sports": ESPN.

By 2003, they finally called—though not without dissension within their ranks.

Mark Shapiro, ESPN's executive vice president for production and programming at the time, insists he didn't know a damn thing about me. Yet seven months after the *Inquirer* named me a general sports columnist in March of that year, Shapiro reached out to bring me to his network's headquarters in Bristol, Connecticut, for an audition. Two of my closest friends had prodded him to do it: Kevin Frazier, then a host of *NBA Shootaround* (and now a host on *Entertainment Tonight*), and Kerry Chandler, head of the network's HR department during that period.

Shapiro took their counsel to heart but not before broaching the matter inside a conference room with more than twenty of his direct reports. According to Shapiro, while going through that day's agenda, he mentioned that he was bringing in Stephen A. Smith for an audition, with the idea of adding me to the network's roster of on-air talent. As soon as he mentioned my name, the room reacted with virtual unanimity:

Nobody wanted my ass there.

The general consensus was that my bombastic, demonstrative style as a contributor to Fox Sports was a turnoff—something they considered beneath ESPN. The lone exception in the room was Norby Williamson, then a senior VP responsible for the network's day-to-day news and information content. But his voice was drowned out.

"He's not what we do," one dissenting underling told Shapiro. "He's not representative of who we are."

Shapiro was stunned. But also intrigued. His gut response: Bring him in!

"I've never been in a room in my life where every single executive and producer unanimously doesn't want someone," Shapiro later explained. "When that happened, I said, 'Fuck this! I've got to see for myself why this guy evokes such a response.'"

I arrived at ESPN headquarters in Bristol on October 14, 2003—my thirty-sixth birthday. From what I could see on my drive into town, Bristol, a Hartford suburb of sixty thousand, consisted of ESPN's campus-like headquarters, a Courtyard by Marriott, a Ruby Tuesday's, a Chili's, and a couple of gas stations. That's about it.

I didn't care. My focus remained on fulfilling the dream Basil had drummed into my head.

"You will work at ESPN one day and you'll become one of the biggest personalities in America, covering the NBA and more," he'd said. "Just wait and see."

Now I was there.

I was greeted first by Fred Brown, a Black executive who worked for years striving to diversify the network's on-air talent, and then by Fred's boss, Al Jaffe, whose kindness and candor would later make him a genuine friend. Jaffe informed me I had eighteen interviews scheduled before my 2 p.m. audition. The recurring theme in every interview was the extent of my commitment to hard work. I was repeatedly reminded that ESPN's in-house nickname was "the car wash," because "this place will run you through it," as Brown put it. "We work our tails off here."

My last and most memorable interview was with Mike McQuade, a no-nonsense senior coordinating producer who's considered one of the best in the business. His nickname preceded him: Darth Vader. A smile on Mike's face qualified as breaking news. He was all business, all the time. He minced few words.

"Right now, you've established a little bit of a name for yourself at Fox Sports," he said. "To us, that's like being a big fish in a little pond. Here, you'd be a little fish in a big pond. How do you think you'd handle that if we hired you?"

I looked around his office as I considered the question, thinking about all the talent that had walked through this building over the years, while also reminding myself that any semblance of cockiness might set off alarms. But I kept in mind another thing Basil used to tell me: "If you don't believe in you, how the hell can you expect anyone else to? There's no excuse for doubt when you've put in the work and know you're qualified and ready."

My gaze returned to McQuade.

"I sincerely mean no disrespect," I told him, "but I'm not about to be a little fish in anybody's pond, sir. Just put me in front of the camera, turn on the lights, and watch me do what I do. Then feel free to be the judge."

McQuade almost seemed to smile.

"All right then," he said, getting up. "Let's go see."

We left his office next to the newsroom and walked down a hallway to a nondescript studio. Any panic or nervousness I might have felt went out the window the minute I stepped through the door and saw Kevin Frazier, the host of *Entertainment Tonight*, waiting for me. The biggest reason K-Frazier, as I called him, insisted I get an audition is because he was unhappy with *NBA Shootaround*, believing it needed some sizzle to go along with the credibility it already had. He thought it needed to be good TV, not just TV that was good for you. "If you really want to win," he told Shapiro, "you need to get this guy to ESPN. Period."

Now here Kevin was, hosting the audition. That was all the loosening up I needed. I talked about Iverson, Kobe Bryant, Shaq, and championship expectations. I dribbled words out of my mouth with the brilliance Isaiah Thomas once showed dribbling a basketball. I was sharp and sharp-tongued, informed and candid. Most of all, I was courageous, willing to say what I truly thought to be true, regardless of who the subject was. Players were no different than coaches. Coaches were no different than executives. Executives were no different than owners. I was an equal-opportunity flatterer and offender. And I didn't give a damn one way or the other.

The audition ended thirty minutes later. I'd waited years for the opportunity, and I thought I'd done pretty well, never thrown off by any subject that was tossed at me. K-Frazier told me afterward, "There's no way in hell you won't have a contract by the end of the week. You were huge." Yet that was just one opinion. I figured I'd know, one way or the other, in a couple weeks.

Ninety minutes into my two-hour drive back to my mother's house in Hollis, my phone rang. The caller ID lit up my phone: Steve Mountain.

My agent.

His first word:

"Congratulations!"

Then:

"We've just reached an agreement with ESPN on a three-year deal, at a base salary of $225,000 per year."

Two weeks after that, on a Friday night, I was live on *NBA Shootaround* with the show's regulars: Frazier and former players Greg Anthony and Bill Laimbeer. They sat together at the studio's main desk, while I sat at a separate desk off to the side, like a guest at their party.

One of that day's hot topics was Kobe Bryant, then in the prime of his career but suddenly under a dark cloud. Bryant had been charged that summer with the sexual assault of a nineteen-year-old woman who worked at a Colorado hotel where he was staying. Bryant admitted to having consensual sex with the woman but denied raping her. The criminal case was dropped when the accuser proved unwilling to testify. That same day, Bryant publicly apologized to her, her family, and his own family. A civil suit filed by the woman was later settled out of court.

Still, it was clear Bryant had marital issues to deal with. He reportedly bought his wife a $4 million ring, and reports circulated that, at age twenty-five, he was contemplating retirement. That prompted numerous commentators, including the main hosts on *Shootaround* that particular Friday night, to express their sentiments about what the NBA would look like without Kobe.

I was having none of it. I joined in with a whole different take.

"Kobe Bryant is not retiring from the game of basketball," I said dismissively. "Either he gets up and goes to work every day to play the game he loves, or he stays home and sticks around all day long face-to-face with the woman he admitted to the world he betrayed. What choice do you think he's making? Stop it!"

The *Shootaround* team chuckled quietly and nodded affirmatively. The producers in my ear chuckled a little bit louder. The next day, everyone was talking about what I'd said.

By Monday, I was informed the side desk was being eliminated and that I'd be sitting at the main desk with the rest of the team.

Figuratively speaking, I'd found my stride. Although my contract obligated me to do 225 appearances a year, at a thousand dollars per appearance, I quickly became an ESPN fixture—a big fish in a big pond, just as I had promised McQuade. All told, that year I made 325 more appearances than my contract called for—a total of 550 appearances on shows across the network, earning me $550,000.

At first, Shapiro, with one eye on the bottom line, wondered what the hell was going on. Producers liked what I brought to whatever table they had, and I was more than willing to sit wherever they asked.

"Morning, noon, or night," one producer told Shapiro, "when we call, he answers. He never sleeps."

I was still writing my column for the Philly *Inquirer*, and in April 2005, I also ventured into sports talk radio, with *The Stephen A. Smith Show* airing every weekday from noon to 2 p.m. on ESPN Radio in New York.

Shapiro's eventual response to me:

"You're unbelievable. You're a fucking machine. I've got plans for you."

Those plans, nearly twenty months after I came on board, turned out to be my own TV show.

And then to everyone's surprise: I balked.

For a moment.

Until my sister Linda called me a bitch!

She didn't mean it. I say that because it's the only time in my life she ever called me that. She was caught up in an emotional moment with her little brother—one she had taught how to read and write, how to fight, how to never succumb to limitations—and now she feared that all her efforts over the years had been in vain. Those efforts would not be in vain, but Linda didn't know it at that moment. All she saw was a little brother who resembled a scared puppy, afraid to embrace the opportunity of a lifetime.

"Oh, so we're a punk now, huh?" she said in my mom's living room, where we were talking. "That's what we are? All these years of hard work. Of crying about how you'll take the industry by storm, just wait and see?" she continued in her mocking voice. "All that shit was just talk, huh? Maybe I shouldn't have called you a punk. I should've called you a bitch instead."

The opportunity that had provoked Linda's fury was at ESPN2, a channel that had been around since 1993 but which was still mostly unwatched. Looking to raise the channel's profile, Shapiro offered me my own nightly show. Shapiro saw a star-in-the-making. I was the guy who busted onto the scene and raised *NBA Shootaround*'s ratings 22 percent during my first month. I was the guy who more than doubled my earnings by showing up on-air more than twice as many times as my contract called for—just in my first year.

To Shapiro, Stephen A. was a replica of himself. Hungry. Determined. Indefatigable. Someone who didn't give a shit about what anybody said. Shapiro was determined to make sure ESPN capitalized on all of those traits with an interview show that put me in front of a live audience as the host.

So he couldn't believe it when I hesitated at his offer.

"What the hell are you scared about?" he asked incredulously, putting it nicer than Linda had. "You're killing it. Folks fucking love you or hate you, but they won't stop watching you, which is the name of the game in this business. They don't turn the channel. So, I don't want to hear shit about your fears. Let's go get this shit!"

To me, it wasn't that simple.

If someone had asked me back in 2005 if I had a vision for a television show, my answer would have been an emphatic no. I was still relatively new to TV. I had zero training and had never hosted anything in my life. Even though I'd worked at CNN/SI and Fox Sports Net as an NBA analyst, I didn't really know what the hell I was doing.

I was an expert on the NBA, had sources in every locker room in the league. I'd played for and covered basketball coaching legends who had taught me the game's nuances, beyond just *X*'s and *O*'s. So, when I went in front of the camera, even without any formal training, I simply acted like myself. Raw and authentic. If someone played well, I said so. If someone played badly, I didn't hold back. If someone was atrocious, I'd spell it out. Getting my true feelings across was my priority. I didn't leave anyone guessing what the hell I felt. As the late, great Georgetown basketball coach John Thompson once deadpanned: "The thing I love about Stephen A. is, if you want to know how he really feels, just ask him."

For me, it wasn't personal. If you put your skills on public display, then you're subject to public scrutiny. Everybody's watching what I'm watching, so if I soft-pedaled an opinion about something I saw, viewers would see right through it and view me as something less than "real," and authenticity has been in short supply throughout the industry for years. That just wasn't me.

On-air presentations that others termed demonstrative and bombastic were simply me being the way I'd always been. When I argued over sports with my father or siblings or neighborhood friends back in Hollis, none of us were timid with our opinions. We came at each other. In the house, at backyard barbecues, waiting around in barbershops—you name it, we verbally sparred all the time. Those sparring sessions were passionate, informative, entertaining—and fun. I wanted that same experience for the viewer. The rules of the game were simple: Be passionate! Mean what the hell you say! Make them laugh! Piss them off!

Annoy and frustrate them! And make sure you give them something they don't know or haven't thought about!

In short, do anything but bore them or lie to them, and you'll be okay.

That was my thinking from the first time I sat in front of the camera for that cable show in Philly through my first year at ESPN. I exuded confidence because, in the end, any show on which I appeared relied on my expertise. Whoever had me on was at my mercy, not the other way around.

But the show Shapiro had in mind was different. Hosting solo, in an interview-format, put me in foreign territory. I didn't know the intricacies of carrying a daily show myself, so I was scared out of my mind. How do you do a "tease"? How do you put together a "rundown"? How do you go in and out of commercial breaks? What do directions like VO (Voice Over) and SOT (Sound on Track) actually mean? If you aren't in the business, you knew as much as I did at the time.

The fact is, they're all basic things you can learn in about five seconds. But when you're a novice to that stuff like I was, you're nervous, because you know just how much you don't know. Along with rabid followers, the audience who watched me was rife with loyal haters ready to pounce on my every mistake. Now they'd have a field day with me.

Linda had zero patience for my nervousness. In her eyes, I was made for this. I'd already overcome poverty, reading disabilities, the negligence and ridicule of my father, the virtual absence of a mother forced to work sixteen-hour days. After all of that, Linda wanted to know what the hell there was to be nervous about.

"Stop being a bitch!" I kept hearing her say. "Stop being a punk!"

Tired of hearing "bitch" in my head, I finally quit being a punk and signed a three-year deal with an annual payout of $1.3 million. My show would be called *Quite Frankly*. This Bronx-born, Hollis-raised Black kid could hardly believe his good fortune.

For me, the three-year contract provided what I call a grace period.

To know that, as long as I showed up for work, I had three years' pay guaranteed was a setup profoundly unfamiliar to me, as it is for most folks, especially most Black folks. It alleviated a level of stress I'd walked around with my entire life, even before I was old enough to know what actually qualified as stress. It would also allow me to pay off my college debt and the house I had bought in 2005 in Hainesport, New Jersey, rent a nice apartment in Manhattan, and build up a legitimate savings account. More important, it also allowed me to do something I could only have dreamed about just a couple of years earlier.

In mid-April 2005, I walked into the ABC headquarters building off 66th Street and Columbus Avenue (ESPN is owned by Disney/ABC), took an elevator up to the tenth floor, then stepped into Shapiro's office to sign the contract right in front of him. I wanted him to look in my eyes and see what he already knew: I would succeed at this or go down swinging.

In that moment, the only thing on my mind was my mother. Janet Smith had toiled for years to make sure her children had a roof over their heads, heat in the house, and food on the table. She had done so with great sacrifice, depriving herself of any pleasures or luxuries to make sure her children were okay.

I would be profoundly reminded of her impact on my own childhood experiences almost a decade later, in 2014, when NBA superstar Kevin Durant paid tribute to his mother in his acceptance speech after winning the league's Most Valuable Player award. During the speech, Durant cried, his mother cried, and, while watching it live on TV, I cried too.

"You'd wake me up in the middle of the night in the summertime," Durant said through tears to his mother, seated in the audience, "making me run up a hill, making me do push-ups. Screaming at me from the sidelines of my games at eight or nine years old. We weren't supposed to be here. You made us believe. You kept us off the street. You put clothes on our backs, food on our table. When you didn't eat, you made sure we ate. You went to sleep hungry. You sacrificed for us. You're the real MVP."

I felt the same way in Shapiro's office after signing that contract. Thoughts of my mom working so hard and starving so that we were less hungry never escaped me. She took the same Q2 bus I had to take to high school every weekday, to the same stop at 169th Street. She walked up the same hill I did to get to Queens General Hospital during the day, then to the nursing home the same evening. She walked alone up that hill early every morning and down that hill late every night, with no assistance from my father.

Only when my mother was robbed by a mugger who held a knife to her throat and threatened to kill her back in the late 1980s, when I was at FIT, did my father even think about the potential danger she braved daily. After the mugging, my father escorted my mom to and from work every day—for a week. Then she was back on her own again.

My father was the only thing that distracted me from her struggles. I spent inordinate amounts of time wondering how any man could subject his wife to such circumstances without even a semblance of guilt. I vacillated between sympathy (for her) and fury (toward him) right up until I signed that multi-year contract to host my own show.

Practically before the ink dried, I left Shapiro's office, got in my car, and sped out of Manhattan—traveling across the Queensboro Bridge to the Long Island Expressway, exiting onto Francis Lewis Boulevard, heading down to 200th Street and 112th Avenue—until I stopped in front of the Police Athletic League (PAL) to give my mother the news. The PAL, where I'd played basketball and other sports but where my mother now worked to earn extra money after retiring from nursing, was packed that afternoon with senior citizens. They came several times a week to play bingo. My mother was in charge of the event. Standing behind a bar area, her eyes popped wide open when she saw me.

"What are you doing here?" she asked, sounding a little annoyed.

"You know I don't like you bothering me when I'm working. What happened?"

I just smiled. Then tears swelled in my eyes; I'd been thinking about this moment since I was a teenager. I put my hand over hers, then looked at the manager of the PAL, standing nearby, and told him, "My mother will not be working here anymore."

My mother looked shell-shocked. She was speechless. She didn't know what was going on. But she followed me as I grabbed her by the hand and walked out.

Once we got in my car, I told her about the show and the contract. I didn't get a signing bonus or anything up front, so I didn't have enough money to just go and buy her a new house in New York or St. Thomas. But I had enough to provide her with the kind of leisure she'd long craved. A few blocks away, I stopped in front of her house on 203rd Street and handed her an envelope.

"Here's two tickets for a cruise to Europe," I said. "I've waited my whole life to be able to do this for you. You won't be paying for cruises, for flights to St. Thomas, or your mortgage any longer. I got you. Enjoy your life. I love you."

Then I added, "It's my turn now."

I saw a tear streak down my mother's cheek for only the second time in my life. (The first was after she found out I lied to her after my father picked me up at the airport with his other family. She never showed us her tears when my brother died.) Mommy saw in my eyes that I wasn't bullshitting. She knew when I told her "it's my turn now" that I was telling her she didn't have to work anymore, didn't have to pay another bill, for the rest of her life.

Yet that also meant I was committed to putting in the work for the rest of my life. I now had to perform at a higher level than ever; just doing the job wasn't going to be good enough, not in this league. I had to excel to the point that if this venture didn't work out, I'd stand out enough that other doors would open to more opportunities. I had to

STEPHEN A. SMITH

do so well that, in this dog-eat-dog business, the decision-makers above would have no choice but to recognize my worth. If I shined brightly enough, the company would shine as well. They'd have to make me part of their long-term plans. That was my thinking.

For all of that to happen, I needed one of those decision-makers in my corner—someone pushing my cause—and I had that, initially, in Shapiro. He's the reason I heeded my sister's words and took the job. I knew he had invested his faith, and the company's dollars, in a Black kid who'd never hosted a show in his life.

"You're fucking worth it," he kept telling me. Then he'd add, only half joking, because he knew the unpredictable nature of television, "You'd better be."

Hell, I had to be worth it if I wanted a future in the business as something more than just a basketball analyst known for being loud and obnoxious. I had to be worth it for Shapiro, who took the chance on me. And I had to be worth it for the Black community, for a multitude of reasons, but especially to help ensure that other Blacks dreaming the same dream would be afforded the same opportunity. For better or worse, I always felt the palpable presence of my community looming over me. I've always said: "White people come to work every single day with a job to do. Black folks come to work with a responsibility." I've never understood why so many people would ask what I meant by that. To me, it was obvious.

From the vantage point of most Black people I've spoken to in corporate America, white folks get up and go to work every day devoid of pressures from the white community to "represent us." Any Black person in a prominent position to speak to the masses will tell you that's not the case for us. With a huge platform comes a huge responsibility, and the Black community is the first to remind you of that.

"Speak out, Stephen A.!"

"Be real, bro!"

"Don't be scared. Say what the hell needs to be said!"

"Don't let us down, man!"

As a reporter and analyst for ESPN, I don't care whether a story entails politics, police brutality, the judicial system, you name it—if it's a subject percolating in the Black community, Black folks want me and every other Black person with a mass platform to be speaking out about that matter which affects our community. Giving voice to the voiceless. Providing the "Black" perspective, consequences be damned. I walked into *Quite Frankly*, with its young staff and diverse guests, knowing I had to have that attitude or risk being stigmatized as an Uncle Tom or a sellout—figuratively stripped of my Blackness. That was simply the cross I bore.

That's what forced me to ask Shapiro one last time, "You sure you want to do this?"

CHAPTER 8

QUITE FRANKLY

Q*uite Frankly* debuted on August 1, 2005, from a studio inside the Penn Hotel, across the street from Madison Square Garden.

My first guest was Allen Iverson, who came to the rescue when Terrell Owens backed out due to what he said was a family matter he had to deal with. Seated in a living-room-like set in front of a live audience, dressed in baggy shorts, a black cap low over his eyes ("Pull your hat up so everyone can see your face," I suggested), and a camo T-shirt with Tupac's image across the front, A.I. gave me, arguably, the most memorable interview of his career—and mine—at one point crying over words that former 76ers coach Larry Brown had expressed about him.

Kobe, by then back on the court, soon sat down with me for his first one-on-one interview since the sexual assault charges against him had been settled. Pete Rose made his case for the MLB Hall of Fame, despite being banned for life for gambling on baseball. Shaq kept his promise to come on by, flying in from Europe.

One of my favorite moments was when Donald Trump, years before he became president, made a grand entrance to the song "For the Love of Money," by the O'Jays, the theme music to his hit NBC show *The*

Apprentice. Then Trump topped it off by letting me touch his hair to prove it wasn't a toupee. Actor Matthew McConaughey had my sisters Carmen and Abigail drooling at the sight of him. Jerry Rice, the greatest wide receiver in NFL history, came on the show following his stint on *Dancing With the Stars* and tried to teach me to do a dance step. He was appallingly unsuccessful.

The guest list went on: Michael Strahan, Senator John McCain, Steve Harvey, Joe Montana, Lawrence Taylor, Wayne Gretzky, Deion Sanders, movie mogul Jerry Bruckheimer, white anti-racism writer Tim Wise, and former president Jimmy Carter. As I told A.I. at the start of that first show: "You got a whole platform here"—a platform I felt would be especially appreciated by Black athletes and Black audiences in particular.

With each passing show, I began to feel I was worth the risk. I loved performing in front of a studio audience. I became addicted to seeing their reactions up close and personal to things I said and to whatever guest came on. It was an interview show that was meant to be lively, provocative, and fun.

But it's difficult to have fun when you're not winning. The early reviews were great, but I had trouble getting traction in the ratings. The long-interview format was problematic. The show's success was predicated almost totally on how interesting the interview subject was. I wanted the show's success to be more dependent on me and my relationship with the viewer.

Shapiro knew this and planned to make *Quite Frankly* more host-oriented. But soon after the show aired, Daniel Snyder, owner of Washington's professional football team, was in the process of buying Six Flags and turned to Shapiro, whom he had known for years, to run it, as well as other parts of his company. Initially, Shapiro turned him down. Then, according to sources familiar with their discussions, Snyder waved a huge check in front of him and said something along the lines of, "It's yours right now, just for saying yes." Shapiro sure as hell didn't say no.

"None of your damn business," Shapiro told me with a smile when I asked him about the offer.

He was gone October 1. With him went my support system; many of those direct reports who'd told him not to hire me in the first place were still around, and taking his place was John Skipper, who for years had run *ESPN: The Magazine*. I knew right then *Quite Frankly*'s days were numbered.

Skipper was not Shapiro. Unlike Shapiro, who focused on creating original content in an effort to avoid being overly dependent on airing live professional sports, Skipper believed in ESPN as the "World Wide Leader" in a literal sense: he wanted the network to have every league contract it could, and he made clear that his emphasis was on live sporting events and live programming. As I saw it, that didn't leave much wiggle room to grow shows like *Quite Frankly*, especially since ratings were low and the production costs—Manhattan studio, large staff— were high.

Weeks after the new regime arrived, the honchos broached the idea to me of moving the show's weeknight time slot from 6:30 to 11. Not only did I oblige, I did so enthusiastically. I was excited as hell to move to late night. But quite frankly—no pun intended—it was a stupid thing to do. As much as anything, the move put my ignorance about the business of TV on full public display.

Late night! Late night! Late night! That's all I could think about. Jay Leno, David Letterman, Jimmy Kimmel—stupidly, arrogantly, I believed that one day I might actually compete with them. I thought I'd have access to more eyeballs in late night and that the skies would be the limit.

As I sit here writing about it in 2022, reflecting on what I was thinking and the decisions I okayed sixteen years earlier, I'm so embarrassed by my level of ignorance that I've actually paused to slap myself.

Seriously!

First off, I didn't have a clue how crucial a lead-in—the show that would air right before mine—is in the world of linear television. In the case of *Quite Frankly,* the late-night lead-ins were not the kinds of programming that drew viewers, particularly the ones who'd stick around for my show.

Instead of professional basketball, football, or baseball games, the lead-ins were events like shark-fishing competitions. And because of their unscripted nature, they rarely ended right at 11 p.m. Instead of a definitive start time that began every weeknight at 6:30 p.m., a floating time replaced it. Our start time could be 11:07 or 11:11 or 11:18—nobody ever really knew exactly when the hell we'd come on. That uncertain starting time was not likely to attract viewers who were getting ready for bed and in no mood to search for a show that should've been on ten or fifteen minutes earlier. Beyond that, my competition throughout that entire hour was ESPN's own 11 p.m. *SportsCenter.*

I never stood a chance. And everyone else involved with programming, especially Skipper, likely knew it. While it would've been easy to accuse Skipper of setting me up to fail, I never blamed him. Despite almost zero marketing, the time-slot obstacles, and a new regime that inherited an upstart show that they had no hand in creating and little interest in seeing succeed, responsibility for making it work still fell on my shoulders.

The good news: I still had a show. The bad news: not enough folks were watching. I knew this because there were times I wasn't even watching my own damn show. I was bored when the subjects were boring. Changes needed to be made.

A year into its run, in August 2006, Skipper signed off on my request to become an executive producer and have a more hands-on role. As ratings slid, the show's executive producers were often pulled off for other assignments, and the rest of the staff was relatively young. So, I decided that if I was going down, I'd go down in my own way.

I still needed help with the intricacies of show-running, so I hired a new right-hand man, from CNN: Galen Gordon, a terrific executive producer who'd eventually become one of my closest friends in the world. We changed the format immediately. To speed up the show and lure viewers, we relied more on my personality and made the interviews shorter. We inserted more opinion and banter. We incorporated a panel of sports reporters. Commentary, commentary, and more commentary—that was our new thing, with me as the ringleader.

The result over the next five months: ratings jumped 22 percent!

I felt good about that, but with about forty staffers in a Midtown Manhattan office, the bump wasn't enough to justify the costs. Skipper canned the show. Two execs showed up one morning to see me at the ESPN Radio offices in Madison Square Garden and told me they were pulling the plug. The opportunity had been given. The only math that mattered was profitability, and I didn't generate enough to keep the show afloat. I got it. I didn't like it, but I got it.

"We're in the win business," I told the two execs. "You're telling me this isn't financially feasible to continue. I'm a big boy, I can take it." Cancellations qualify as business-as-usual in TV, just as they are a daily part of the sports business I've made a career out of covering.

I had only one request: take care of my staff. They'd given their hearts and souls to help create a new show. I asked that instead of the three weeks of severance pay the company was offering that they be given three months. The bosses agreed. I'd already made sure when I brought in Galen Gordon from CNN to help me retool the show that he would have a landing spot at ESPN if things went sideways.

Thirty-six hours later, the show went dark. The last episode was taped on January 11, 2007. *Quite Frankly* had lasted eighteen months—327 shows, 780 guests.

Though there wasn't much fuss or friction over the cancellation, there was plenty of second-guessing about why it didn't work.

"I'm a white guy," a buddy and former ESPN colleague, Gerry Matalon, would later tell me. "I love you. But watching *Quite Frankly*, as a white guy, I never felt like I was invited by you."

He was right. That was one reason it failed. I was fixated on "representing my people"—the Black community.

Foolishly, I thought that Black folks didn't support the show, which in my mind meant that they didn't support me, either. For a minute, I was mad at us, believing I should have been supported no matter what. After all, how many Black hosts were there at the time on national TV? Then I settled down and lectured myself:

"Wait a damn minute! I sit here and hold folks accountable for their performance every day, regardless of their ethnicity. So who the hell am I to think it's supposed to be different for me?"

Black folks did to *Quite Frankly* what I do every day: called it like they saw it. If they weren't feeling the show, they just weren't feeling it. That's not on my community, that's on me. I needed to know my business before I could handle the business. I had to learn the tricks of the trade, master my profession.

Shapiro knew what he was doing by putting me on at 6:30 every night. You'd catch me every night, rain or shine; there wasn't variable lead-in programming to alter our start times. As a result, folks would know exactly where and when to see me. That's how you become appointment viewing and build an audience.

Pardon the Interruption, with my buddies Tony Kornheiser and Michael Wilbon, has always been box office. *Quite Frankly* was never box office.

I'd entered a business that I was a natural at but knew little about. I'd paid too little attention to ratings and revenue. My definition of success was people screaming and cheering my name on the street or seeing myself, bigger than life, on billboards along the highway as I drove into Manhattan each day from my home in New Jersey. It was just me stroking my ego.

The show's cancellation proved how much I had to learn. I'd gone from being the toast of the town eighteen months earlier to wondering what kind of future I had. My obituary was being written by radio talk-show hosts and newspaper columnists across the country, even though I still had a job at ESPN, on radio, and as an NBA analyst.

"Stephen A. blew it!"

"Stephen A. is done!"

That's what I heard in the immediate aftermath of the show's demise. I finally got a taste of how professional athletes felt all these years when I called it like I saw it. It hurt like hell, but since I had dished it out I knew it came with the job, and I was determined to take it.

Yet any thoughts of a quick resurrection, of a public salivating for more of me on another show, evaporated one day as I was walking down Fashion Avenue in Manhattan. A fan ran up to ask for my autograph. While I stood there writing my name on whatever he handed me, the guy said, "I love you, man. I love your show so much. I watch it all the time. I never miss it."

I knew he was full of shit. The show had been canceled four months earlier.

I would learn what I needed to learn, eventually. Because of that epiphany, I'm now hell to deal with when it comes to business. I know what I'm doing a hell of a lot more than I did while trying to save that first show, more than fifteen years ago, and I plan on keeping it that way.

But back then, I still didn't know what awaited me.

I had no idea that the worst was yet to come.

CHAPTER 9

PERSONA NON GRATA

When *Quite Frankly* was canceled, in April 2007, my ESPN contract was a couple of months away from expiring. Renegotiations started and, because I had raised the ratings on *Quite Frankly* significantly once I had become an executive producer, I actually thought I was in a good place despite the show's cancellation. I was still hosting my ESPN Radio show, plus I had spent the previous three years on *NBA Shootaround*. So, I held some cachet, at least in my own eyes.

Yet, after some haggling back and forth, ESPN offered me a three-year deal for $1.7 million per year–$400,000 per year more than what I was getting paid at the time. I was not happy. I'd heard of several colleagues getting well over $3 million. My feeling was that my workload was unmatched, and my talent was apparent. I was also insulted because no specifics were provided as to what my job description would be. Maybe I'd do a radio show; maybe not. Would I go back to covering the NBA? *We'll see!* Could I do *SportCenters*? *Sure, you can do* Sports-Centers. Well, how many? They weren't sure.

All of that led to my saying no to the contract offer. I found it unacceptable.

I know $1.7 million sounds like a lot of money—and it *is* a lot of money. But like the athletes I cover, it's all about the market. Given what I'd accomplished, the ground I'd broken, and what others with my level of visibility were pulling in, I thought I was worth more, both in salary and security. And I told them so in turning down their offer.

I thought the negotiations would continue, but instead, they stalled. And as they stalled, I trusted everyone less and less. I made it personal. I shifted blame to my longtime agent, Steve Mountain. I loved Steve, a sharp Philly guy who was a master negotiator and had represented me well for years. But as hard as Steve worked—his phone seemed permanently attached to his ear—he rarely traveled outside of Philadelphia, and I thought, stupidly, that I now needed someone better connected nationally.

After all, I was in the big time!

So, I bolted to the William Morris Agency, a huge firm (which would get even bigger when it merged with Endeavor in 2009 to create WME). It was a haphazard, immature, and, in hindsight, desperate move on my part. The last thing you want to do while negotiating is to look desperate, and I was playing right into ESPN's experienced hands, losing leverage with each passing day. I was still covering the NBA as an insider, making numerous appearances on *SportsCenter*. I'd written a few articles for ESPN.com and the magazine and I was doing ESPN Radio. But *Quite Frankly* no longer existed, and I had no permanent time slot where I could be found on television.

Finally, in the spring of 2008, ESPN came to me with a take-it-or-leave-it offer. That pushy approach in itself was bothersome. What made it worse was that it was for $1.1 million, more than half a million dollars a year less than their original offer—and $200,000 less than I was making on my old contract. The final insulting blow was that this take-it-or-leave-it offer was a one-year deal, not the three that I was told I would be offered. I was also informed that instead of being able to do both television and radio, I would need to decide between them. It was an odd demand, for sure, but one with a predictable choice. I picked TV, which, it turned out, is just what they'd hoped I'd do. A couple hours later I ran into John Skipper by the cafeteria on the ESPN campus. I said I'd like to cover boxing, thinking of yet another way to diversify my portfolio and make me more marketable down the line. His body language and the look on his face was completely dismissive.

I knew in my heart right then that I'd be gone by 2009—no matter how much I tried to deny it to myself. Agreeing to a one-year contract was equivalent to my signing my name on the dotted line as Dead Man Walking. I signed the deal anyway

Assignments immediately started to dry up. So did invites to appear on *SportsCenter.* The staff clearly took its cues from above: keep Stephen A. off the air. For the entirety of my one-year contract, I did practically nothing. A concerted effort was being made to assure I was viewed as a malcontent. When I bitched about the situation, as they knew I would, rumors flew:

Stephen A. is tough to work with!

Stephen A. won't cooperate!

Stephen A. isn't a team player!

The less screen time I got, the more frustrated and madder I became, which only gave the rumors more substance. I viewed myself as the righteous one in a battle with a few mid-level ESPN producers who were chirping behind my back. That righteousness only led me to overreact at times and see myself as bigger and more influential than I was. I wasn't aware of my foolishness, of course, and my stock plummeted big-time because of it. The handwriting was on the wall. ESPN is a place that'll work you until the wheels come off, so if they're not doing that, your days are definitely numbered.

I felt it was all part of a plan to teach me a lesson. My arrogant ass, as it was being described behind my back, would finally get humbled. Who the hell did I think I was, turning down $1.7 million? To Black folks, that's code for: "You unappreciative bitch. How many Black folks are making that kind of money? To hell with what you *think* you've *earned*. You should be *GRATEFUL!*"

One of the things Black people lament most are the false narratives often created around us. Those who perpetuate those narratives often don't even realize that their reactions are triggered by our skin color, and they get defensive, or even take offense, when it's brought up. But it's real. In my business, if you're white and you're loud, you're viewed as passionate. If you're Black and you're loud, you're called angry or arrogant.

The message that came through loud and clear in this case is that I should've been appreciative of the money I was offered. When I balked and said I thought I deserved more, I encountered resentment. The underlying sentiment was "We gave this to you," not "You earned it."

That feeling was intensified around the same time at the *Philadelphia Inquirer*, where I'd continued to write my column. A new regime had been installed there as well and I was in the throes of battle with them. They were making cuts as the newspaper business was continuing to shrink, and they wanted me out. I didn't have much of a beef with that, but I did think that after all I'd done for the paper, helping put them in the forefront of NBA coverage in a basketball-mad town, that I deserved severance. A new editor thought otherwise:

"You're over there at ESPN, working for them too," he said to me during our lone one-on-one conversation. "I think you've earned enough money."

That was the worst thing he could possibly have said to me.

Here's the thing: I would not have taken offense if he was talking about the money I'd made over the years at the *Inquirer*. But he was talking about ESPN. In my mind, he was really telling me, "Your Black ass has made enough money in this business." It felt personal with him. To me, he was clearly on a mission to bring me down to size.

I wasn't backing down. I knew I was right. I notified the newspaper union, went through arbitration—and won! They had to give me my job back. I left ten months later anyway, but my point was made.

In April 2009, one of the ESPN bosses emailed me out of the blue to ask me to lunch. I sensed what was up but didn't want to admit it to myself.

The boss picked a restaurant about forty-five minutes from Bristol, inside a Marriott Hotel. I was driving there when a colleague phoned me. It wasn't good news.

"They're about to let you go," he said in a hushed tone. "That's why he's meeting with you. Sorry."

Despite all of my certainty over the past year that this day would be coming, I still couldn't believe it. I drove for a minute in silence, my colleague still on the line, lost in my own thoughts. My fear of unemployment was real. I finally regained my composure and thanked my pal for the heads-up. For the rest of the drive, it was like I was going to my own funeral. Actually, it was more like I was headed to my own execution. I still had to act like I had no idea what was coming. If I gave away that I already knew why the exec was meeting with me, he could probably figure out who'd told me. One execution that day was enough.

I arrived at the Marriott lobby first. Five minutes later, the ESPN boss walked in. We shook hands and sat down at a table inside the mostly empty restaurant. It was just he and I and the waitstaff. He got straight to the point.

"We're letting you go" he said, practically before I could put a napkin in my lap. "We're not going to renew your contract. It was not a unilateral decision."

He never gave any reason for the decision. Never even said he—or they—were sorry things had regressed to the point of my being let go. He just told me my last day on the air would be midway through the first round of the NBA playoffs. That date would be May 9, 2009. The last day of my contract was June 30, 2009. They didn't care. The date was nonnegotiable.

My hands shook. I swallowed hard. My voice nearly cracked when I spoke. I actually fought back tears, engulfed by a combination of sadness, fury, and utter embarrassment. I wanted to do something harmful to anyone who played a role in this decision. I knew names. But I also knew it would be career suicide to react like some petulant child, lashing out at executives.

It's hard to know how much time went by before I responded. Every second felt like a minute. I took a deep breath and thanked the executive for giving me the news straight up. I even went so far as to add: "Who knows? Maybe I'll be back someday." Then I told him I harbored no ill feelings.

I lied my ass off.

I heard the exec say: "I know you drove all the way over here. You want to order something to eat?" Still shell-shocked, I replied, "Yeah, I'd like that," and ordered a Caesar salad. I assumed he'd sit there with me as I ate, that he'd at least converse and express his good wishes for whatever future endeavors I might pursue. Instead, he volunteered to pay for the meal, then pushed away from the table and walked off to the other side of the room. He stood by the wall working on his phone until I got up to leave.

Executions don't get much weirder than that.

I left the Marriott without saying another word.

While driving home on Route 15, I had to pull over. I needed gas, but more than that I needed to get the hell off the road and settle down. I exited at a rest stop with a Mobil station but never left my car. I sat there with my head buried in my hands—devastated! I didn't cry, though I don't know why not. I sure as hell wanted to.

Eventually, I called my sister Carmen to let her know what happened. She did what a big sis is supposed to do at a time like that: assured me everything would be all right. Next I called Dave Roberts, who at that time oversaw ESPN News, and who would later become my boss and guardian angel. I felt a kinship with Dave that I didn't feel with many other ESPN execs back then. He was the ultimate straight shooter and he shot straight when I called: he was pissed, told me he disagreed with the decision, and that he would stay in touch. With Dave, I knew that wasn't just lip service. My last call was to the colleague who'd tipped me off on my drive over. I let him know that it all went down just like he said. He told me to keep my head up and stay strong. It was nice to have those people in my corner at a moment when I felt totally abandoned. It helped snap me out of my stupor.

I'd worked my tail off, and I knew that my work ethic and production was not a reason for my dismissal, despite the rumors and behind-my-back whispers that suggested otherwise. I honestly believed I didn't deserve what was happening. To lose the goodwill I'd accumulated from all the work I'd done at ESPN, only a year after I thought I was due a long-term deal, was incomprehensible to me. I felt completely screwed over. Betrayed! Like this was all planned and plotted. The fix, as I called it, had been executed to perfection. This was corporate knife fighting at its nastiest and bloodiest. The takedown was complete.

I had become a dad in the last year and needed to support my daughter Samantha. After she was born, I was no longer working just for myself.

Sitting at that rest stop parking lot in the middle of Connecticut, fear and embarrassment started to mix with my rage, welling up inside me, suffocating me. All the slights I had chosen to ignore during the past year suddenly came into focus. All the sly smirks and uncomfortable silences around the office had been telling me what I refused to hear: "We'll be just fine without you." ESPN was the behemoth. No individual was bigger than that four-letter brand.

Even worse: I knew they were right.

Meanwhile, friends encouraged me to look for something elsewhere, but my new agents informed me that nobody was interested. My notoriety was fading fast—I was out of sight, out of mind. Other networks noticed I wasn't on-air as much as I had been, and seemed to me to be likely thinking the worst thing possible: that I was too much of a headache to be worth the trouble. Employing me simply wasn't worth the headache. No one was kicking down my door to say, "We want you! Come with us!"

Not Fox.

Not NBC.

Not CBS.

Not a single cable network. Not even Black Entertainment Television (BET) or TV One.

Not radio. Not digital.

The realization hit me like a ton of bricks that it wasn't just my ESPN career that could be over, but possibly my career as a sports journalist. In 2009, ESPN was not known for bringing back anyone they'd pushed out. When they said "goodbye," that was followed by an unspoken "Don't let the screen door hit your sorry ass on the way out!" It felt like ESPN was in the process of sending an emphatic message to the rest of the sports world: "We don't want Stephen A. and none of you should want him, either."

ESPN couldn't care less; they weren't worried about me at all. I felt like the loneliest person in the world. I was a lost soul.

During the month between taking my last bite of Caesar salad at the Marriott and my last day of work for ESPN covering the NBA playoffs, the sports press got wind of my demise. They had a field day. It seemed like a daily topic for discussion on sports talk radio.

The only thing that lifted me from the abyss of self-pity I'd plunged into—an abyss probably better described as simple depression—came subsequent to my last assignment for ESPN. Following Game Five of the Atlanta-Miami playoff series in Atlanta's Philips Arena (now State Farm Arena), I headed to the Heat's locker room deep in the cinder block bowels of the arena to say goodbye to some of the players and staff I'd covered. As I was about to enter, the Heat's team president, Pat Riley, was striding out.

As always, Riley was dressed to the nines. His designer suit and slicked-back hair only accentuated the no-bullshit confidence that's made him a multi-title-winning player, coach, and executive, from L.A. to Miami. All of that came through full force when I informed him that this was my last night for ESPN and that it had been great covering him. We'd been cordial over the years, some friendly sparring sometimes, away from the cameras and microphones, but that was about it. I wished him good luck in the future, then extended my hand as a final goodbye.

Riley just left me hanging. He refused to shake my hand. I stood there frozen, vulnerable as hell, feeling like this was yet another in a series of slaps in my face over the previous months by several people.

Riley sighed. Then he looked me straight in the eye, like he might look at one of his players in the locker room after a tough defeat, and snapped, "Put your damn hand down. I'm not shaking your hand. You're acting like this is over, like you're finished. Well, you're not finished. Lift your head up and save the handshakes for when you come back. Because you will come back."

That was it. He said what he had to say and strode off. At some point, I finally put my hand down.

Riley's tough-love coach-speak on that day, April 29, 2009, prevented me from taking a turn for the worse, from surrendering all the fight, all the never-say-die attitude, that was left in me. "You will be back." Those were the words I held on to. Those four words saved my career and, possibly, my life. Years later, every time I think of Riley or run across him, I still remember them.

After talking to Riley, I wondered where the swaggering dude I'd been during the good times at ESPN had gone. *How did I lose myself the last two years?* I wondered. And more important: *Would I have even noticed the erosion of my own state of mind had it not been for Pat Riley's spurning my handshake, and the words he spoke afterward?*

Riley's reinforcement of my determination to overcome my challenges was especially important because the hard times weren't about to immediately evaporate. I had made too many unforced errors to overcome as easily as that. Plus, I still had some more sulking to do.

Whenever I got low—really low—I headed to my mother's house in Hollis. After I was officially out at ESPN, I laid up there for three days. I already owned a 5,500-square-foot house in South Jersey, with a huge master bedroom, yet my childhood bedroom—the one I'd shared with my brother, Basil, and then my sister Carmen after Basil left for the army—was where I wanted to be.

That bunk bed inside that tiny space of a bedroom the size of a jail cell, with nothing in it but a dresser drawer and a thirteen-inch TV, was the most comforting place I knew. I loved lounging in the same bunk bed I'd slept in growing up. I loved it even more when my mother would bring me my usual breakfast: toasted plain bagel with extra butter, scrambled eggs, and a hot tea with milk and honey. What I loved most, however, was just being around her. Mommy was my safe haven.

I didn't make or take any calls for those three days. I rarely left my old bedroom except to go to the bathroom down the hall. My dad, now home because of age and oncoming symptoms of Parkinson's disease (and no mistress to lean on since she had passed away years earlier), was always in front of the TV, watching baseball and those Westerns. My mother was there if I needed something to eat, but otherwise she pretty much left me alone.

So I wasn't prepared for what she had in store when she came through the door on my third morning there with a tray piled with my usual breakfast. There was the bagel, eggs, and hot tea. This time, however, she'd also placed a new item on the tray: a hand mirror.

"What's this?" I asked, holding it up, a bit annoyed.

"You know what it is," she snapped back. "I put it there because I'm wondering when you're going to start looking at yourself."

Of course, that provoked an argument. And, of course, the argument was one-sided: her side!

My mother proceeded to rip me a new one. She challenged my "audacity" for feeling victimized. Mommy didn't know a thing about sports. She never had, but she knew her baby boy. That means she knew what a headache I must have been to ESPN. Mommy had often heard me on the phone with one honcho or another in her kitchen or living room during the negotiations, debating, challenging, questioning one decision after another. She knew how I'd consistently thrown accusations their way that they were marginzalizing me, and that I'd accused them of not exactly having my best interests at heart. It wasn't so much what I said to them that she didn't like, it was my tone.

Mommy reminded me of all that, adding how I'd occasionally gripe about the role race and prejudice played in limiting my prospects. She just let me have it.

"Why should [ESPN] want somebody like that working for them?" she asked, her accent rising and falling. "Who needs that headache? You don't like anyone questioning your decisions and you're not even a boss, so why should they like you doing it? I'm not saying they should've fired you, but how would you feel if you were them? You're not blameless here."

It hurt to hear all that. Yet it was the truth, which coming from anybody, let alone your mother, can hurt like hell.

As she spoke, I reflected back on an exchange from just a few weeks earlier. I'd gotten into an argument with some executives about my not being allowed to go on different networks, like CNN and Fox News, to debate politics and social issues. My attitude was that while I worked for ESPN, they didn't own me and they shouldn't act like they did. Talking about politics and non-sports issues didn't conflict with my responsibilities as a sports personality, so I should be able to go on TV elsewhere and talk about those things anytime I damn well pleased. I felt that ESPN's domination over my life was beyond annoying.

But my mother's words forced me to realize I'd forgotten some things I'd learned about working in corporate America over the years. I'd forgotten the lessons from my days at the *Daily News*; to ask myself if what I want is consistent with the bottom line of the company that's paying me. If the answer is no, then the only thing you can do is accept the rules of the game until you gain enough influence to change them.

I'd forgotten the Golden Rule: those who have the gold make the rules.

Love it or hate it, that's the reality I'd come face-to-face with, because I had failed to recall—and follow—the golden rule on a number of occasions.

That realization left me feeling that I'd been incredibly immature.

More like a dumbass, actually.

Now I saw the blowup I'd had with ESPN execs over my appearances on other channels in a new light. ESPN was paying me, not the other networks. My contract was with ESPN and I'd signed it voluntarily—in fact, I'd done everything I could to get that contract. Any views I expressed on another outlet would inevitably be attached to ESPN. It was the same as if I got arrested for speeding or anything else. The headline would invariably start "ESPN's Stephen A. Smith . . ." I was no longer just some dude named Stephen Smith.

It didn't mean I had to be a puppet. No one has ever accused me of that. But when you play for the man, the brand comes first. You help build the brand, then you build your wallet. That's another lesson I'd forgotten in the midst of one spat after another.

The end result: I concluded that I was the one ultimately responsible for perpetuating a false narrative about myself. I'd allowed my bombastic and demonstrative diatribes on TV to become one with my interactions with others off the air, and this had happened often enough that the perception of me as bombastic had seeped through the screen and into executive offices throughout the business. I was now persona non grata because of it.

I had to change that narrative—and fast. It wasn't who I was, as a professional or as a man. I was determined that my career wouldn't end like this.

My firing would not be my epitaph. There would be a new beginning. I'd see to it.

CHAPTER 10

THE BEGINNING OF MY RESURRECTION

Before I could reach out to anybody about a new job, I got the most unexpected call I could have imagined: from George Bodenheimer, then president of ESPN and ABC Sports. He asked me to come to his office just days after my official exit.

If there's a nicer executive in this cutthroat business, I haven't met him. Bodenheimer started in the mailroom at ESPN, so he always seemed to have a bottom-up feel for the place. He was incredibly unassuming; for a guy who held the kind of power he did, he never came across as somebody who was anxious to use it. He was smart, fair-minded, and totally committed to the well-being of the company.

No one has treated me with more respect and decency in my entire career than Bodenheimer. He was like that from the moment I met him, just weeks after I started at ESPN. He'd made it clear then that he believed I would do big things for the company. As our relationship continued to develop, he would remind me from time to time that folks at ESPN believed in me, and with that belief came expectations and responsibilities.

My interpretation of what he said was that trust would play a big role in how successful anyone is in this business. That no matter how big the talent, if that person was seen as someone who wouldn't hesitate to throw a colleague under the bus when things got tough, that person should expect a hard time getting to wherever he or she wanted to go. So when I received the call from Bodenheimer, I didn't know what to expect.

I immediately thought back to the last time Bodenheimer called me to his office, ten months earlier, in June 2008, weeks after my contract negotiations stalled. He'd summoned me there from Boston, where I was working the NBA finals between the Celtics and Lakers. He wanted to have a heart-to-heart about things he was hearing concerning my feelings and behavior toward some of his subordinates—the honchos running the day-to-day operations at ESPN.

In his spacious office, Bodenheimer listened intently as I explained myself and all the underhanded rhetoric being spewed about me. He acknowledged a few of my points, admitting he could see how I'd drawn some of my conclusions. He then pointed out the flip side—the side my mother later pointed out to me when I fled to her home after my firing.

"A lot of what you're expressing is how you feel, it's your perception," Bodenheimer began. "But what about what others are saying? They're entitled to their perceptions of you, just like you have your perceptions of them. And if they're your bosses, with negative thoughts about you, where do you think that's going to get you?"

Where it got me is back inside Bodenheimer's tenth-floor office, only now as an ex-employee. I didn't blame him for any of it, of course. After all, he'd tried to warn me, indirectly, of what might happen nearly a year earlier. Considering his position, he must have known which way things were heading. And in conversations we'd had over the years, he always made it clear to me that good executives let their subordinates do their jobs. In my case, Bodenheimer would have asked for an explanation from his direct reports as to why I was being let go, but he wasn't likely to overrule them, at least not at that stage of my career. If you're a headache to the bosses, you had better be worth it. At that time, frankly, I wasn't.

So when the honchos under him wanted me gone, I was gone. Period.

Yet our relationship was too important to me not to go hear whatever he had to say. So, when he asked to see me at his office instead of just having a conversation over the phone, I jumped at the chance. I knew something positive would come of it, that I would walk away enlightened. That was the case anytime I was in his presence.

Bodenheimer made small talk for a minute, but quickly got down to business. He wasn't angry or upset, he didn't come at me like that. He seemed almost melancholy, like he was sad it had come to this.

"I'm disappointed you won't be with us," he said. "I imagine you're incredibly disappointed as well. But I don't think you're totally surprised by all this."

For the next fifteen minutes or so, we went back and forth about what had happened. Then he uttered words that both shocked and energized me.

"Just remember this," he said. "This is only one chapter. The book is not closed on your time with us. I truly believe that."

For a minute, I couldn't even respond. It was a huge moment for me. It was then that I knew I'd have a chance to return to ESPN someday. His words meant I was still respected by someone who mattered. It also meant ESPN just might alter its history by keeping an open mind about bringing back a talent they once cast away.

Bodenheimer could have easily told me, "See ya. It was nice knowing ya." That's the attitude a few of his underlings showed me in the months *leading up* to my departure and leaned into even more once I was gone. Instead, Bodenheimer did the opposite. He sounded more hopeful than I could ever have imagined.

I wasn't a lost cause after all.

*   *   *

"Man up," I told myself. "You got yourself in this situation. Now get yourself back on track."

That was easier said than done. Networks weren't calling me with job offers. It was months before I even got something freelance.

Driving in my white Cadillac Escalade up and down the New Jersey Turnpike, flipping from one channel to another, I'd periodically hear someone on talk radio going on about my fall from grace. Hosts portrayed me as the standard of what not to be, attacking my character, even implying the industry was better without me. I had become a punching bag, a gag line. Their vitriol was accentuated by laughter, and their utter satisfaction with my demise oozed through their microphones.

Now, all that did was motivate me.

I could always take the heat. The skepticism. The occasional attacks. I knew that being well known in this business wouldn't come without critics. To me, it was essential to my rise that I be able to take criticism, because I sure as hell never hesitated to dish it out. I wasn't going to bitch about somebody who said I couldn't write or questioned my credibility or my presentation as a commentator and pundit when I was just as quick to say somebody couldn't play, or coach, or run a team. As long as the attacks weren't personal, and fell within the lines of the business, I was cool. I always am.

However, while many people were happy about my fall, far more were supportive. They sent encouraging words and kept in touch. Those connections came through when I needed them most.

The first big assist came from Steve Mountain, the agent I'd foolishly let go. As the summer of 2009 came and went without anyone reaching out with a job offer—leaving me feeling completely blackballed—I humbled myself and reached out to him, asking for his help in getting me back on track. Mountain could have easily told me, "Go fuck yourself." And he would have been justified. He had believed in me, and I had snubbed him. Yet, instead of harboring hard feelings, Mountain, proving that he's simply one of the good guys, said, "Everybody makes mistakes. You weren't the first. You won't be the last. I know you're a good guy. Let's move forward," and immediately went to work for me.

Within a couple months, as of January 4, 2010, I was back in the business as a morning host at Fox Sports Radio. The job was from 6 to 9 a.m. EST (3 to 6 a.m. PST) every weekday morning. It required me to get up at 3:15 a.m., be on the road by 3:45, and drive 87 miles each way, from Hainesport, New Jersey, to the studio around the corner from Rockefeller Center, five days a week.

The morning drive was a nightmare for me. There are few things in life I hate more than early wakeup calls, primarily because I'm a night owl. My ideal schedule is going to bed around 2 a.m. and waking up about six hours later. That lifestyle helped ensure my early success in journalism. I'd cover games, then head out to wherever the athletes, coaches, or executives and their various crews hung out afterward without worrying about having to get up early the next morning.

Now I woke up at 3:15 a.m., went to work, and was a zombie en route back home. On the return commute, I often pulled over two or three times at rest stops on the New Jersey Turnpike to take naps, because I just couldn't make the drive without nodding off. Sometimes I'd think about how Michael Jordan's father was killed under similar circumstances: asleep in his car at a North Carolina rest stop, oblivious to his surroundings. Those stops could stretch that two-hour commute into a four-hour marathon.

I had no choice but to endure. I couldn't wait around for other offers. Unemployed for nearly a year, with a new daughter and another on the way, I was running out of money. Although Sonny Hill, the longtime basketball legend and sports-radio personality in Philadelphia, implored me when I lived there and was doing well to "save and invest, save and invest," I hadn't saved nearly enough. The salary Fox Sports Radio offered was less than a third of what I made at ESPN, and I had mouths to feed.

Not only was my future at stake, but also the future of my daughters. Plain and simple.

Though I hated the early mornings and long commute to and from my gig at Fox Sports Radio, the job was terrific, just what I needed back then. I had a great boss in Don Martin, a total pro who valued talent, and fun, and I had welcoming coworkers and a great team in Jake Warner, Michael "Ty Eli" Pearson, and Deb Carson. I was back in the game, talking sports and making connections. Oprah Winfrey even called in for an interview one day, as a courtesy to our mutual friend, *CBS This Morning* host Gayle King.

Fox Sports Radio opened doors I'd never paid attention to while at ESPN. I fostered relationships at Premiere Radio, the largest syndication company in the country, and executives there such as Julie Talbott and Jennifer Leimgruber. They were nearly as committed as I was to my comeback, bestowing their audio expertise upon me with such grace and candor, I actually grew comfortable with the thought of working with them for decades to come.

But the most important relationship I made while I was at Fox Sports Radio was Mike McVay, a widely acknowledged genius of talk radio. Introduced to me by my friend Terry Fox who worked at ESPN at the time, McVay was consulting for ClearChannel (which owned Fox Sports Radio). He spent nearly ten months tutoring me—right up until he took over content and programming at radio giant Cumulus Media— literally giving me private coaching. He not only taught me how to host a radio show, he educated me about the business of radio.

During my time at ESPN, I had based my value on how many cheers and jeers I got—all those people hollering at me on the street. McVay just waved them off.

"Cheers and screams don't provide intel," McVay would say. "Numbers do!"

Ratings! Revenue! Ad sales! Q-scores (a measure of on-air talent's appeal)! The things that distinguish one person's market value compared to another's were the things I was most clueless about until McVay took me under his wing. He left no stone unturned. He taught me not only how to be a better host, but where and how to best devote my energy and, even more important, decipher my market value. He had a next-level understanding of ratings, breaking them down to teach me what really mattered. He showed me how to prioritize one market over another, and what contributed to ad sales and what didn't—which, overall, is what truly defined success in the eyes of radio executives.

McVay told me I should build a radio career, that I could compete with, and even surpass, the likes of Jim Rome, Mike Francesa, and Chris "Mad Dog" Russo, if I was truly committed to making a long-term investment in the industry.

Years later, as the podcast boom took hold, he'd still throw out names like Joe Rogan, Bill Simmons, et al. "I wouldn't bet against you with anyone in the audio world," McVay told me, years after I had returned to ESPN. "You are that special."

He made knowing my self-worth a priority.

McVay also made me appreciate the importance of mentorship. I started to shape and define for myself what a future mentor should be. Just the process alone worked wonders for me. Someone with knowledge of the business to guide me was one component. Someone cheering me on was the other.

The only other thing I needed was a mentor with the power to make decisions that could help my career. Little did I know that person had already found me.

*   *   *

Dave Roberts was the ultimate straight shooter. I'd called from the car right after I talked to my sister Carmen on my drive back from the Marriott where I'd been told I was being fired. A ferocious competitor who'd earned his reputation while working as a news director at TV stations in Baltimore, Atlanta, and Washington, D.C., he was now general manager of 1050 ESPN Radio, in New York. He had gotten to know me and respect me at ESPN, as I did him, even when we disagreed. I trusted the hell out of him. He was fully aware of the internal politics that got me exiled—he was both a savvy exec and a rare Black man in a decision-making position who understood all that it entailed. He could see my being Black for what it was: complicated. That resonated with me. When I got fired, he had promised me he'd call me every month to check in. He'd done exactly that.

Dave is never ambiguous. If there's a problem, he tells you, no bullshit. If there's an issue, he tackles it head-on. He doesn't pass the buck. He's accountable. He's tyrannical about winning—which can cause headaches, at times, especially for talent—but it's something any talent under him needs to get over, because he doesn't apologize for it. He never will.

In February 2011, less than two years after ESPN kicked me aside, Dave engineered my return. His approach to bringing me back into the ESPN family was calculated and deliberate. It had to be. While some folks wanted me back, there was also plenty of resistance. Enough of those direct reports who'd balked when Mark Shapiro had raised my name when I was first hired were still around, as were a few producers who had undermined me before I left.

Roberts believed that ESPN Radio in New York was the perfect outlet from which to stage my return. I'd had a successful run there from 2005 to 2008—I later learned that 62 percent of the audience in my afternoon time slot vanished after I left—and I was a native New Yorker.

I was also kicking ass during morning drive time right down the street, at Fox.

But from a business perspective, I was viewed as high-risk, high-reward. That meant it was possible folks above Roberts would balk at his push for my return. He sold them the potential reward—the network would recoup the big audience that disappeared after I left. And no matter what anyone asked about me as a risk—Will he work hard? Will he get distracted?—his answer was almost always in my favor. Any negativity was something he confronted me with directly as a professional and as a man. I never had to hear anything third-hand or through the grapevine, which is a talent's dream.

ESPN also lessened its risk by making a low offer. I would do four hours of radio daily: two different two-hour shows in the country's two largest markets. The first would air from 6 to 8 p.m. EST in New York, followed by a show from 6 to 8 p.m. PST in Los Angeles, which meant no more early mornings for me. That was a big plus. But on the significant downside, at the time, hosts in those markets were getting $400,000 to $500,000 per year per show. The total compensation they offered me for both shows: $400,000. It was also strictly a radio deal—no TV. I was not allowed back on television.

"I know the numbers and the opportunities are not exactly what you want," Roberts told me, seeing how taken aback I was by the limitations. "You deserve better. I'm telling you that. But this is your chance to get back in. I need you to accept this, to come back here and show us what you're made of. You do that and the rest will take care of itself. I'll see to that."

I trusted Roberts and did what he asked me to do.

And because I listened to him, I've made millions.

We became partners. Roberts didn't tell me to shut up and dribble. All he asked was that I go on the air, do my job, and be the best. He gave me the chance to be more involved, asking for my input on almost every decision being made about anything involving me. Roberts made the final calls—I always knew who the boss was—but there was very little he did that he wouldn't ask me about first. My sense that I didn't have anyone at the network who would stand up for me disappeared. Our relationship remains the same to this day.

As a result, over time, other execs treated me the same way as Roberts was doing, including John Skipper, Norby Williamson, the now-retired Traug Keller, and—one of my all-time favorites—John Wildhack, who I'll always respect and revere and is now the athletic director at Syracuse University. Roberts's willingness to validate me as a team player helped make these other people more receptive. They opened up because of it, compelling me to do the same, helping to create and foster relationships that have benefitted me to this day.

But the bosses weren't the only ones to whom Roberts spoke up on my behalf. He did it with everyone. When advertisers and sponsors wanted to do business with me, Roberts cosigned. When additional opportunities presented themselves with ESPN Radio and Mad Dog Sports Radio on SiriusXM, Roberts cosigned.

I was always considered a workaholic and I never shied away from the workload. But to know I had a manager "championing" me like this only made me want to work harder, both to validate his faith in me and to avoid what I considered the worst thing possible: making a liar out of him. When you have a boss who volunteers for the role of "mentor" purely through his actions, and he also happens to be your biggest cheerleader, it doesn't get any better for an employee. Roberts put his reputation on the line to vouch for me. He told the other bosses, "I'll deal with him. Let me worry about him. Y'all judge his work." And I'm where I am today because of it.

Because I had a champion.

Opportunities flowed my way because Roberts paved the way for me to be fixated on the work, not bureaucratic nonsense. He was fearless in taking care of everything else. Rumors and innuendo would no longer derail my progress. Lies wouldn't gain traction. All I had to do was put my head down and perform. His presence helped me overcome the trauma of having been fired.

Even with his tireless support, he never failed to remind me of potential pitfalls. He knew one of my Achilles' heels was becoming preoccupied with bosses who spent their time elevating folks they got along with at the expense of those who actually produced.

"That's going to exist wherever you go," Roberts told me. "Get the hell over it. You will never find a job in this world where that problem doesn't exist. Adapt and overcome by focusing on what you do and performing. In the end, all bosses appreciate talent with that attitude. Especially a talent like you, because I'm here to tell you: you are the fucking best!"

I listened and learned. And I woke up every morning first thinking about my daughters, and then continued with two thoughts regarding my performance at work.

First: How to make my bosses more money.

Second: How to get some of it for myself and my family!

I knew if I kept that attitude, I'd never fail. Not ESPN. Not Dave Roberts. Not anyone I'd do business with in the future.

Most important, I wouldn't fail myself.

CHAPTER 11

THE BLESSINGS—AND PERILS—
OF FATHERHOOD

Fatherhood is the greatest blessing I've ever received. From the moment my daughters were born, I immediately recognized that I was madly in love. That I'd never known love like this. And that every thought in my life revolved around them.

Yet that incomparable love, that unwavering devotion, is also a *curse*. At least in certain respects. It's a curse in that that love breeds a complete absence of peace, a persistent and incessant worrying, and virtual panic about everything involving—in my case—two beautiful daughters.

Every day, I wondered: *How did they feel when they woke up this morning? Did they eat their breakfast and get to school on time? What did they learn in school today? Did they get home safely once school was over? What do they need?* The list went on and on.

I didn't sleep unless I knew they were comfortable. It's still that way today. I'm not comfortable unless I know they're safe. If they're hungry, it's because I'm starving.

Samantha and Nyla are simply *my everything!*

They are the reason I feel like a man at all.

Before I became a daddy, I was honestly a shell of the man I am today.

I've never been married for a reason: I was promiscuous into my early thirties, with few exceptions, and unapologetic about it for years. I avoided commitment like the plague and never hid it from anyone. I fought and beat back love throughout my adult life, the way Mike Tyson used to destroy opponents. I was even engaged once, and I ruined that within six months.

Why? Because I was a coward, that's why!

I was afraid to care. I was afraid to be distracted. *Be successful,* I thought, *and finding the right woman won't be a problem.* Plenty of men have lost money chasing women, but few have lost women chasing money!

I was held back by the thought filling my psyche, memories of starving for food, being laughed at for wearing the same outfit two to three times per week, of the time in the seventh grade I sent the class into hysterics because I showed up to school in fifty-degree weather wearing a short-sleeved dashiki.

"I'm never going back to being poor," I'd chant to myself. "I'm never going back."

That was the sort of immaturity my thoughts were defined by, justifying my unwillingness to commit and invest in someone emotionally. If I was going to get *caught up* by being a father, it damn sure wasn't going to happen voluntarily.

Now look at me.

Before my daughters were born, I strictly went about enjoying myself. Doing what I wanted to do. Although I was honest about my actions, I didn't give much thought about how I'd made ladies feel because we were all adults and they knew I was interested in being married to my work only. Fourteen years later, I'm barely recognizable. All I think about now is my daughters and their well-being. Imagining the idea of them getting into a relationship with someone like I was once makes me grimace a lot these days.

Some folks call it God's revenge.

It's not like the world we live in makes parenting easy.

Social media is the latest craze to steer a child's interest away from the guidance of his or her parents. TikTok, the phenomenon that has swept the nation, has become more valuable to many kids than teachers, not to mention Twitter, Facebook, and Instagram.

Mass shootings have occurred not only in malls and at concerts but in elementary and high schools.

Blacks, whites, Hispanics, and Asians have been attacked. In Colorado. In Buffalo. In Florida. In Uvalde, Texas. The mayhem seems to be spreading instead of subsiding, and not even children are being spared.

Fair elections labeled as rigged by power-hungry politicians have divided instead of galvanized. Cable networks have become partisan outlets, eager to take sides and polarize, generating ratings at the expense of civility and decorum.

The divisiveness that exists throughout America has only made adults more fearful, with the natural fearlessness of children—*"We know what we're doing, Dad! Stop worrying!"*—only contributing to our fright.

As a father, I can't help but be scared all the time, praying my counsel is profound enough, repetitive enough, to be so ingrained in Samantha's and Nyla's brains that they'll hear me talking to them even when I'm not around.

Mommy would always tell me, "You better pray you never have daughters. You'll never be the same if you do."

Amen!

My mother was prophetic, in more ways than she ever realized.

Once single and proud, and happy to be childless, a permanent alteration took place in my life once my girls were born.

Work wasn't my priority anymore. Neither were women. Ensuring my children were having a good time and living well became my priority; my having a good time took a back seat.

I prayed more. I spoke to my pastor more, A. R. Bernard from the Christian Cultural Center in Brooklyn, whom I consider a spiritual father. I quelled my insatiable appetite for beautiful women. Almost instantly, I went from being someone who always wanted to be where the ladies were to receiving satisfaction from simply hearing my daughters' voices.

For a couple of their formative years, there was no greater joy I felt in my entire life than coming home and watching my youngest daughter greet me by throwing clothes on my head from the top of the stairwell; or her big sister sneaking up on me from behind to punch me in my back just so I could chase her around the house.

That's when they were younger.

As they've gotten older, Nyla, a voracious reader, looks destined to become a lawyer or venture into politics. She already out-debates me by simply refusing to believe she is wrong. Samantha, a brilliant student with a vibrant personality, is convinced she'll be the next Viola Davis or Alfre Woodard, destined to be a star actress in Hollywood someday.

I've been sorry about a lot of things in my lifetime.

I've never been more grateful for anything as much as I am for having them.

I recall one time about seven years ago when I had to go from Los Angeles to Dallas for an event, but I hadn't seen them in ten days. It killed me to be away from them for that long, so I flew home on the red-eye from L.A. to New York just to see them for three hours before having to head right back out to Dallas.

Hugs and kisses abounded as we laughed and joked around, right up until the moment I said, "Okay, Daddy's got to head out of town now." All I heard was a big *"WHAT?!"* from my daughter Nyla. The second I tried to explain, both busted out in tears and screams, completely distraught that I had to leave town again.

Neither of them would talk to me for the rest of the day. They were furious with me.

It made me blush.

"They love their daddy," Aunt Carmen would say. "They really do."

It's nothing compared to how much I love them.

They are the reason I breathe, even while they take my breath away. Their happiness is my happiness. That's where it all starts for me these days.

When my mother cried in my arms when I was a teenager, when she told me *"just don't be like your father,"* I had always assumed she meant to be faithful, honest, and honorable in my commitments. Although I'm sure that was a part of it, I came to realize she'd meant something more.

Be animalistic in my approach toward my children. Protect them the way a bear would protect her cubs. Nurture them in ways any devoted father would nurture his own.

Take them to work with you. On the road with you. In the streets with you. Figuratively, not literally. It's about having them in your heart and mind wherever you go.

"Nothing compares to the love a loving parent has for their child," Mommy would say. "You'll do anything for them. Anything to protect them. You'll be a better person because of them, and miserable without them."

I learn that anew every single day.

No matter what I go through or what I'm enduring, no matter the medicine required or the rest that comes with it, nothing makes me feel better than hearing one word:

"DADDY!!!"

Too bad I waited until I was forty years old to become one.

I should have embraced fatherhood much earlier in life.

A lot of happiness would have arrived a lot earlier.

CHAPTER 12

SKIP BAYLESS AND *FIRST TAKE*

When Skip Bayless approached me in March 2012 in the parking lot outside of building four at ESPN headquarters in Bristol, Connecticut, to ask that I join him as a partner on his show, *First Take*, there were two good reasons to think it would never work out: I didn't want to do it, and ESPN didn't want me on television.

So my answer to Skip Bayless was going to be no. Bayless brushed all that off and made an attempt anyway. And I had to give it to him, his argument was compelling.

"Look, I know you're reluctant to do this, because you have your own plans," he said. "But I've been told there's no way you're getting your own show anytime soon here. Come on, we've talked about this for years."

Bayless was right about all of it. I wanted to get back to TV and host my own show, and I was trying to find ways to do it. I never liked the idea of having an on-air partner in television, of attaching my potential success, my destiny, to someone else's work ethic, commitment, and production. But that was currently beyond my grasp. The restrictions on my return to ESPN meant I was not allowed to have any scheduled appearances on TV at all. Skip thought that he, and his boss Jamie Horowitz, with approval and encouragement from Dave Roberts, could get around that and get me on *First Take*.

We also had a history together, and Skip was reminding me that our pairing on a regular show together was long overdue. Skip and I had done a pilot show for Fox Sports back in 2000 called *Sports in Black & White*. It came down to the eleventh hour of being green-lit, before a Fox Sports boss, David Lee, nixed the pilot. Had it been okayed, we would've gone up against two of my favorite buddies in the business, Tony Kornheiser and Michael Wilbon from ESPN's *Pardon the Interruption*.

Later, in 2004 and 2005, Skip and I had done a segment called "Old School/New School" on *SportsCenter* every Sunday morning, hosted by anchor Bob Ley.

I remembered how one Sunday morning in 2005, perturbed by the shenanigans a few athletes had found themselves in, Bayless went nuclear. After discussing athletes' penchant for getting into trouble, he declared—in front of a live national television audience—that all professional athletes should be contractually obligated to "avoid nightclubs." He added: "they should also have an 11 p.m. curfew throughout their respective seasons, even on off days."

After laughing hysterically at how ludicrous that suggestion was, I screamed into the television, "How old are you, Skip? How old are you?"

The thing I'd always liked most about Skip was that he was no caricature; he believed what the hell he said, which was a mandatory condition for both of us to work under. Neither of us could stand phony-ass people. I had never known him to mess around or just make arguments for effect. But in that instant I questioned if he was actually joking.

Outside the studio I told Skip: "Good job, my man. Only you would say something that crazy." He came up close to me, looked me right in my eyes and said: "Hey, man, you're laughing, and I get that. But I want you to know, I am dead serious. These athletes should be contractually obligated to avoid nightclubs. And they should have an 11 p.m. curfew. Every single one of them. Nothing good happens when you're out after 11 at night. Nothing!"

My mouth dropped. I just stood there for a second, staring at his face to make sure he was as serious as he appeared. Bayless did not blink once. He was not playing. I thought he was nuts, affectionately speaking. But damn if he wasn't great television. Because of his conviction—and mine—I recognized at that moment there would be fireworks anytime we were on the air together. Call it the defense against the prosecution: two individuals dogged in their beliefs and their commitment to staying-the-course and sticking to it, regardless of what others may feel.

So, in 2012, when Skip told me "we've talked about this for years," he had a point. "I need an everyday partner I can trust, and to me, there's only one person I know I can depend on," he said. "All I need from you is three years. I think we'll knock this out of the park."

I slept on Skip's proposal, turning over in my mind what he said he'd heard from the higher-ups about there being no way I was getting my own show. I knew it was true. So I started fantasizing about the impact the two of us could have together. Thinking back on our history, I felt we'd beat any show on the planet we got put up against in a debate format. I decided I wanted to do the show.

But there was still the other problem: ESPN's desire to keep me off television altogether, paired with my own cynicism toward those folks. It would take someone other than Bayless to convince me we had a chance at success. In my opinion, even the people who didn't support me inside of ESPN knew that once I returned to the airwaves, I'd have an impact, and the demand for me would grow. The public would take notice. My stock within the company would increase because the ratings would increase. ESPN would make money as a result. But so would I, and I believed there were those in positions of power who preferred that

I remain marginalized—those who elected to let me go in the first place would look quite silly if I returned and did so in a huge way—rather than maximize my potential for the sake of the company.

Jamie Horowitz was the clincher. He made things happen.

Horowitz had been the *First Take* boss since 2012. White, balding, standing about six feet four and built like Snoop Dogg, he was not the typical executive. Yes, he wanted his way. He could be demanding. But very few executives in television, I came to find, were as forthcoming, as talent-friendly, and as committed to capturing an audience as Horowitz.

When the show first originated, in 2003, it was called *Cold Pizza*. A conventional morning talk show consisting of interviews, features, and games, it was hosted by the talented trio of Jay Crawford, Kit Hoover, and Thea Andrews. Dana Jacobson, a brilliant sports mind in her own right, came on in 2005, and Hoover and Andrews left.

Bayless started appearing on the show in 2006 and brought a debate element to the program. But his appearances were too infrequent to really gain traction for that side of the show. It was not truly a debate show. When *Cold Pizza* changed its name to *First Take*, in May 2007— and filming moved to Bristol from New York—the format stayed untouched. It wasn't really until Horowitz's arrival, in 2010, that everything changed. He rolled the dice and adjusted the entire format from a conventional morning sports show into an all-debate fest.

His rationale for the change was based on ratings research and audience focus groups, which confirmed his suspicions: the audience wanted more debate, which meant they wanted more Skip Bayless. "Ask around. Talk to people on the streets," he later explained to me. "You quickly learned that everything was about Skip. What he said. What he felt. Where he stood with his opinions. And who he polarized. It was clear the audience wanted more Skip Bayless, and I wasn't about to deny them that."

Horowitz didn't make many friends by changing the format of the show, but he truly did not care. "As far as I'm concerned, the audience made the call," Horowitz said to me.

At Bayless's pleading, Horowitz brought me on to cohost *First Take* for one Wednesday in 2012. He knew I was prohibited from doing television but agreed to take a risk and do it anyway—to see if it would work. And once he saw Skip and me together, he didn't need any more convincing. He took it upon himself to persuade the bosses to change course and allow my return to television on a more permanent basis. Of course, it wasn't easy—some people at ESPN disliked Skip almost as much as they disliked me, so there were plenty of critics, appalled at the thought that such obnoxious back-and-forth bantering between two "unlikeable characters" could potentially sully the *SportsCenter* brand, or even the overall ESPN brand. Critics were saying, "Is Stephen A. really back? I thought he was finished. It's bad enough we have to deal with Bayless, but the both of them? Damn!"

Horowitz didn't worry about that or listen to the doubters. All that mattered to him was the show. And he started to get his way. I came on the show weekly. Within two months, he made an offer to me to triple my salary from what I was making on radio and become Skip's permanent cohost five days a week.

My official arrival as the *First Take* cohost was May 7, 2012. As expected, Skip and I got along right away. We genuinely liked each other. We believed in putting in the work. We detested those who only pretended to work hard for the sake of the optics. Both of us had journalistic backgrounds, having spent years in press boxes and locker rooms. Although folks would try to question our credibility whenever we said something they didn't like, we had the credentials to render those assertions weak. We were writers. We did interviews. We broke stories. The critics didn't have a leg to stand on.

And for a debate show, our chemistry was perfect. No matter the subject, we were so certain we would *not* see eye to eye, preparation wasn't even necessary. As long as we were discussing relevant matters the audience wanted to hear opinions about, all you had to do was let us loose. We were polar opposites, a walking embodiment of *The Odd Couple.*

After what I had endured years earlier—feeling like I'd been sabotaged back in 2009, nearly having my career ruined—I was compelled to make sure my mind-set was about winning the marathon, not a sprint. My salary was not my main concern. I was all about long-term sustainability instead of immediate gratification. It was far more important for me to be a part of a winning situation, proving that I was an asset, not a liability, proving that I moved the needle and drew ratings. I had learned my lesson: likability damn sure wasn't going to be my calling card; ratings were the only thing that would provide long-term success. And that meant working well with others. Sustained success was not something I could achieve by myself. Corporate America didn't believe in lone rangers.

There always needed to be someone who'd benefit from my success, preferably someone in a position of power. In my case, and Skip's, that was Horowitz. He was just as committed to winning as we were and was not about to let petty personal biases—or a need to let everyone know he was the boss—get in the way of achieving our bottom-line goals. He didn't feel the need to control the talent. He left us alone to be all we could be. That didn't mean Horowitz didn't have plenty of good ideas, which he made the case for and executed on. One was his belief that the audience cared to know that Skip and I were actually friends, even though we genuinely disagreed about just about everything. He wanted us to come across as guys enjoying ourselves while jostling with each other. He went so far as to develop a marketing campaign to demonstrate that Skip and I were friends.

I didn't think it was necessary, because Skip and I were tight. It didn't need to be advertised. But Horowitz felt differently and pleaded with us to engage. So we played along.

Horowitz was right. It turned out to be successful. People really did not believe Skip and I got along as well as we did until they saw the campaign. Once they saw it for themselves, it elevated our profiles, our relationship with each other, and, ultimately, the show's popularity.

The single issue I ever had on *First Take* under Horowitz's steward-ship was a lack of diversity, and it was quickly addressed. After Galen Gordon—one of the best producers I've known, and one of my best friends in the world—moved on to another show at ESPN, called *Numbers Never Lie*, in May 2012, there were no Black people on the production side. The second I went to Horowitz and Bayless to insist on the issue being addressed, producer Antoine Lewis from *SportsCenter* was brought on within two weeks as *First Take*'s coordinating producer. Diversity has never again been an issue at *First Take*.

By June 2012, two months after I came on as a permanent host, *First Take* had catapulted from a show execs struggled to embrace to the number one morning sports show—even though we were on ESPN2 instead of ESPN. We outrated everyone in the morning, including *SportsCenter*. At times, we outrated the 6 p.m. *SportsCenter*—unheard of once upon a time.

Love us or hate us, the sports world couldn't get enough of Skip Bayless and Stephen A.

I've spent a lot of time dissecting what made *First Take* work in its first year with me and Skip Bayless. To me, it comes down to two things: the similarities in our approach to work, and the differences in our beliefs.

Skip and I both got our starts as newspaper journalists. Skip worked in Miami, L.A., Dallas, and Chicago. We had to find sources and back up our stories. We had to study history and get our facts straight. We broke news. We had our writing copyedited, then re-edited. We had executives to answer to and a bureaucracy to oversee us. We pounded the prover-bial pavement for years, and only then did we earn the right to become general sports columnists, as we both had risen to, and editorialize and provide our opinions. That was a pinnacle very few had reached.

In other words: we were not bloggers or social media commentators. Because of our newspaper background, we didn't just spew thoughts devoid of facts or informed perspectives.

There is simply no one more versed on sports than Skip Bayless. Before I got on *First Take*, most of the folks he debated (look and see for yourself! I'm not saying their names) made the crucial mistake of trying to attack his facts. He was always ready. They were his prey. They never realized it wasn't his information they should be attacking, just his perspective. He loved the fact they couldn't figure him out.

With me, it was different. I was aware of his tricks before I started doing *First Take*. I knew his facts were in order. So I focused on his vulnerabilities: his assumptions that he knew the perspectives of others; his unwillingness to ever admit he was wrong or misguided; his occasional jadedness.

LeBron! Bosh-Spice! West-Brick! Tebow!

Only in the world of Skip Bayless would Tebow get seen in a greater light as a professional athlete than LeBron James, Chris Bosh, or Russell Westbrook.

That gamesmanship, that back-and-forth banter and chemistry, was what made *First Take*. It never made Skip angry. It made him smile.

Our newspaper backgrounds and savviness about debate were the building blocks. The real differences of our opinions and personalities were what supercharged it.

Bayless was a white Oklahoma native in his early sixties; I was a Black man from Queens in my forties.

Skip graduated from Vanderbilt, which didn't accept its first Black student until 1964; I graduated from an HBCU.

Bayless never discussed politics; I loved talking about politics.

To Bayless, only one Super Bowl existed.

To me, there were actually two: the NFL championship and presidential debates. I loved them as much as I loved Super Bowls.

I hated jogging; Bayless ran five miles a day, minimum.

Bayless's only vice was—and still is—Diet Mountain Dew; I had quite a few vices over the years, particularly sweets, red meat, and women.

Years ago, while he was still single, Bayless admitted to the *Washington Post* that he told a woman on their first date: "Let's get this out of the way right now: You will never come before my job. It will always come first."

That woman's name was Ernestine Sclafani— a lovely, fiery, loyal-to-the-core lady if ever there was one—who'd ultimately become Mrs. Skip Bayless.

I would never say such a thing to a woman—before, during, or once I loved them. Not in a million years.

Bayless is also a born contrarian. Someone who relishes taking an opposite point of view. Except he means what he says. Perhaps the greatest thing about partnering with him was the gamesmanship we engaged in, no matter what we discussed.

From segment to segment, minute to minute, hour to hour, you didn't know who was going to get the better of whom. Bayless wasn't budging. And neither was I.

Bob/Weave.

Punch/Counterpunch.

Left/Right.

Then both of our hands got raised.

At a time when it was difficult to get folks to sit in front of their televisions to watch twenty minutes of a show, our time-spent-viewing at one point reached over forty-two minutes. Our viewers were also diverse as hell: half white, and half Black, Hispanic, and other folks of color.

"Anyone who has something to say to me can come right here on [*First Take*] and say it," he said. "I'm here."

And they sure as hell showed up, everyone from athletes like Chris Bosh, Ryan Clark, and Chad Ochocinco, to rappers like Lil Wayne, Common, Snoop Dogg, Ice Cube, Fat Joe, Wale, and Bow Wow.

First Take was box office. Bayless was a household name. My career was resurrected. Then came the Seattle Seahawks' young, trash-talking, All-Pro cornerback Richard Sherman. He nearly ended *First Take* for both of us.

The afternoon of March 7, 2013, was a day that could have easily lived in infamy for *First Take*.

After nearly a year with me and Skip, the show having gained major traction and establishing itself as the number one morning sports show, Horowitz had decided we were due more prime television real estate. Already on ESPN2 at 10 each weekday morning for two hours, a thirty-minute slot became available, just for a couple of days, one particular week on the main ESPN channel.

Horowitz snatched it, believing it would expose us to a different audience, expecting it to help the *First Take* brand grow.

That afternoon, our scheduled guest was Richard Sherman.

Two months earlier, the Seattle Seahawks, having completed an 11-5 record in the regular season, had lost to the Atlanta Falcons in the divisional playoffs in a thriller. Sherman, however, had established himself as one of the premiere cornerbacks in the league. Everyone knew this, of course. But Bayless the contrarian questioned Sherman's stature in NFL history compared to the likes of Darrell Revis and Deion "Prime Time" Sanders. He felt Sherman wasn't worthy of being mentioned in the same breath as those two.

It proved to be all the fuel Sherman needed to come at Skip in a way no one ever had on live television.

"Skip, whenever you refer to me, whenever you speak to me, whenever you address me, address me as 'All-Pro Stanford graduate,' because those are some accomplishments you can aspire to, but you will never accomplish," said Sherman, attacking Bayless right out of the gate, the second he appeared live on-air. "You have never accomplished anything."

When Bayless didn't back down, and replied, "I think I've accomplished more in my field than you have in yours," Sherman's venom intensified.

"I'm at the top of my field," Sherman declared. "I'm an All-Pro. I'm one of the best twenty-two players in the NFL. You're gonna brush it off. But I don't think you're the best twenty-two at anything. In sports, in media, in anything. I think you think more of yourself than you can actually prove. In my twenty-four years of life, I'm better at life than you."

Sherman went on to call Bayless "pompous and ignorant," among other things.

Skip kept his cool, but Sherman's words were damaging. While their exchange should have been seen as exactly the kind of fireworks *First Take* was positioned to make, the very reason our ratings were through the roof, Sherman had come on our show and given voice to all of Skip's most powerful and determined haters. He'd hit a nerve among some of the executives at ESPN, who held Skip responsible for the denigration that had been aimed in the company's direction, about *First Take* specifically, and ESPN more broadly, ruining sports media. Bayless and I had been called an embarrassment to the sports media business by critics. Never mind that debate shows had been in existence since the days of *The McLaughlin Report* and *Firing Line* and opinions had become television's preferred commodity. We were the ones deemed at fault.

According to Horowitz—and internal word of mouth—folks within the walls of ESPN basically celebrated Sherman for his willingness to call Skip out so publicly. They talked about Skip's years of "excessive criticism"—aimed at Sherman, LeBron James, and Terrell Owens, to name just a few—lamented his unapologetic tendencies, and concluded Bayless had no place being employed at ESPN.

Horowitz, emphatically supporting Bayless throughout the ordeal, was utterly disgusted, even going so far as to blame *me* for "sitting there and not saying anything" while Sherman was on the show. Only after I pushed back, reminding Horowitz that before the show Skip had specifically asked me to let Sherman vent, did Horowitz relent and let it go.

Horowitz's dismay ultimately proved to be valid when he divulged that the ESPN brass were actually contemplating canceling the show. I never directly confirmed with the honchos above Horowitz whether that was true or not, but I'll be damned if I didn't believe him.

First Take with Skip and me—two loud, obnoxious individuals bantering back and forth with debates on a daily basis—was the antithesis of the *SportsCenter* brand ESPN had created over the previous thirty-plus years. That our show might be more memorable than the network's biggest brand scared many internally.

Bayless and I knew this. We took pride in it. And we didn't give a shit what anyone thought about it.

In the end, we knew we were feeding the audience, and the bottom line. We were growing. And winning. The show didn't get canceled. And we marched on.

CHAPTER 13

NO SAFETY NET

Sports have always been bigger than the games for me. I always saw they had an impact beyond the playing field. Think of Jackie Robinson breaking baseball's color barrier in 1947, Billie Jean King's fight for gender equality in her tennis spectacle with Bobby Riggs in 1973, Magic Johnson's public revelation that he was HIV-positive back in 1991. More recently, after a series of deaths of unarmed Black folks at the hands of the police, athletes took knees during the National Anthem in support of social justice—four years after Colin Kaepernick was basically fired for doing the same damn thing.

Politics, race, gender: all of it connects with the games we love, whether we want it to or not. And as modern media has given everyone a louder voice, that wide impact sports has is more potent today than ever.

As sports have changed, so has sports journalism. In the world of debate, particularly a sports-debate show like *First Take*, it's even more apparent. For two hours, the show moves through twelve to fifteen different segments whose subjects are determined by newsworthiness. My job is to sit in the middle of where the issues and the games meet, then give viewers a rapid-fire, in-the-moment take. The goal is for that opinion to be as fresh, informed, unafraid, and entertaining as possible, given both the limits and dangers inherent in live TV.

Since I started on *First Take* in 2012, I've spouted approximately 3,500 takes a year! Each take—every single one of them!—has been blurted out live. No tape delays, not even a seven-second delay (as is common in radio). You talk, listen, argue, all in rapid-fire mode. You can barely pause for air: silence on live TV is death. So, while you're arguing with somebody else, you're also working against time; you have thirty seconds, ten seconds, one second! You need to make your point but keep up the pace before cutting to the next segment, the next issue, the next commercial.

In short, no safety net.

As I've religiously told family, friends, and loved ones throughout the years: "You want to really imagine the life I lead? Contemplate this: Every single day of my career, spanning years, I've awakened knowing I have to take one side or the other, guaranteeing that I'll make someone unhappy. I've had to piss off someone *every single day.* I make enemies daily."

Sometimes the antagonism comes from folks in the Black community—my community. I was called a "fucking coon" when I pointed out how ineffective Colin Kaepernick was in strategizing his attempt to return to the NFL. I was called a "sellout" due to repeatedly imploring the Black athlete to "Stay off the weeeeeeed!" Things got so bad for me at one point that Hall of Fame wide receiver Terrell Owens— a person I supported for years, dating back to 2004 during his days with the Philadelphia Eagles—actually came on *First Take* in November 2019 and said, "Dang, Stephen A.! Max [Kellerman] almost seems Blacker than you!"

And don't get me started regarding the heat I was forced to absorb when I had the temerity to demand that Brooklyn Nets superstar guard Kyrie Irving—who spent his first three seasons in Brooklyn missing more games than he played, while still pocketing an average salary of over $30 million per season in recent years—should be paid one year at a time to ensure he actually shows up and plays for the team he's supposed to represent.

People attack my friendships and my politics, too. I'm not a Republican, but I'm friends with people I don't agree with on most issues, including Sean Hannity and Mark Levin from Fox News. Acknowledging that I know them pretty well and consider them both good men—not racists—who simply share a different ideology from me, apparently makes me a complete sellout! (And, by the way, they also happen to be right about things far more often than they're given credit for from the Black community.)

"Don't ever forget, the biggest trick racists ever played on Black people was teaching us to strip each other of our Blackness whenever we disagree," said Trevor Noah, former host of *The Daily Show*. He said that—with class—in response to insults directed at him by Kanye West, but he was also talking to Black people in general.

If you're successful, you can't be real. If you're a Republican, you can't possibly care about the Black community. If you decry smoking weed, acts of violence, or you're against defunding the police—which I am, because I know most Black folks are dialing 911 when they sense trouble at their doorsteps—you're disowned. As if someone owned you in the first place.

What other community spews such venom over a difference in opinion? It's racism one minute, fighting among each other the next. No matter what, there's always a damn fight. In saying that, I'm not talking about "them" as if I'm distancing myself from my own community. When I say that Black people have a problem, I'm talking about me and everyone else to whom I'm connected by virtue of our Blackness. There isn't a Black person I've met who isn't proud to be Black. Especially myself. There is simply nothing on earth I am more unapologetic about than being a Black man. But that doesn't mean we're devoid of moments when Black folks will look at one another, wag our fingers, and say among ourselves what one of my best friends, Jeff Brown (who is Black), says all the time:

"See: That's why I can't hang with y'all."

We may look the part—"Black don't crack"—but a life spent fighting with your own is beyond exhausting.

As rap mogul Snoop Dogg once declared, after calling into my radio show unsolicited to speak on my behalf back in 2016: "Let me say this to your audience out there. Stephen A. ain't selling out. He's looking out. He's tipping you off about the obstacles that are out there, giving you a heads-up about what to look out for. Wake up!"

After all these years, the amazing part is that folks still appear oblivious about my intent whenever I tackle issues. They assume I'm just talking. They have no clue that there's a method to my presumed madness on television: positively affecting the lives of the many, even if it's at the expense of a few.

I never liked making enemies; I just don't care if I have any. *First Take* has given me what I've always cared about most: the platform to speak up and speak out on what I believed to be true. If feathers have to be ruffled along the way, so long as I'm fair, I've never given a damn. Because here's my little secret I've kept from everyone but my family throughout career:

I never wanted to get into sports journalism just for the purpose of talking sports!

The more serious and socially riveting the issue, the happier I was to talk about it, knowing a mass audience—Black, white, Hispanic, Asian, and otherwise—would be transfixed on every syllable I uttered. I knew there were few who'd speak as fluidly and with as much conviction as I would. And I knew I had the courage and intestinal fortitude to speak up and speak out on behalf of those who couldn't or wouldn't speak up for themselves, or on behalf of those less fortunate. My commitment is to truly make a difference by calling it like I see it.

Please don't get me wrong. Since I was a child, I've loved talking basketball and boxing. I grew up loving Muhammad Ali. I idolized Bill Russell and Kareem Abdul-Jabbar. And although the Immaculate Reception—when Franco Harris grabbed a ball that had ricocheted off a teammate to score a winning touchdown for the Pittsburgh Steelers in their Super Bowl effort against the Oakland Raiders in 1972—made me like the Steelers, it didn't change the fact that I've been a lifelong fan of the running great Jim Brown, who retired from football a year before I was born.

But notice the common denominator? Ali! Russell! Jabbar! Brown! Not to mention Jackie Robinson, Curt Flood, Oscar Robertson, and a host of others who stood tall in the face of flagrant prejudice and racism.

They were all activists in their own right. They were committed to civil rights for Black people and minorities, in America and throughout the world. Afraid or not, they were going to fight. They all knew they were serving a higher purpose. And if career-altering—or career-ending—consequences came with it, that was the price they were willing to pay.

As I found out, someone like me, who absolutely lives for the opportunity to tackle hard-core, issue-related matters relevant to the masses, no matter how risky the subject matter may be, could confront the same kind of hot water in the sports-media world. If you speak your mind long enough, you're going to step in some shit. It's a lesson everyone in the sports-talk business eventually learns.

I'm no exception!

Among the thousands of takes I've put out there over more than a decade for millions of intensely involved viewers—it's not a stretch to imagine them shouting back at me through their screens—a handful have dumped me atop a mountain of shit high enough to prompt viewers and non-viewers alike to call for my head, or frame me as misogynistic, xenophobic, or just downright despicable and irresponsible. It's happened when there are more sensitive issues to discuss, transcendent subjects in news and culture that demand dialogue and banter that venture beyond the court or field of play: including race, social-justice, and gender-equity issues.

Athletes have to get back up every time they get knocked down. I've never met an elite athlete—a winner—who didn't tell me they ultimately wound up on top because they failed, lost, and made mistakes, yet persevered and came back stronger. I wasn't good enough to be a professional athlete. Hell, I wasn't good enough to be an elite college athlete. But I always knew I'd have to do something similar in journalism and broadcasting.

The question was: How was I going to handle it?

Once upon a time, star NFL running back Ray Rice was seen as a good man.

A rough and rugged running back, undersized in a land of giants, yet playing every bit as one himself, Rice was beloved in the city of Baltimore for more than just ten-yard runs for first downs or colliding with bodies for three-yard touchdown runs. He was also revered for his philanthropy.

Rice would share the money he had. He'd give to the desolate and impoverished. To him, the struggles of the less fortunate of Baltimore's citizens were his struggles, too. And his willingness to feel their pain—and to give so much of his time and energy to alleviate that pain for so many—led a local magazine to name him the city's most charitable person in 2012.

Then on February 19, 2014, Rice began his descent from being a pillar of the Baltimore community to being the ugly face of domestic violence. The transformation happened within a few dozen frames of a grainy, soundless surveillance video taken inside an Atlantic City casino that was posted in two parts, over the course of eight months, on the website TMZ.

Four days before the first posting, Rice and his then fiancée (now his wife), Janay Palmer, had gotten into an argument at the casino after a night of heavy drinking. Palmer got up from the blackjack table where the couple had been sitting and headed for an elevator to go back to their room. Rice split from the table right after her and followed her onto the elevator.

The footage from the hallway security camera showed Rice dragging—not lifting—the unconscious Palmer out of the elevator, after the door opened on their floor. Then it showed him standing over Palmer's motionless body as she lay facedown, like a boxer over an opponent he'd just KO'd. Rice looked like he couldn't figure out what to do next to get Palmer up and out of sight, as he kept peeking around the vicinity to see who was around or who was coming.

The one thing Rice didn't do: look like he gave a shit about Palmer's condition.

After an investigation into the matter, the NFL handed down a two-game suspension to Rice on July 24.

Then on September 8, TMZ released a second video. Once this video was shown, it would rock the foundation of the NFL forever.

This was the footage from the security camera inside the elevator. On the tape, words—obscenities—were exchanged. At one point, Rice looked as if he spit in Palmer's face. After Palmer seemingly jerked away from the spit for a second, she then moved toward Rice. The next thing the video showed was Rice, the 205-pound, two-time All-Pro, throw a check-left hook to his fiancée's face. Palmer's head immediately snapped sideways before it crashed violently into the elevator's handlebars.

Palmer lay still on the floor, out cold.

This time, the media was aghast. Rice was written and spoken about as a pariah whose NFL career should be over.

Naturally, NFL commissioner Roger Goodell came under fire for the two-game suspension he'd given, which now looked like a slap on the wrist for a professional football player caught on video distributing a one-punch KO to his woman.

Goodell said he hadn't seen the whole video when he handed out the earlier suspension, but many critics declared that that assertion was utter bullshit. The belief was that a multi-billion-dollar conglomerate, with well-informed and well-connected former law enforcement officials draped all over their security payroll, had to have been aware of the video long before it was released. The NFL was covering its collective ass, critics asserted, because they knew such an incident would be a stain on the NFL shield.

Women were apoplectic. Advertisers and sponsors would react emphatically, affecting the NFL's precious bottom line. Politicians got involved, pointing to reports of other acts against women having been ignored by the NFL for years and calling for the NFL to do more to address domestic violence.

That maelstrom of criticism left Goodell and the NFL with no choice but to suspend Rice immediately and indefinitely. Some critics even called for Goodell to resign.

Eventually, the critics wanted my resignation, too.

Skip Bayless and I could see that if ever there was a story that crossed into territory occupied by both the game and society at large, this was it, so we took it on. The day that Rice's initial two-day suspension was handed down by the NFL, July 24, Skip did his take on the horrors of domestic violence, and then the issue was thrown to me.

In my response, I said:

"There is never an excuse to put your hands on a woman . . . at the same time, we also have to make sure that we learn as much as we can about elements of provocation. Not that there's real provocation, but the elements of provocation, you've got to make sure that you address them because we've got to do what we can to try to prevent the situation from happening in any way. And I don't think that's broached enough, is all I'm saying. No point of blame."

All hell broke loose.

Michelle Beadle, my former colleague at ESPN, immediately erupted on Twitter:

"So I was just forced to watch this morning's *First Take*. A) I'll never feel clean again and, B) I'm now aware that I can provoke my own beating . . . Violence isn't the victim's issue. It's the abuser's. To insinuate otherwise is irresponsible and disgusting."

More of the same followed from all corners of the media and the Twitterverse. Some print, radio, and TV pundits called for my dismissal. A colleague I revered and looked up to for years, then *New York Times* sports columnist Bill Rhoden, wrote that he could only "hope" I would learn from this and that it would be a "teachable moment" for me.

Not one single critic called me directly.

No one reached out to ask what I meant, what I was thinking, or how I felt. Folks just saw the opportunity to pounce and didn't hesitate.

It didn't take me long to understand the magnitude of the controversy. Domestic violence is a profoundly serious issue. The obvious point to emphasize was that women are the victims far more often than not.

The challenge I would learn from is that if you're sitting across from Skip Bayless, Max Kellerman, Michael Irvin, or anyone else, that is on *First Take*, you have to stick to the format of the debate show. The audience just heard their take, now they want to hear mine, and they don't want to hear me say the same damn thing. If I come back with something we completely agree on, where do we go from there? At the same time, in my standard ESPN contract, there's a clause noting that anything I say on the air that jeopardizes or impinges the integrity of the brand is grounds for dismissal. My former agent once brought up the inherent contradiction in that stipulation when applied to a show such as *First Take*:

On a show like *First Take*, or any live debate show, something that causes an uproar happens almost every day. The objective of these shows is to have opposite points of view.

To be candid: We capitalize on the kind of polarization people supposedly abhor.

That's the way it's been since the inception of debate shows. It's not about to change anytime soon.

Reflecting back on all I said regarding Ray Rice, the issue wasn't whether Rice was right or wrong. Hell yeah, he was wrong. That was obvious. My focus was on what can we all take away from it.

Skip went off first with a diatribe about the horror of domestic violence and how the NFL needed to hold its players more accountable.

I could not have agreed more. Any man who strikes a woman is the worst kind of man; this is what I was taught since I came out of the womb by the five women who raised me.

But since Skip said what he'd said already, what was I going to add to the conversation?

When the camera turned to me the instant Skip finished, my first thought was of all the women whom I've loved in my life. As the son of the world's greatest mom, a little brother to four older sisters, an uncle to nine nieces, and a father to two daughters, my thoughts veered in a direction no one else was thinking about, in my mind. I was thinking: How can a woman protect herself in the moment from a disgusting man willing to physically abuse her?

My answer to that question in that split second: keep things as calm as possible until you're removed from that situation in that moment. The farthest thing from my mind was blaming any woman who found herself in circumstances clearly forced upon her.

But that was not how it came out of my mouth. And I paid a price because of my inexplicable ambiguity.

Then ESPN president John Skipper called me two days later, on a Sunday night, and I immediately apologized for all the noise I had created. I knew he was probably being pressured internally and by media outlets to address the matter. Skipper responded by telling me: "Don't worry about it. I saw what you said, and I understand you had no malicious intent. Just apologize and let's move past this."

He then added, knowing I knew folks were calling for my head: "I am not going to suspend you."

I felt an apology was the least I could do. As a professional who makes a damn good living by spouting off opinions to the masses, it's my responsibility to elocute my words clearly enough to avoid any confusion. I didn't do that this time around. I knew it. I accepted it. In addition, I felt compelled to make clear to all the women who had been subjected to domestic violence what my position was, and has been my entire life.

So, I apologized on the show the next morning, though not the way I wanted to. Against my own gut instinct, I followed a script prepared by ESPN—both PR and Human Resources—at their insistence, instead of simply speaking from my heart extemporaneously, as I almost always do.

I read it and assumed that would be the end of it.

Little did I know it was the start of something much bigger.

After reading the apology that Monday morning, the next day—a little more than twenty-four hours later—Skipper called, while I was hosting an event in South Carolina for 2007 former NBA coach of the year Sam Mitchell, a dear friend of mine. Skipper called to apologize. When I asked why, he said, "Things have changed, Stephen."

He went on to say, "I'm fully aware of what I told you on Sunday, but I've had a change of heart. This thing has taken on a life of its own, and it has left me no choice. I have to suspend you."

The suspension was for a week. I wasn't allowed on any ESPN platforms. Regardless of what I meant, of my stated apology, Skipper felt compelled to distance me from ESPN and Walt Disney.

I was totally pissed.

And the statement issued by Skipper about an hour after our phone call only made it worse for me. Sent via internal email, the first paragraph announced that I would not appear on either *First Take* or ESPN Radio until the following Wednesday, a weeklong layoff. Then it went on:

"As many of you know, there has been substantial news coverage in the past few days related to comments Stephen A. made last Friday in the wake of the NFL's decision to suspend Baltimore Ravens running back Ray Rice for two games following charges of assaulting his then fiancée, now wife, a few months ago," it began.

"We've said publicly and in this space that those remarks did not reflect our company's point of view, or our values. They certainly don't reflect my personal beliefs."

But then Skipper continued:

"We have been engaged in thoughtful discussion about appropriate next steps. Those conversations have involved a diverse group of women and men in our company. Our women's ERG [Employee Resource Group, designed to give voice to underrepresented employees] has added to the conversation going forward, I know they will help us continue constructive discussion on this and related issues."

Then, near the end, he added:

"Stephen has called what took place 'the most egregious mistake' of his career. I believe his apology was sincere and that he and we have learned from what we've collectively experienced."

I understood the situation and told Skipper that after I read his statement. The day after my suspension was announced, I flew to St. Thomas, my motherland, to chill out in the hot sun and mull over the storm I'd walked into. At that moment, I felt as alone as I'd felt when I was let go in 2009. Friends, coworkers, peers in the industry—a strong-willed bunch of folks—were avoiding me like a toxic waste site. At least it seemed that way. I knew I'd messed up with my words, but I was also concerned about being restricted when I came back. No one seemed to share that worry: there was no concept of "if it's him today, it could be me tomorrow." No one I heard had discussed publicly how a suspension, initiated by the misuse of one word ("provocation"), could affect their careers, their livelihoods, and the whole business of sports talk down the road.

The only person at ESPN who seemed concerned about restricting what any of us could say on the air was the same guy who sat opposite me when I said what I said about the Ray Rice incident:

Skip Bayless.

✳   ✳   ✳

Skip never called nor texted me with his support.

Instead, the man who'd brought me on board *First Take* two years earlier finished the show on the day of my suspension without me, stepped off the set—then refused to come back until my suspension was over.

"I'll be back when my brother returns," I'd ultimately learn he told the bosses.

And that's exactly what Skip Bayless did: He didn't return to *First Take* until the following Wednesday, when I returned to the airwaves.

We were already close. From that moment on, we were brothers for life.

Although there were no repercussions for Skip for the position he took, he didn't have to do it. Skip could have declared my problems were—well, exactly that, my problems—and then went on about his business. Skip stood up and stood out, instead, making it clear there was no *First Take* for him without me. He challenged folks inside the network to remember what *First Take* was supposed to be all about: a debate show, with dissenting opinions that shouldn't require folks' approval or comfort.

I spent my time in St. Thomas breathing in that immaculate ocean air and giving myself time to contemplate my error. I realized a number of important things.

On the one hand, Skipper answered not only to ESPN but to its parent company, Disney. Beyond the moral standards upheld by any company, bad headlines are kryptonite to advertisers, shareholders, and board members—and ultimately to the bottom line. It was the obligation of Skipper and the Disney honchos in Burbank, California, to diffuse any compromising situation as best they could, as is always the case. Had I articulated my point of view better, my words would not have been misinterpreted and none of this would have happened, I surmised.

The suspension elevated my awareness of what minefields to avoid. It heightened my sensitivity.

On the flip side, I never hit a woman in my life—I'd made a mistake with my verbiage. So to see some folks' willingness to stigmatize me as someone who'd remotely condone domestic violence still amounts—to my mind—to the greatest insult I've ever received in my career.

I could deal with the hate, the jealousy and envy, even the inclination contemporaries who didn't like me may have had to capitalize on my dicey situation with ESPN at the time. Hell, I would not have cared if folks called for my resignation just for being inarticulate regarding such a sensitive subject.

"It's not what you've done, Stephen A., it's what you said." I could live with that.

But to imply I condoned domestic violence, that I was okay with a woman being knocked unconscious, just because I uttered the word "provocation," showed me how low folks were willing to go to take me down.

"Do not let them break you," I told myself as I re-gathered myself on the beach, trying to put all the pieces of me back together again. "You were made for this shit! Hate ain't nothing but a thing impact players have to deal with."

For everyone who wanted to take me down—this Black dude from the streets of Hollis, Queens, who couldn't even ball well enough to earn a Division-I scholarship—there were fans who'd become advocates because I spoke their language. Cynics didn't understand that fans wanted me to *intensify* my bantering, not tamp things down. I had become their trusted voice. I speak my mind as if I'm hanging in the backyard chillin' with friends and family. I speak a language a lot of folks find familiar. I'd slipped up with a misspoken word in the Ray Rice situation, but 99.9 percent of the time I said things that provided an honest perspective the audience could relate to, either because it was what they believed and wanted to say but didn't have the courage to verbalize, or because it was a perspective they disagreed with but needed to hear.

I realized there's no attribute more valuable than being seen as trustworthy. There's no fake in me—for better or worse. I never did things for effect. I've always respected every viewer, reader, and listener. I believe they all have an inherent sixth sense about who is authentic and who is full of shit.

Viewers didn't think I was full of shit!

Viewers just thought I was a piece of shit. Hell, some still do, but I get it. I always have.

I loved that I was speaking to millions every day, and everyone knew it was me. I loved that no one could avoid hearing what I had to say, due to my volume, energy, and content. Although I love my Black people, viewers know I live by this credo: "I'm not interested in Black appeal. I'm interested in mass appeal. I want EVERYBODY. Not just a few."

I loved how in this field I've chosen to be in, millions couldn't help but respond to things I'd said—on Twitter, on Facebook, and especially in papers who'd passed on the opportunity to hire me, like *USA Today*, the *Washington Post*, and the *New York Times*.

When you read my work, heard me on the radio, or watched me on TV, I made it clear I meant business. From the way I dressed to the way I walked and talked.

I wasn't playing damn games.

When you do that, you have to expect more enemies than friends will come in your direction.

Folks love to hate the player when they can't play the game.

That's what I felt the attacks against me were about, at least somewhat, with the Ray Rice episode. The aftermath didn't leave me worried, however. I was on a mission. Everyone seemed to know it, and it appeared to petrify folks.

That mentality of refusing to be broken, of using hate as a motivation, got me this far—got me from 203rd Street in Hollis to being beamed into living rooms all over the world.

I would not let this suspension stop me.

It would chasten me. It would instruct me. But it also would propel me. It ignited a spark in me, a spark folks usually assume becomes slowly defused by the comfort one can develop from being on top.

It was time for me to get back to business.

My biggest regret from the suspension was that my on-air apology was not in my own thoughts, my own words, my own style. I surrendered that to the hands of my employer, at the behest of John Skipper.

ESPN meant well. Skipper meant well. They were actually trying to protect me from myself, as difficult as that is for an employee to believe sometimes. Still, there was no excuse for allowing myself to be convinced that a corporation could do a better job of protecting me than I could myself.

In the end, with that pathetically choreographed apology, I failed to give the audience exactly what I vowed to give them from the moment I entered this business: a true and authentic Stephen A. Smith.

Not a perfect Stephen A. Just a true one.

That would be the last damn time that happened.

Instead of coming back from my suspension angry and bitter, I returned enlightened and hyped about my future. My critics had done me a favor. The ordeal of getting myself suspended, and pilloried in the court of public opinion, would only make me stronger and better at my job.

CHAPTER 14

BURIED BY A CURRY (NOT NAMED STEPH)

I had learned a hell of a lot from the Ray Rice suspension, but not everything. In the business of sports talk, controversy is inevitable. Two years later, in 2016, I stepped in it again.

My transgression this time: pissing off Ayesha Curry, wife of the NBA's reigning superstar, Steph Curry.

I arrived at the 2016 NBA finals in Cleveland fantasizing about my future. The month before, I'd run into Skipper at the annual "upfronts" in New York—the spring presentations all the networks put on for advertisers to highlight their fall lineups. While I waited to go onstage to talk up *First Take*, Skipper came up to me in a hallway and confided: "Congratulations! You'll be the new host for the six p.m. *SportsCenter* in the fall. Things need to be worked out contractually, but we're going to give it to you. We'll talk to you about it soon."

I was ecstatic. Paired with my cohosting duties on *First Take*, already the number-one morning sports show, a prominent role on *SportsCenter*, or better yet hosting it solo, would give more visibility than just about anyone else covering sports on TV. I'd dominate the mornings, then I'd set the stage each night for the evenings' sporting events. If you want cachet in sports, it doesn't get any more significant than that.

So, when Skipper came up to me and told me it was mine, I shared the info with family and loved ones, but otherwise kept it under wraps, knowing nothing's official until the contracts are signed on the dotted line.

On June 16, 2016, near the end of Game 6 of NBA Finals series, with the Golden State Warriors trailing the Cleveland Cavaliers in the fourth quarter, 99–87, Steph Curry, frustrated from being in foul trouble throughout most of the game, got tangled up with LeBron James on a loose ball and was called for his sixth foul by referee Jason Phillips, ending Curry's night.

Uncharacteristically for him, he went ballistic. Curry, as visibly furious as he's ever been seen in his career, spit his mouthguard into his hand and launched it into the court-side seats, accidentally hitting a fan. He then jumped into Phillips's face, waving his arms and screaming "bullshit!" over and over until teammates Klay Thompson and Shaun Livingston had to restrain him.

With Curry gone and the Warriors down 12 with 4:22 left, it would have been safe to predict that the game was over. The Warriors, once holding an insurmountable 3–1 series lead, now found the series tied 3–3, and were in danger of becoming the first team to surrender such a lead and subsequently lose in the NBA Finals. Worse, it was occurring in a year when they had gone an all-time-NBA-best 73–9 during the regular season.

That only made the pressure more palpable. And it showed in more than one Curry!

After the game, Ayesha Curry went off herself—on Twitter. She called the game "rigged" and blasted the officials and the NBA for the unfavorable treatment of her husband. Her tweets went viral, with every news outlet picking them up, including *First Take*.

The morning after the game, I opened the segment:

"I'm trying to sound as appropriate as I possibly can. You are the wife of Steph Curry. What you do is a reflection on him. What you do is a reflection on the organization he works for. You have to be mindful of that. You can't get caught up in your own individual emotions and having this zest to speak out to the point where it compromises your husband."

Of course, Skip Bayless's stance was totally different. He didn't blame Ayesha one bit for feeling the way she did and saying so publicly. He pointed out the level of scrutiny her husband was under, and how justified her actions were because her husband was getting screwed over by the officiating.

I was having none of it. The debate was on!

I'd spent years listening to Skip hold LeBron accountable for everything, practically down to the color of his fingernails, for Christ's sake. I genuinely believed that if LeBron's wife had done the same thing, Skip would have blasted her for it. So I continued my diatribe:

"If that was Savannah, LeBron's wife . . . if that were Gloria, LeBron's mother, what would we be saying?" I asked Skip rhetorically. "LeBron James has a mom, has a wife, has kids. He's a great guy, an even greater ambassador of the game than Steph Curry, because he's done it over the test of time. He's a wonderful, beautiful father, by all accounts. And I've got news for you. As beautiful as everyone wants to say Ayesha Curry is—and she is—Savannah is something special.

"I'm here to tell you something right now," I went on. "Ain't a man alive, particularly a Black man, that's going to look at LeBron James's wife and not say that that woman ain't wonderful inside and out. She never tweets and goes out there and calls out the league and stuff like that . . . Nobody is more scrutinized than her husband. But yet she thinks about how she represents him. As a result, she doesn't do that."

Trouble was on its way.

Ayesha Curry didn't take kindly to what I said. She immediately went on social media and called me out. "Pitting two Black women against each other like that?" she wrote. "You're the one that's out of pocket."

I thought her claim was bullshit. Just her claim, mind you, not her as a person. Ayesha Curry is wonderful. She's an incredible role model for young women, and not just a family woman but a businesswoman as well. Speaking strictly about her take on the issue, I was simply pointing out that if you're someone in the public eye, the folks in your inner circle have an obligation to look out for you by not placing themselves in the spotlight, particularly because of your foolishness, in a way that makes the situation even worse. I don't believe she looked out for Steph Curry in that instance, that's all. A couple members of the Warriors even called to tell me that not one of them had a damn problem with what I said.

It didn't matter.

In the span of just over a month, I went from the highest of highs—being promised the host slot of the 6 p.m. *SportsCenter* while I still cohosted *First Take*—to landing atop another mountain of shit. This time, I'd come away with a whole new trove of knowledge and an understanding that continued to make me better, as a journalist and as a man.

Women inside ESPN, specifically at ESPNW—the platform created to give a woman's perspective on stories and issues around sports—vehemently objected to my comments. They didn't speak to me: they went directly upstairs to Skipper to voice their discontent over what I said.

Right after Game 7 of the NBA Finals concluded on Sunday, June 19, 2016, I returned home. I was back in Bristol that Tuesday, June 21, to do *First Take* when I stopped by the office of Rob King, a senior VP who oversaw the 6 p.m. *SportsCenter* at the time.

King, a brilliant mind, a dear friend, and my former deputy sports editor at the *Philadelphia Inquirer*—whom I've known for more than twenty-five years—was straightforward with me.

"A lot of folks are not happy with you right now," King began. "What you said, man . . . that was an incredibly bad look for you. Women are offended by what you said. I honestly can't say that I know what's going to come of all of this right now, but it's not good. A lot of ladies in this building are highly upset with you."

I was completely caught off guard.

First of all, I honestly felt I didn't say anything particularly wrong. Perhaps the only thing I lamented about my diatribe directed at Mrs. Curry was that I didn't bring up Hillary Rodham Clinton. Since the former First Lady and New York senator was now running for the presidency at the time, I harbored the same belief about former president Bill Clinton that I had articulated about Ayesha Curry:

With Hillary running for the presidency and, by virtue of that, living in the public eye, I believe Bill Clinton had an inherent responsibility to look out for her; to make sure that anything he did during the campaign didn't amount to a negative reflection on his wife, that could jeopardize her election aspirations.

My take on the matter had absolutely nothing to do with *gender*. It had everything to do with the role I believe any loving, supportive spouse has an obligation to play as the partner to someone in the public eye.

King understood this when I explained, but accurately pointed out that I failed to make that point on *First Take*. And since he didn't hear me articulate it that way, neither did others.

That reality left King shaking his head with apprehension and doubt when I asked if this was going to cost me the 6 p.m. *SportsCenter*. Clearly, he suspected all was not well. But he said nothing definitive.

In the end, King didn't have to say anything at all.

I never heard a word from Skipper again about hosting the 6 p.m. *SportsCenter*.

In fact, nearly three weeks passed after the NBA Finals were over before I heard a word from anyone. The person who finally contacted me was Ed Erhardt, president of global sales and marketing for ESPN at the time, who was always one of my biggest supporters and advisers and someone whose counsel I will embrace for the rest of my career.

STEPHEN A. SMITH

Erhardt met with me at Gabriel's Restaurant near Columbus Circle in New York City after the Fourth of July weekend to break the news to me as delicately but directly as he could:

"I've got some bad news for you, buddy. Stuff you probably already know. They've decided to go in a different direction with the six p.m. *SportsCenter*."

It was another shot to the kidney for me. Anger and disappointment engulfed me once more. It would have been nice to nab the *SportsCenter* job, but jobs come and go. That was not my issue. It was more that purportedly the criticism generated by colleagues that helped get me suspended over the Ray Rice incident was behind this latest development as well. Here we were again.

I'd later learn that my former colleagues Michael Smith and Jemele Hill would be coanchoring the 6 p.m. *SportsCenter*. The rationale behind the decision was that they hosted the show *Numbers Never Lie* together, and both had a strong social media following. I was genuinely happy for them for two reasons:

1) They are colleagues I respect a great deal, who were more than qualified for the job and who worked their tails off for the opportunity.

2) They are both Black.

I vehemently believed that someone Black needed to be a part of the 6 p.m. *SportsCenter*, in position to set the stage for each evening's sporting events. A successful Black in that position would only open doors for more Blacks. And I'd said so repeatedly to Rob King throughout the months preceding the decision on that role.

But while I was happy for Michael and Jemele, fury doesn't begin to describe what I felt about the stigma of having *SportsCenter* given to me then taken away attached to me.

Only my family could calm me down. Immediately, I went right back to Hollis to Mommy's house. I explained what happened to her, along with my sisters Linda, Arlyne, and Abigail, and later to Carmen at her house in Long Island. Unlike nearly eight years earlier, when my mother handed me breakfast on a tray, along with a mirror so I could look at myself, this time she agreed with me. So did my sisters.

My family's belief coincided with my own: Skipper's word should have taken precedence. I wasn't being fired or suspended. I wasn't taken off *First Take*. So why take away a job that was promised to me just months earlier? Worse, why were Rob King and Ed Erhardt left to talk to me about it instead of Skipper himself?

I just felt totally disrespected.

(Note. Something any Black person will tell white America is that the one thing consistently missed is the importance of RESPECT. Opportunities come and go. Change happens, as well as the changing of minds. We may not like it. We may abhor it. But in the end, when we're looked in the eye and told of decisions, coupled with rational explanations, whether we like it or not we can live with it. R-E-S-P-E-C-T was sung by the late, great Aretha Franklin for a reason. That shit matters!!!)

Skipper's decision led me to take some actions.

First, I parted ways with my agent at the time (Lou Oppenheim of Headline Media; Steve and I had parted amicably years earlier).

Secondly, I committed myself to saying absolutely nothing about my anger to any executive outside of Dave Roberts. Again, he was the lone executive I trusted to understand that my feelings were justified. Quite honestly, I was afraid of what I was going to say to Skipper, and I knew it wasn't in my best interest for anyone to see me as angry as I was in that moment. It simply would have been counterproductive; I couldn't preach about being about my business, then act contrary to the advice I had given to colleagues, contemporaries, and to audiences throughout the lecture circuits I had been on.

The last thing I did was hire an agent from the Creative Artists Agency named Nick Khan.

Khan was a shrewd operator, to put it mildly. There didn't seem to be anyone he didn't know, no one that he didn't have some sort of relationship with, and no issue he was devoid of knowledge about.

Simply put, Khan was considered the best agent in our business, with the best relationships.

When Skipper and I ultimately met face-to-face at a restaurant in Bristol three months later, in October, it was Khan who made it happen. Skipper was joined by then Content Executive Connor Schell and Senior Vice President of Audio Traug Keller.

What was foremost on my mind was ESPNW. In my mind at the time, a few women, none of whom had ever spoken to me directly up to that point, took issue with what I had said and expressed their ire upstairs to Skipper. I was highly offended that he purportedly listened to what they had to say without gathering any input from me.

By this time, the combination of revenue, ratings, and focus-group data made it clear I was the number one talent at ESPN, according to some executives and Khan himelf. Because of my worth to the company, simply put, I felt I deserved a better handling of the situation than what Skipper had put forth.

When I finally got in front of Skipper and expressed as much, he did acknowledge that he "understood" how I could feel that way. He apologized for not speaking to me directly about it sooner. Still, my initial thought was to feel insulted, sensing he was just placating me, because I thought his first response was garbage. Then Skipper got as real with me as he's ever been:

"This job isn't easy," he explained. "Regardless of your value to this company, you're not the only one to be appeased. There are lots of others. Honestly, there are lots of issues that are even bigger than you, and the one you found yourself in—not me—was one of them. I had to take a lot into consideration. So I'm asking that you at least understand that."

Then Skipper added an interesting twist that had never been presented to me before. "Why don't you talk to Laura Gentile of ESPNW," he said. "I'd really like you to do that. Maybe then you might have a better understanding of where I was coming from—and gather a level of understanding you may need to have moving forward in your career."

I approached my meeting with Laura Gentile, the senior VP overseeing marketing, social media, and business for ESPNW, with nothing but cynicism and annoyance. But since I had already promised Skipper I'd do it, I had to follow through.

Gentile, to her credit, happily obliged. The meeting took place approximately a month later, at Restaurant Asiate, on the thirty-fifth floor of the Mandarin Oriental Hotel in Manhattan.

Due to the many murmurs I'd heard regarding her communications about me with Skipper over the previous couple of years—and the fact that she never reached out to me personally— I expected a tense meeting at best, an ambush at worst. So I showed up to the meeting with a major attitude.

Laura disarmed me within the first five minutes.

She could not have been kinder, or more honest and forthcoming, about her position. Plus, I appreciated her acknowledgment that we both shared the failure to communicate with each other long before these issues had ever unfolded.

Laura admitted immediately and directly that she was not a fan of my words or perspective regarding the Ayesha Curry matter. Her main point: the discussion that caused such an uproar might have come across in an entirely different light had there been a woman from ESPNW there to join in.

Her sentiment about ESPNW was no surprise. But what she articulated next left me speechless.

"I heard you address tough topics many times, Stephen, and you never hesitate to point out the importance of inclusion," she said, as we dined within the restaurant's plush atmosphere, Central Park glittering below.

"Well, where was the inclusion then?" she went on. "You talked about Ayesha Curry and how she should have acted. You brought up how LeBron's wife, Savannah, would have acted. You implied, essentially, how both should have acted. And two men—you and Skip Bayless— were discussing this without any input from a woman to debate the issue. Why wouldn't I have a problem with that? Why wouldn't any woman have a problem with that?"

Damn! Laura Gentile was dead right, and I knew it!

Although Molly Qerim had been hosting the show since 2015, she served almost exclusively as the moderator. That host role was different back then, especially with Skip at the helm. Debaters debated. Hosts moderated, moving the conversation along without really joining in. That's the way Skip insisted the show should be when he was there. So Molly's presence didn't take away from Laura's point.

But Mina Kimes was at ESPN and could have been brought on to debate the segment with us. So was Cari Champion. So was Jemele Hill. And Basketball Hall-of Fame broadcaster Doris Burke. And Maria Taylor. And Sarah Spain. And Sage Steele. Elle Duncan had just arrived, with stardom conspicuously on her horizon.

All those women were accomplished, intelligent, thoughtful, and credible, with strong opinions suitable for holding their own in the kind of format *First Take* had become known for. Not to mention Molly herself, who can spar with anybody—if she'd been unleashed to do so.

One of Laura's biggest points was that, yes, I'm a star now. Sure, Skip Bayless was the patriarch of the show, but I had major say as to who appeared on *First Take* as well. I could make a difference. And up to that point, what had I really done to address the concerns she expressed?

To ensure that all bases were covered when we'd debate these sensitive matters?

The answer: nothing!

All I could do was acknowledge Laura Gentile's point of view, reiterate that I never meant to come across the way I did, and assure her that it wouldn't happen again. She accepted that with visible, sincere appreciation. With both of us now at ease with the other, we continued talking like trusted colleagues for the next hour and a half, discussing the importance of women in our industry and how they could best be utilized on multiple platforms at ESPN.

I left dinner that night feeling edified and refreshed, stoked by the insight I'd just gained from our dinner. I realized that while I knew what I meant when I talked about Ayesha Curry, others did not. Included in that group was probably millions of young women, watching Skip and me go back and forth about an issue that had far less to do with men than with women. To them, I was degrading one woman for not meeting a standard set by another woman—a standard set eons ago by men.

I was mansplaining!

And women like Laura Gentile, quite simply, were tired of it. And justifiably so.

Until Laura spoke to me about it directly, I didn't get it. I never thought about women salivating at the opportunity to express themselves on a lot of these issues, just like men do. I simply thought about what I had to say—not the role I needed to play to ensure others got their bite at the proverbial apple, too.

But Skipper did get it.

In the end, I understood he was right. And more mature. And more responsible on the particular issue.

And the actions that he took forced me to be better, because they reminded me of the power of my words and the responsibility that comes with it.

Over the years, whenever I've gotten frustrated at ESPN, and by extension Disney, I've thought about jumping ship. It's the nature of the business, particularly with a company that can be so restrictive and consumed by public perception far too often. But when folks ask why I've stayed all these years, my answer is simple:

I'd rather work for a place with standards than a place in search of standards.

Mistakes happen. Flaws are exposed. But the bottom line is that when you're forced to perfect your language and your tenor and your perspective—to say what you mean while considering everyone who's listening—it turns out that it's not censorship. It's being responsible. It's just speaking to people the way you mean to, not just the way you want to. It's about committing yourself to actually being heard, not just listened to.

My dinner with Laura made me look at Skipper and ESPN in a different light and drop any lingering resentment entirely. It challenged me and emboldened me, forcing me to become more educated about things I never deemed important in the past. It made me far more accountable.

CHAPTER 15

NATURAL-BORN CONTRARIANS

As the success of *First Take* continued, Skip and I grew closer. We were grateful to each other: he had put his trust in me, brought me on *First Take*, and believed I would catapult it into the stratosphere. He was also appreciative of my work ethic, my willingness to do reporting, to travel to games, to go inside the locker rooms and talk to players, coaches, and executives, and bring those perspectives right back to the airwaves of *First Take* so we'd both gain. Traveling, going to games, and recruiting folks to come on the show were all the things Bayless wasn't looking to do any longer, after years of paying his dues as a foot soldier in print journalism. I understood, and respected all things Skip, in ways no other contemporary ever could. That yin and yang made us successful and connected us at the hip.

As the summer of 2016 approached, though, with the NBA playoffs taking shape from May into June, Bayless became a bit distant. Sure, he showed up to work every day, always performing when the lights came on. But there was something different about him.

He wasn't as talkative about the show anymore, on-air or off-air. He wasn't as forthcoming with ideas of what would make subjects and segments better, or the show overall. It wasn't that Bayless didn't care, because apathy and indifference were impossible emotions for him to possess—he cares too much about anything he does. But to say he was distracted would be an understatement.

The fallout from the Richard Sherman show, and the bosses' reaction to it, ate at him over time. And then there was another important matter, which had to do with me, albeit indirectly.

Just a year earlier, in 2015, after all the drama I'd endured for years working for ESPN, I had finally re-upped with a new six-year, multi-million-dollar contract extension. No one was happier for me than Skip.

"You deserve this, my man," he said to me at the time. "You truly do. This is long overdue."

What he didn't say—what he didn't need to say—is that he was supposed to be next.

That following year was Bayless's turn to nab a big-time contract. No matter how popular I had become, it was all made possible by Bayless.

It was Bayless whom audiences looked forward to seeing from the days of *Cold Pizza*. It was Bayless who held down the fort when the show moved from New York to Bristol and was renamed *First Take*.

When folks became leery of conventional sports shows, and interest had dissipated in conventional news and interview formats, it was Bayless's debates they looked forward to, clung to, and eventually turned to permanently once the show became an all-debate format. And it was Bayless who served as the daily debate foil for any and all comers, before finally choosing me to be his permanent partner.

Despite the millions I had signed for, and the noise emanating from the sports world about *me* being the star of the show, Basketball Hall of Famer Isaiah Thomas would always remind me: "I love the way you never fail to give Skip Bayless credit. You never fail to express your love and appreciation for him on the air."

I was glad Thomas noticed it. My gratitude and appreciation for

Bayless never diminished or wavered. Yet my respect for him was even more palpable. Because in doing *First Take*, I knew what level of commitment it took to formulate a show like that every day, then show up and be the lead performer.

A natural-born contrarian—nobody played the role better than Skip. He was an invaluable commodity ESPN did not need to lose.

Skip felt this.

I did too, and various executives I'd spoken to echoed as much. But that's not what he was hearing during contract negotiations.

"I am not happy," Skip finally confided in me, after I approached him one day to ask what was wrong. "I'm happy for you and the contract you got. You know that. But I'm valuable too. And essentially they're giving me a take-it-or-leave-it offer nowhere close to what I'm getting offered elsewhere. They're saying, 'Hey, we've got Stephen A.! So we'll be just fine without you.' That is not right, man. That is not right!"

You're damn right it wasn't.

Bayless deserved better, especially after all the years he'd given to the company, the commitment he'd shown. In fact, I always believed that Bayless should get paid more for *First Take* than me, since he'd driven it for so long.

First Take wasn't just a show I didn't *want* to do without Skip Bayless. *First Take* was a show I didn't believe I *could* do without Skip Bayless.

Where the hell was I going to find someone who instinctually disagreed with me? Someone I could debate for two hours per day, ten hours per week on live television, knowing we wouldn't miss a beat?

Where was I going to find someone who was guaranteed to make headlines? Who was fearless in creating those headlines over the things he was willing to say? And was adroit at knowing what would generate buzz and ratings?

I raced upstairs to talk to the honchos after my conversation with Skip. "Skip needs to stay," I said. "We cannot lose him. If there is a way to keep him, will you guys please find it and get it done?"

It was too late. Skip wasn't kidding about having a big offer elsewhere. Ultimately, that fact, plus the harsh reality that the ESPN bosses didn't think highly enough of him to do what it took to keep him, made it a done deal.

In 2015, Fox Sports 1 (FS1) had acquired themselves a new bigwig executive: Bayless's number one champion, Jamie Horowitz. The first order of business when Horowitz arrived at Fox Studios off Pico Boulevard and Avenue of the Stars in Los Angeles was to establish FS1 by replicating what had already worked for him at ESPN. What better way to pull that off than by prying Skip Bayless away? Stealing Bayless would break up the most dynamic duo in morning sports talk, a duo who had dominated the a.m. hours for the previous four years.

Bayless's champion was in L.A. now. The money Horowitz committed to paying him at FS1 was reportedly $30 million over five years with a $6 million signing bonus. ESPN didn't even think about matching those numbers.

During the 2016 NBA Finals, in the parking lot on ESPN's campus, Skip told me he'd made his decision, and explained why. "Horowitz believed in me. He's supported me. I am where I am today because of him. And, boy, has he offered me 'unthinkable' money. I just couldn't say no. It's life-changing money, man. I just couldn't say no."

I was happy for Bayless. He deserved the money. It all added up, and it made perfect sense for him to say goodbye.

"On this show, I've gone from that crazy Woody Paige, in New York City on *Cold Pizza*, to my man right here, Stephen A. Smith," Skip said, during his final on-air goodbye from *First Take* on June 21, 2016, two days after LeBron and the Cavs had overcome a 3–1 NBA Finals' deficit to deliver a championship to Cleveland for the first time in fifty-two years.

"[Stephen A.'s] here today for me and I love him for that. We've had our battles on this show, we fight like brothers, we get mad, we love each other. And I'm going to miss him more than he has any concept of."

Bayless was right. We did fight like hell, but we did love each other. We still do and always will. I knew I was going to miss him.

But I also knew a harsh, unavoidable, reality: Bayless was the competition now. And so was Jamie Horowitz.

My mind-set had to shift. Skip and Jamie, naturally hungry individuals, always in pursuit of success, were coming to take me down. There was no other way to look at it. Their hunger and ire were aimed at ESPN, specifically *First Take*, and I *was First Take* now.

Bayless's show would be called *Undisputed*, and would air from 9:30 to noon, right up against *First Take*'s 10 to noon slot. Horowitz would pit Bayless right up against me—feeding off the momentum Bayless and I had built over the years.

"Hey, folks," Horowitz was essentially saying to the audience. "Skip is gone now. Stephen A. is over there and we're over here. Make a decision! You have to pick one!"

It was a smart strategy; divide and conquer. Not a surprise at all for an astute executive looking to make noise.

Bayless and Horowitz would be formidable competitors. They had taken most of the weapons with them to *Undisputed* that had served *First Take* well over the years, in producers, editors, researchers—and a former contributor and NFL Hall of Famer in Shannon Sharpe. Losing Sharpe—a smart, passionate, and good brother who is also a graduate of an HBCU (Savannah State) and whose sports credential couldn't be questioned—that would matter during NFL seasons, especially. And it was expected to sting *First Take*.

Bayless was also salivating at the opportunity to come right at us, not only feeling that ESPN had short-changed him but further annoyed at being forced to stay off television for nearly three months—from June 21 to September 6—until his ESPN contract had officially expired.

On Bayless's first day on the new job, September 6, 2016, he said the following:

"I'll be the first to admit to you, I'm going to miss my brother, Stephen A. Smith. I'm going to always root for him, and I will always be there for him, as I was a few years back when ESPN let him go."

Then the kicker:

"But as Stephen A. knows, I have always belonged right here on Fox. Fox isn't owned and operated by Walt Disney. And here on FS1, I'm gonna be a little more free to give all of me. And now I'm going to be reunited with the man and the team who, six years ago at ESPN, turned *First Take* into an all-debate show, every day for two live hours, and the rest was television history. Thank you, Jamie Horowitz."

There you had it.

Bayless had departed for an outlet that made him more armed and dangerous. He was proclaiming that we hadn't seen him at his best because he had been restrained. Now he would be unleashed.

To Bayless, ESPN had dismissed his significance as "out of sight, out of mind." That made it personal for him.

Against ESPN, that is. Not me!

But I was the man in the lion's den. *First Take* was officially mine now. If *Undisputed* succeeded and *First Take* failed, the headlines to come would be obvious. Everyone knew whose name would be illuminated and emblazoned as the fall guy.

Stephen A. flops! Takes First Take *down with him!*

I couldn't let that happen.

It was officially my fight, whether I liked it or not.

I had to get ready.

Or else!

CHAPTER 16

"WHAT IS YOUR POINT?"

Although quite a few folks at ESPN were happy Skip Bayless was gone, they were equally dismayed that the reins of *First Take* had been handed to me.

It was my show now, the responsibility resting squarely on my shoulders. Win, and the credit would be spread around to everyone involved, especially the producers and executives behind the scenes. Falter, and I would be on my own!

"We're here to support you," John Skipper would say. "You are not in this alone."

But I felt that, essentially, I *was* alone.

While it felt like the success of the show was up to me, the job of finding and approving Bayless's successor was not. Contractually, ESPN had to grant me input, which meant, basically, that I had to be brought into the conversation prior to any firm decisions being made—but the bosses had final say, and the decision was not really in my hands.

Contrary to what some may have believed based on my history at ESPN, I could not have been happier with those circumstances.

Rewind the clock eight years earlier and I would have felt totally different. The Stephen A. from 2008 to 2009 would have insisted on making that call. I would have fought for it.

"It's my future," I would have declared. "I'm the one who has to sit across from this person for two hours per day, ten hours per week, and we all know I'm the one who'll be held accountable if things go awry. So I don't want to hear shit! The final call should be mine."

But I was all grown up now.

The 2016 version of Stephen A. was an entirely different person.

That version wanted *First Take* off ESPN2 and onto ESPN. ESPN was a household brand. It magnetized sports viewers to its channel. After all those years in existence, ESPN2 never captured the level of cachet of ESPN. That meant fewer viewers, less visibility if we stayed on ESPN2. ESPN was clearly the better option.

I wanted to take *First Take* on the road, just as we had done in previous years when we'd gone to the Super Bowl, the NFL draft, NBA All-Star weekend, and the NBA Finals. I wanted the show marketed and promoted.

It costs money to do those things. There was a budget to consider, and those dollars required executive approval, which comes easier when they enthusiastically support you. That support doesn't arrive if you're a talent that's all about you, unwilling to take management's concerns into consideration. If I had learned nothing else over the years, it was that you can't acquire allies unless you're demonstrating an interest in the concerns of your employer. That knowledge would come in handy while trying to pick the right replacement for Bayless.

What did the bosses think would ensure success for *First Take* in the future, and get us from ESPN2 onto ESPN? What were they looking for in a cohost? Who would they support?

In my opinion, we'd need another natural contrarian like Skip, someone with strong and independent beliefs and perspectives. We needed an individual who not only played the role of villain to perfection but enjoyed the reaction it provoked—even if it was anger and dis-gust, bordering on hatred.

But, above all, chemistry and cohesiveness—not only between me and my new host but also between me and the ESPN executives—was needed to solidify *First Take*'s future. The right successor to Bayless would ensure that *First Take* received the necessary support, so long as management and I were on the same page as to who that should be.

Thankfully, we were!

By early July 2016, less than a month after Bayless departed, we had our man.

His name was Max Kellerman.

Max Kellerman wasn't the first choice to become *First Take*'s new cohost. He was the only choice.

At forty-two, he was young enough and brash enough. He was supremely confident, and exceptionally well educated, an Ivy League grad (he majored in history at Columbia). He'd been on TV and radio for nearly twenty years, including as an original host of ESPN's *Around the Horn* in 2002; a regular contributor to Tucker Carlson's early talk show on MSNBC, and a commentator on sports and popular culture issues at CNN. He was an expert on boxing—he'd started at ESPN right out of college as a boxing analyst on *Friday Night Fights*, and later worked ringside for HBO. He was knowledgeable about basketball and brilliant on baseball. He was the lone available individual on the ESPN roster perceived internally as already having his own audience.

He was also white.

Kellerman's ethnicity certainly didn't diminish his appeal with the bosses for the *First Take* job, but it was very important to me, as well. Half of our audience was white, half was Black and other people of color. Research had convinced me that replacing Bayless with a Black cohost would have alienated nearly half the *First Take* audience—the white audience—at that particular moment in time.

Bayless is a white man. I am an unapologetic Black man. And when we opened our mouths, regardless of our takes or the support we received from one ethnic group or another, a significant part of our success was the flagrancy of our Black vs. white dynamic.

When folks tune into the "World-Wide Leader," they want to see a mixture, a mosaic, over the course of two hours. They didn't want one monolithic perspective patrolling the airwaves.

Especially if I was playing the lead provocateur.

The audience, through research, had basically said as much. The network knew as much. I had no choice but to acknowledge as much.

I flew to L.A. and met with Max at the JW Marriott at L.A. Live downtown, verbalizing my support to him face-to-face.

Kellerman was doing well there on radio for ESPN 710, while also being a part of the ESPN show *SportsNation*, which aired every weekday afternoon. Like many others, he was thoroughly enjoying the lifestyle of sunshine and warm weather that comes with residing in Southern California.

To do *First Take*, the Bronx-born Kellerman had to relocate his family, with his three young daughters, back to the Big Apple. Despite being a native New Yorker, returning home from the life he'd built for himself was a tall ask. A major sacrifice!

I was sensitive to that. I was also aware of my promise to him; telling him upfront we'd do *First Take* together for a minimum of three years—but no more than five—before I'd look to move on to some other opportunity at ESPN, ideally on my own show in the afternoon or evening. I was hell-bent on catapulting beyond the confines of *First Take*, despite how successful and culturally impactful the show had become, and was dreaming of doing a late-night show, among other things.

"The goal is for us to knock this out of the park, bro! That'll put me in a position to move on, and I can hand the reins to you," I told him.

*   *   *

Kellerman's first day on *First Take* was July 25, 2016.

In his debut, he declared that Tom Brady was a bum, that he was on the verge of "falling off a cliff," stating that Brady was closer to being a JAG (Just Another Guy) than he was to becoming a Super Bowl champion again.

By the next day, he apologized for it.

I immediately realized the show was going to have issues. Kellerman's problem wasn't being wrong in his prediction, it was backtracking from calling Tom Brady a bum.

Kellerman wasn't wrong in any way. It's just that the *First Take* audience was not used to seeing that wishy-washiness from Skip Bayless. So they damn sure didn't want to see a mea culpa from his replacement after his debut show. Reaction via social media at the time validated as much, as the audience seemed to be saying: "If you think he's a bum and that's what you said, what the hell are you apologizing for?"

Kellerman's apology, completely unsolicited but totally understandable, was an indication of things to come. It would be the first of many times I believed he came across as someone who equivocated far too much on the airwaves instead of simply saying what he felt and why without worrying about what kind of reaction he'd get.

"I do what the facts tell me," Kellerman said on the air within two weeks on the job. "I'm not married to any opinion. If the facts tell me differently, I'll happily change my mind."

Kellerman knew his stuff. He knew how to defend his point of view. But I thought he would overdo it, seemingly fixated on showing how knowledgeable he was so he could cover all bases. That caused the audience to wonder, *What exactly is your point? What are you trying to say?*

Within a month, their questions became my own, and I was repeatedly forced to ask, "What is your point, Max?" Soon, every contributor on the show would ask, "Max, what the hell are you trying to say?"

Ultimately, it defined who Max was in the public eye.

Kellerman's "safe" approach wasn't some intentional act he committed to hurt the show. It was just his natural disposition. He cares a lot. He's decent at his core. He's as fair-minded as they come.

The problem, however, was that Kellerman's equivocating prompted questions as to whether or not *First Take* was living up to its debate-show mantra of letting the audience know how you feel and leaving them to pick a side. It brought the very essence of *First Take* into question, since the show's success was predicated on a cohost's willingness to let folks come at them. Even berate them.

In terms of ratings, *First Take* was holding on to its number one ranking in the mornings, but the show wasn't generating many headlines, not much buzz. The audience had embraced me; now I needed that audience to embrace *us*. Usually anything they had to say about Max involved clarification, not opposition, to what he had to say. After about a year, we started to become stale. It prompted management to hire focus groups and gather data, placing an emphasis on our chemistry, on whether or not we worked well as a cohesive pair.

We realized that on too many occasions, the chemistry just wasn't there. The standard Skip Bayless and me set had gone out the window. Both Kellerman and I worked hard. But I honestly felt the distinct differences in our personalities impeded our ability to live up to what *First Take* was supposed to be.

On a debate show, the one impossible feat is being able to debate yourself. It simply cannot happen. You need a true partner. So, when Dave Roberts, who had become the VP in charge of *First Take* day-to-day in November 2016, repeatedly tried to tell me that the chief responsibility for our chemistry issues lay at my feet, telling me that I was the star and harbored the most culpability, I protested.

I said, "Nobody's doing anything wrong here, Boss! We just don't have it. You can't manufacture chemistry. You either have it or you don't."

To be fair, I eventually saw that I had been coming off in a certain unfortunate way toward Kellerman on the show. I was aware that critics and focus groups alike honed in on the idea that I was a bit harsh toward Kellerman, that I came across as someone who didn't like him too much. Even friends of mine noticed.

It wasn't true, but perception is reality sometimes.

I have a recurring role on the soap opera *General Hospital*, and I'm very close friends with the actor Maurice Benard, who plays Sonny Corinthos on that show, and Eric Braeden, who plays Victor Newman on *The Young and the Restless*. Maurice and Sonny are two of the biggest soap opera stars in American history. In separate conversations with each of them, they both described watching me go at Kellerman as an "uncomfortable" watch—saying that I appeared cruel—concluding it was on *me* to do a better job on camera.

Everyone was totally right about how things *looked*. But folks were wrong about how I *felt* toward Kellerman.

I actually liked Kellerman a great deal as a person. I harbored no ill will toward him.

This was the same guy who uprooted his family to come to New York. Consistently, he was supportive of anything I wanted to do pertaining to my personal ambitions and, frankly, he's an all-around great guy. Things weren't all bad.

One of my favorite on-air moments with Max was when he hid away from the camera after I one-upped him on a debate involving Kawhi Leonard. It was absolutely hysterical television.

There were times when he found the natural contrarian quality too. His diatribes about the perpetual ineptitude of my favored New York Knicks were brilliant. His opinion about how the Lakers had overpaid the late Kobe Bryant after he sustained an Achilles tear was a profoundly different one than I would ever have uttered. And he disagreed with my takes about Colin Kaepernick in compelling ways. His incredible eloquence on issues with regard to race, social justice, and politics were second to none.

Above all else, what I appreciated about Max was that dead space never occurred on the air with him. He always had something to say, which made my day-to-day job significantly easier.

Had there never been a Skip and Stephen A. combination that spoiled an audience into expecting a certain type of daily confrontation, perhaps things would have been different. But a standard was set for four years before Max ever arrived. We had a mandate to live up to it, and we couldn't pull it off.

So I just reached a point where I knew we couldn't live up to what the audience demanded and didn't want to work with Kellerman on a debate show any longer. We were not ideal sparring partners. That was all! I had to depend on him in a debate format, and I grew to believe that was something I could not do.

I prided myself on caring about the success of *First Take*. In my eyes, Kellerman prided himself on caring about how he came across on *First Take*. By no means am I trying to imply that Kellerman did not care about the show, because he did. But in the world of debate television, the successful ones are those who don't fixate on how they look. They just tell you what they believe and stand by it.

To paraphrase Kellerman, as he once said himself during an interview at a Knicks game inside Madison Square Garden: Stephen A. tells you exactly what's on his mind and where he stands, and doesn't care what you think. I, on the other hand, am shocked when anyone would disagree with me, so I spend time trying to convince you to see the error of your ways.

Kellerman was right on the money with his assessment. But it was a glaring difference I grew to believe zapped *First Take* of its appeal in the months and years to follow.

I would have felt much differently if we were commentating on a boxing match or were part of a UFC panel together. Those are platforms for actual discussions, not debates. So my success would not have been dependent on him, at all. But *First Take* didn't provide that comfort zone. I felt *First Take* needed more from him and just didn't get it, no matter how hard he may have tried.

For three years, from 2017 to 2020, there were an inordinate amount of conversations with the honchos about my and Max's lack of chemistry—not about ratings (we were still number one), just how uncomfortable it became watching us together.

Lost in all the tumult was the effect this was having on Molly Qerim—a true victim in all that we had to endure. As the host of *First Take*, Molly was assigned to moderate and, essentially, keep things moving smoothly, but the lack of vibe and cohesiveness between Max and me—unintentionally, of course—made her life incredibly difficult. The fact that Molly endured this headache practically every day, coming to work wondering what would happen next, not only elevated my respect and admiration for her. It simply cemented the fact of her being an invaluable asset I had zero interest in doing *First Take* without. The pairing of Max and I ultimately regressed to being a hopeless cause. I was convinced he and I could not work and—although she'd never say so—I truly believed Molly felt that way as well.

But I told Dave Roberts that while I did hold a lot responsibility for the success of the show, it was on the bosses too, if they stood idly by and did nothing while knowing a change needed to be made.

I was happy to place the onus on the bosses to decide what to do.

I made no demands. At no time did I threaten to quit or dishonor the commitments I had made contractually. Anyone who knows me knows I am not made of that cloth.

As Janet Smith's child, you were raised understanding that if "you make a commitment, you honor it. Period! Otherwise, don't ever expect to be trusted."

CHAPTER 17

FINISH THE JOB

The night my mother died, I collapsed onto the bed with her. Then the tears started streaming. They kept going, seemingly forever. Five minutes. Ten minutes. Fifteen minutes. Twenty minutes. I have no idea how long I was crying. All I know is that my sisters and my nephew Josh told me I didn't stop crying for a long, long time.

They know I still cry today.

Janet Smith is simply the greatest woman I've ever known. She is the reason I believe in God! She's the reason I believe that there really is a heaven. Because of her undying devotion to her children, her compassion for her fellow man and woman, her patience, her tolerance—her strength—in the face of more adversity than any woman should ever be subjected to, she is the embodiment of an angel to me.

She worked so her family would be taken care of. She starved so we wouldn't be hungry.

She was miserable far too often, just so we could find a way to happiness. She deprived herself, so we'd be fulfilled.

Once all my emotions came flooding out of me and I managed to get up and go downstairs to sit in the kitchen, Josh walked into the kitchen right behind me and said, "It's on you now, Uncle Steve. You've got to hold all of us together. You're the leader of the family now."

I staggered as I walked back to my car at about 1:30 a.m., knowing Hollis, Queens, would never possess the same allure for me again. As I drove back to New Jersey, slowly, probably for the first time in my life, certain images remained stuck in my head. I've worked in a visual medium for years, so the power of seeing—as opposed to hearing or reading—is strong for me. I replayed the tears flowing as if out of faucets from the faces of my family members, the image of my mother lying motionless in her bed, the scene of the funeral-home people pulling up to my mother's driveway to pick up her body, and the thick, black leather body bag they placed her in and zipped up right in front of me before taking her away. The images were just too vivid to let go of.

The world learned of my mother's passing the following morning because of a beautiful tribute put together by the staff of *First Take*—led by Dave Roberts and producer Antoine Lewis—and played on the show, presented beautifully by Molly Qerim, which immediately left me bawling in tears all over again. The condolence calls came pouring in.

The first was from Shaquille O'Neal at about 6:30 a.m.; he was the one who actually woke me up, as I'd finally fallen asleep for a couple of hours.

The second call was from Momma Shaq (Lucille O'Neal), followed by several members of the NBA Mom's fraternity.

The next call was from the late, great Kobe Bryant. All before 7 EST that morning.

By the time *First Take* came on and the world found out that Stephen A.'s mom had passed away, the calls and text messages came from everywhere. Players, coaches, reporters, executives from various sports, including NBA commissioner Adam Silver, and the one and only Michael Jordan, himself. And, of course, Omari Hardwick, former star of Starz's *Power*, who had been a guest on *First Take* that morning and who has been an incredible friend over the years.

As devastated as I was, the calls, the thoughtful words, sensing how so many people genuinely cared, meant the world to me. It helped the tears stop for a few moments, though it would take a lot more time and reflection before I'd really get out of the malaise of this grief.

I hated my mother's funeral. And there was no one but the Smith family to blame for it. That included me.

Having spent decades attending this small, dilapidated church a couple blocks off Jamaica Avenue on 168th Street in Queens, my mother had insisted before she died that it was where she wanted her funeral to take place.

This insistence was expressed to everyone but me. She knew I would have changed her mind.

As the youngest of six—her baby boy—Janet Smith pretty much gave me whatever I wanted. This is why the faces of all my sisters would shrivel up with envy; I simply got things out of my mother no one else could.

Once she retired, my mother swore she'd never cook for her grown children again—yet she walked straight to the kitchen anytime I entered the house for a visit. Every single time. If there was food, but not enough left over for everyone, they couldn't have it.

"That's for Stephen," she'd say. (Smile!!!)

Mommy knew I had a proclivity for two dishes: her beef patties and coconut tarts. Both were meals she'd made from scratch. At times, there would be ten to twelve people in the house, compelling my mother to make about thirty beef patties. At least ten of the patties were set aside for *me*. The other fifteen to twenty had to be divided among the rest.

As for the coconut tart, Mommy wouldn't make them—knowing my sisters salivated over them—unless she knew I was coming through to see her.

"That's ridiculous," my sister Abigail would complain to Mommy, shaking her head in utter disgust. "He's so damn spoiled," she'd mutter time and time again.

I'd respond, "I *am* the baby, after all."

"Be quiet," Mommy would respond. "There's the stove. Nobody's stopping you from using it to make stuff yourself." (Smile!!!)

So, if I had been there when my mother was alive, and she insisted that her funeral would be in a church with just a 120-person capacity, I would have killed that notion right away. I would have reminded her of all her friends and loved ones, all of those close to her children who'd want to come and support us, not to mention those from the Hollis neighborhood. And if that hadn't worked, I would have simply brought up my job:

"Mommy," I would have told her. "Do you have any idea who will come to your funeral just on my behalf? Executives and colleagues, people folks see on television all the time. If that is what you want the image of your funeral service to be—folks crammed inside, most standing up on the side because there's not enough seating?"

My mother would have caved immediately!

Carmen and I found out about the particulars of the funeral three days before, when it was too late. We weren't happy about it at all.

The funeral touched my heart, but it also provoked shame in me. Half the people who arrived had nowhere to sit or stand. Dave Roberts was there. So were Connor Schell, David Brofsky, and other ESPN executives. Max Kellerman was kind enough to show up. My wonderful former doctor and the biggest sports fan I know, Dr. Steven Charno, was in attendance. My friend, the great boxing analyst Teddy Atlas, was there. ESPN colleagues and friends like Michael Kay, Don LaGreca, along with SiriusXM host Dan Graca. All of my closest college buddies from Winston-Salem State arrived in unison. And, of course, my spiritual father, Pastor A. R. Bernard, showed up too.

Shockingly, my childhood buddy Poolie came out of nowhere. His appearance surprised me. Poolie was a transit worker in New York City, driving a bus at that time, and he literally parked the bus across the street from my mother's church—with passengers on board—to run in during the funeral service just to give me a hug and tell me, "I love you, kid! I'll be here whenever you need me."

I'm eternally grateful to all the people who came. And during my mother's funeral, surrounded by so many friends and family members, I thought for the first time of all the funerals I had missed over the years. I almost never attended them after 1992, because I was concerned that all I would think about was my brother, Basil's, death. That would instantly make me depressed, and I wanted to do everything in my power to avoid those feelings.

But seeing all those folks at my mother's funeral, there to support me, I realized how incredibly *selfish* I had been. Who wants to go to a funeral? Even a memorial service? The answer is: Nobody! The moral of the story is you don't do it for yourself. You do it to support the people you care about—to let them know they are in your heart at a time when they need that comfort the most.

The toughest part of my mother's funeral, as is the case for practically everyone, I'd imagine, was when we went to the cemetery and the casket was lowered into the ground. That's when it hits you that it's really over.

Naturally, my heart sank. Somehow, I gumptioned up the strength to hug my sisters and let them know I was there for them, but I was in a complete daze. Even with Samantha's mother, Stephanie, by my side, doing all she could to comfort me as I tried to fight back tears time and again, I still felt lifeless!

It was as if the end had arrived for me too.

But then, as if Mommy decided to send the message "you will not be alone," a few other ladies came to the rescue.

Karen Hunter, a sensational host for the SiriusXM Urban View radio channel, whom I've known for thirty years, was there. So was NBA executive Leah Wilcox, a dear friend for nearly just as long. ESPN's former head of HR Kerry Chandler was right there, of course, as well. The same went for my financial adviser, Stacy Robinson, whom I've trusted with my money and my friendship for over twenty-five years.

To me, I don't have four sisters. I have eight. (Nine, really, once you count Nina, my buddy Jeff Brown's wife.) Because all three of these women mean that much to me. Each are bold, generous, strong, and as caring as they come. Each look at me as their brother—and my love for them knows no limits.

They were all there, comforting me when I doubted I could be comforted. And after seeing them, I literally looked up to the sky and nodded at Mommy. "I see you, Mommy!" I said to myself. "I got it."

Back at my mother's house, as the family just sat in the living room saying nothing, my sister Linda finally broke the silence and asked me, "So when are you going back to work?"

I lifted my head up, saw all four of my sisters' faces locked in on me, and told them I wasn't going back.

"What the hell is wrong with you?" Linda said. The other three chimed in with similar messages.

"Imma say it again: What the hell is wrong with you?" Linda fumed. "This is what you do. These are the NBA Finals. [Game 3 between the Golden State Warriors and Cleveland Cavs was coming up.] *First Take* is on the air. We saw that crowd before Game 1 when they *thought* you were going to be there, before everyone disappeared once they saw you were gone because Mommy died. There's nothing to do here.

"The funeral is over. And you know damn well what Mommy would say: 'Finish the job! You've got all summer to mourn me.' That's exactly what she would say, and you know it. So get your ass back to work, bro. You gotta finish the job."

I didn't say a word. Because I couldn't.

I knew my mother. Obviously, so did my sisters. When Linda uttered what Mommy would have said, each of my other sisters nodded in affirmation. Not only were there games to cover, I also had to reappear on *First Take*.

"You go to work," Carmen implored. "That's how we were raised. That's what Mommy did every day of her life."

Totally true!

So I called Sumatra Hawkins, my personal assistant since 2005—and one of my most trusted confidantes in the world—as she was driving home from the cemetery and told her to make the arrangements for me to get to Cleveland for Game 3.

"I can't believe you're here," said my boss, Dave Roberts, stunned, when he saw me in Cleveland. "You just buried your mother yesterday. Are you sure about this?"

No, I wasn't.

Molly greeted me with a hug. Max Kellerman was very supportive, as was the rest of the *First Take* staff, making every effort to keep things as normal as possible for me. The roar of the crowd was deafening when they saw me, tugging on my emotional strings.

Even the bloggers could not have been more decent. I was both grateful and relieved.

At no time in my life had I ever been as vulnerable, so easy to hurt emotionally, as I was upon my return to work. I was still struggling, visibly.

After running into Warriors' coach Steve Kerr while entering the arena, who was especially gracious in expressing his condolences, I found myself very worried. For the first time in my career, I didn't want to be at a game. I was petrified that I would break down and cry at some point, because the agony was just immense.

I nearly broke down when I saw my friend Chris Broussard, again when I saw Dr. Michael Eric Dyson, and when Sage Steele came over, she nearly broke down and cried herself once she'd laid eyes on me, seeing the misery flowing from my face.

Jesse Jackson hugged me, then led a prayer on the basketball court with Broussard and Dr. Dyson. I had to get the hell out of there. At least get myself off the court, out of public view.

I hustled back to a back room designated for ESPN and tried to hide from everyone, including when former NBA players Chauncey Billups and Paul Pierce, both working for ESPN at that moment, came over to express their condolences.

But then another person came over and tapped me on the shoulder, informing me that someone was waiting to see me at the door. When I turned around, Wanda Durant—Kevin Durant's mother—was waiting at the door for me.

Uh-oh.

Nearly eleven months earlier, I had declared her son's decision to depart Oklahoma City and take his talents to Golden State "the weakest move by a superstar I've seen in sports history." Fiercely devoted to her son, and never shy about expressing it, Mama Durant might not have been too happy with what I had said, but that didn't appear to be on her mind at the moment.

She stood there with her arms extended. Not a frown. When I walked up to her, she just gave me this massive hug. It was the kind of hug a son with a loving mother could easily identify. That hug, and her words— "We [the NBA Moms] love you. And we're here for you. I am here for you."—were the first moment in the thirty-six hours since I'd buried my mother that I actually believed things would be okay, eventually.

Then she added:

"I'm still going to get you for what you said about my boy, though," before both of us broke out in laughter. It marked the first time in weeks I had laughed about anything, and I took no issue with what she said.

I've never called her anything but Mama Durant ever since.

Her presence and soothing words reminded me of how my mother chastised me, somewhat, one evening in the waning weeks of her life.

"Why are you looking so sad?" she said. "You love me, don't you?

Because if you do, you don't want the alternative. You don't want me sitting here, bracing myself to lose you. This is the way it's supposed to be. I'm supposed to leave this earth before you. It's not supposed to be the other way around. I've prepared you for this. You know what you have to do from here."

Recalling my mother's waning days, I reminisced on how comfortable she appeared. While sadness and quiet engulfed my sisters and me, she was alarmingly calm and cool.

Mommy was a devout Christian. She believed there was a better place than here on earth and that she had a pretty good chance of ending up there. That's why she resigned herself to 2017 being her final year on this earth long before any of us had reached that conclusion. She was barely concerned at all.

"If it's God's will, there's nothing I can do, so why worry about it," she'd said. "I lived a good life. All my children are grown now, and I know you know what to do. I'm okay And you'd better be, too. You can't just lay down and stop living."

It took me a long time to feel that way.

I spent the summer of 2017 reflecting on her passing, the role I'd have to play with the family moving forward, and what I would do with myself.

On several occasions, when I'd spoken to my mother about what I wanted to do with my life, she asked questions to get all the details she craved, then deliver her advice on each topic.

About my sisters? Keep the family together!

My daughters? Just don't be like your father!

On ESPN? Do your best, always. But don't limit yourself to just them.

My entrepreneurial aspirations? Go for it! That challenge will make you happy.

I was proud that my mother had seen her Black child born and

raised in poverty in Hollis ascend to being, arguably, the most prominent sports media personality in the world. And because of it, she went
from being a hard-working mother who couldn't afford life's luxuries
to retiring with her mortgage paid, to touring the world on cruises and
living a life of affluence at her choosing.

In the end, she died happy because her children were accomplished,
law-abiding, and happy themselves. Still, she expected more once she
was gone.

"I prepared you for life without me," she reminded us. "You know
what I want." It was whatever I wanted for myself, but what was that?

I had an idea, and an awful lot of work to put in. That would make
Mommy smile.

She loved hard work, and a mission. It meant you were never standing still.

When my sister Arlyne called in August 2018 to tell me that our father
had died—a little more than fourteen months after our mother had
passed away—my emotions were mixed. I was genuinely sad, but I
didn't cry. Most of all, I just felt overwhelmed.

What does make me cry is reflecting on the unnecessary things my
siblings and I had had to endure in our childhood due to my father's
negligence. I weep because, regardless of all the trifling tendencies my
father exhibited, he was still my dad. I loved him. But I hated the choices
he made and the impact they had had on our lives.

Among them was something that happened in 1996. My father and
I still hadn't talked much. But even years later, the death of my brother
was still devastating to us all. The ruling on a lawsuit, regarding compensation over how he died, had arrived months earlier. Monetary compensation would not only go to his two daughters, Shanelle and Candace,
but also to both of my parents. The amount was about $400K.

The presumption was that the funds my parents received would be split between them and my four sisters (I didn't need the money and made that clear to everyone).

My father had other ideas.

First, he made it clear that he had no intention of splitting his take with any of my siblings. Worse, however, he ultimately convinced my mother to give him her share, as well—supposedly to invest in property on St. Thomas, U.S. Virgin Islands.

When my mother acknowledged what she'd done, we all pounced on her verbally, asking her why would she do such a thing?

"I didn't want to be bothered with him bugging me all the time for the money," she said. "Y'all don't have to hear his mouth all the time. I do. I just didn't want to be bothered."

When Basil died in 1992, my sister Linda sobbed on several occasions. "He died believing Dad never loved him at all," she lamented.

She was talking about the neglect my father had exhibited toward us all, but more about the profound impact it had had on my brother, who suffered from having what was virtually an absentee father his whole life.

So in March 1996, as my father was set to head to St. Thomas from JFK International Airport in New York, I volunteered to take him there myself from my mother's house, about fifteen minutes away.

Once in the car, I informed him I was aware of his stance on keeping all the money for himself; of his refusal to share it with Mommy or my sisters. He responded with complete silence, so I spoke up further.

"You know that Basil died believing you never loved him, right? You know this! You know you never did anything for him. Now, not only are you going to profit from his death but you're going to keep it all for yourself when you know he would've wanted Mommy and his sisters to have their share? What's the matter with you?"

"Your mother gave me the money, so it's mine," he responded. "I'm investing in property in St. Thomas. When I'm gone, y'all will have something to call your own. You want an answer? That's the answer I'm giving you."

Stupidly, I was shocked. Just when I thought I had figured out the depths of his selfishness, Dad had shown another level. I just couldn't take it anymore.

"Just when I thought you couldn't go any lower, you show me you can," I said, right as I pulled up to the curb of the American Airlines terminal at JFK. "But I'm going to tell you this right now: If you take this money all for yourself, doing nothing for Mommy and the family with it—things you know Basil would have wanted you to do—you didn't lose just one son, you will have lost two. Because you'll be dead to me."

My father then turned to his left from the passenger's seat inside my car, looked me dead in my face, and said: "Okay! So be it." Then he hopped out the car without saying goodbye and never looked back as he walked into the terminal. My mother told me he'd always assumed I'd get over it. That's just how he thought.

I didn't!

I never said anything more than "hi" and "bye" to my father for the next eighteen years. That was the summer of 2014, when we learned his health was debilitating. My mother had begged me to let "bygones be bygones!"

The only reason I relented is because she begged me to.

Unlike my mother, who died surrounded by family members in the comfort of a bedroom she'd slept in for almost fifty years, my father's final breath was taken alone, inside a nursing home right across the street from Jamaica Hospital. He spent about a month there. Ironically, in the thirteen months before that, he had been home more than ever. The daughters he never took care of collaborated to take care of him. They fed him. They cleaned his room. Although he wouldn't admit it, his spirit had clearly left once my mother was gone.

My sisters and I (with the exception of Carmen) had visited him in the nursing home before he passed, but none of us were with him for his last moments. It was a privilege we weren't inclined to afford him.

My last visit with Dad was three days before the end, when I'd gone to make sure all outstanding bills were paid, that he was comfortable and relatively pain free, and that he wasn't in need of anything. I stayed for about an hour. When he was awake, all we did was talk about his Yankees.

No apologies. No sad goodbyes. No mea culpas. No in-depth personal conversations. It was a struggle for him to talk at all at that point, but I doubt it would have been any different if he had been able to. To my mind, our time for discussions had come and gone years earlier.

Carmen, who despised my dad most among us siblings, ended up being the one to help me make our father's funeral arrangements (Linda and Arlyne felt as if they had done enough for him while he was alive; Abigail knew Carmen and I had it covered).

We chose the same funeral home on Linden Boulevard in Queens where our brother, Basil's, funeral service had been held nearly twenty-six years earlier. Our father was then buried right next to our mother, in Queens, because we knew that's precisely what my mother would have wanted.

My animus toward my dad was really punctuated the morning of his funeral. I decided to ignore my siblings' advice to the contrary and go ahead and eulogize him. My sisters were in panic mode when I called to let them know of my decision. They were scared to death.

"What are you gonna say?" Carmen's voice quavered.

"You'll find out when I speak," I said.

"Oh God, Steve . . . please don't act up . . . Please," she pleaded. "Think! What would Mommy want? How would she feel about whatever you're about to do?"

I did not care!

In my mind, it was time for friends, neighbors, and all the locals in attendance to finally learn who my dad truly was. I wanted them to know that the praise accorded to folks when they've passed away wasn't warranted on this particular morning. I wanted them to realize all the hell he purposefully put his children and especially my mother through: forcing her to struggle to pay bills to ensure our survival, smiling at everyone and giving the impression he was so much more than he actually was.

But then something overtook me. I kept hearing the biblical words in my head: "Honor thy father and thy mother." Those words indicated to me that I needed guidance—so I called Pastor A. R. Bernard to get some.

We spent nearly an hour on the phone. After I told him what was on my mind, I felt relief because Pastor Bernard assured me it was perfectly within my right to express my dismay and ill feelings toward my father.

"Speak your truth," he said.

But Pastor Bernard didn't leave it at that. He also spoke to the emotional tumult I was going through and reminded me of the importance of grace and forgiveness. "Remember those things when you're talking about your father," he said. "Even when you're recalling all the hurt and pain he caused, the rest will come to you. I can assure you of that."

Sure enough, it did.

I started my dad's eulogy saying, "To y'all, he was a fun-loving, good man. To my family, we have an entirely different story." And I did express some of the truths about him that I wanted people to hear.

But with Pastor Bernard's help, I'd realized something else, too. To have such a woman as my mother love my father so much meant there must have been something very special about him. After all, no one made my mother laugh like my dad. No one could dance like him, sing like him, serenade her like him. Dare I say, make my mother quiver with excitement and joy the way he could. He did that from one decade to the next.

That's why I was able to end the eulogy by saying:

"I wish things were different between us, but he was still my dad. I loved him. And I always will."

I would not have reached that emotional accord that morning had it not been for Pastor Bernard, a man of God whom I love and trust unequivocally. It got me through that moment.

I often contemplate how I would have felt if my last words consisted of the cruel, harsh thoughts I was aching to express. It would have scarred me forever and left me feeling bitter. I thank the Good Lord and Pastor Bernard that I didn't follow through and heeded my pastor's words instead.

CHAPTER 18

LESSONS LEARNED

Learning from our mistakes is a constant process, and in July 2021, I got another opportunity to do that when I screwed up on-air again. This time, I slapped myself in the mouth with my foot, courtesy of an inarticulate diatribe about Los Angeles Angels superstar Shohei Ohtani. From my past experiences, I'd learned that if the cover-up to your mistake appears to be worse than the crime, so to speak—if the apology sounds self-serving or even worse than the gaffe—it's simply because you're trying to escape culpability. When that happens, folks know your heart isn't in the right place. It disgusts them. They'll turn on you.

So I didn't mess with all the woe-is-me bullshit this go-around. And it saved me a lot of trouble.

The morning before the annual All-Star Game, Max Kellerman and I discussed whether it was in decline and why. At our regular 7:30 a.m. meeting with all the producers and hosts, two and a half hours before we were going on-air, we talked about whether the sport was reluctant to promote the Japanese-born Ohtani, a generational superstar who was both a prolific home run hitter and an overpowering pitcher—something not seen since Babe Ruth, almost a century ago.

The feeling was that despite Ohtani's greatness, Major League Baseball still pined for someone who would appeal to the older white audience that's made up the huge chunk of its fan base for decades, not a player from another country who used an interpreter during interviews.

My intent was a bottom-line, dollars-and-sense take, an indictment not of Ohtani but of the sport that employed him.

"When you talk about an audience gravitating to the tube or to the ballpark to actually watch you," I said when we went on the air, "I don't think it helps that the number one face of baseball is a dude that needs an interpreter so you can understand what the hell he's saying, in this country."

I was in Milwaukee at the time for the NBA Finals. By the time I'd traveled back to New York that afternoon, an uproar over that statement was in progress.

Some folks wanted me suspended right away. Others, like former ESPN anchor Keith Olbermann, who I consider one of the all-time great TV sports hosts, wanted me fired—a hilarious take considering the number of times over the decades Olbermann has been reprimanded after backlash surrounding the outrageous things he's said.

I could have gone after those who, like Olbermann, were calling for my job. Admittedly, I was tempted to do so, to have temporarily gotten my own back on those looking to take me down because they hated the fact that I was blessed with a perch in this business. But I quickly checked myself.

I thought back to the shooting spree at three separate spas or massage parlors in Atlanta the previous March that left eight people dead—six of them Asian women. I also remembered all the Asian and Asian American community had absorbed since the pandemic began. When news that the virus originated in Wuhan, China, had emerged while a presidential election loomed, President Trump had repeatedly deflected questions about the pandemic by saying, "Don't ask me! Ask China!"

He repeatedly referred to COVID-19 as the "China virus" or, worse, "the Kung Flu."

Many Americans were anxiously looking for a place to point the finger of blame. Though the former president wasn't the only one fueling vitriol toward the Asian and Asian American community, there's no arguing that he certainly didn't make things any easier for them at that moment.

Set in that context, and given the transcendent season that Ohtani was having with the Los Angeles Angels, my words were especially ignorant and irresponsible. The fact that Ohtani could actually speak English—he used an interpreter with the press to make sure there was no confusion about reporters' questions or his answers—only made what I had said worse.

Right then, I simply said to myself, "Damn, Steve! What the hell were you thinking?"

Since I clearly wasn't thinking enough about the magnitude of such words when I spoke them earlier, I definitely wasn't going to make that mistake again. Unlike previous times, when I'd acquiesce to ESPN's need to get involved and guide my response, I wasn't having that this time around.

This time, I handled the response myself, and in my own way. I'd learned something. Finally!

Part of the problem in the past was allowing ESPN to dictate a response while they were in panic mode. With Ray Rice, they'd forced me to read their apology from a prompter, which, albeit unintentional, only served to make me look to viewers like some disingenuous phony. With Ayesha Curry, I hadn't included voices of the real afflicted party in that brouhaha: women.

This time, when word quickly circulated that Joon Lee, an ESPN baseball writer and an Asian American, was upset by my comments, Dave Roberts suggested I talk with him.

I called Lee that night to express my regret. I told him the intent of my remarks was that Major League Baseball wouldn't promote Ohtani, not that they shouldn't! I also expressed—which I firmly believe—that is why Major League Baseball is behind the curve connecting with a younger audience. They have simply failed to ingratiate themselves with the 18-to-34 demographic, or even the 25-to-49 demo.

Lee was understanding, but still candid in his dismay over what I'd said. He allowed that the problem was less about me specifically than the impact of my words feeding so much Asian hate roiling through America, especially at that moment.

Lee's concern was the bigger picture: the importance of addressing and eradicating the hate and suspicion his community was being exposed to. He was committed to calling on everyone to join in to help eliminate the vitriol directed at his community, and he said he wanted to come on *First Take* to express as much.

I told him that was no problem. If he wanted to debunk me to make his point, I was absolutely fine with that.

Lee's words that night, as well as his personal attachment to them, affected me more than anything. They were one of the main inspirations for my unscripted mea culpa to open the next morning's show. I didn't need ESPN public relations, a script, or a teleprompter. All I needed was me, and a camera to look into, to tell America I was wrong.

"I want to express my sincere apologies to the Asian community and the Asian American community," I said to everyone watching at home. "I am a Black man. I religiously go off about minorities being marginalized in this nation. As an African American, keenly aware of the damage stereotyping has done to many in this country, it should've elevated my sensitivities even more.

"I screwed up," I went on. "In this day and age, with all the violence being perpetrated against the Asian community, my comments—albeit unintentional—were clearly insensitive and regrettable. I'm sincerely sorry for any angst I've caused with my comments."

Then Lee, as well as another ESPN baseball writer, Jeff Passan, were given the floor. If they wanted to undress me in front of God and everybody, so be it.

"So many of us in the media, particularly at ESPN, are so unprepared to talk about Asian Americans in a nuanced way," Lee told *First Take* viewers, most of whom knew he was simultaneously addressing me. "We all need to do better."

Passan was just as unsparing in his criticism of both me and the network.

"Ohtani is the sort of person who this show, who this network, who this country should be embracing," he said. "We are not the ones who should be trafficking in ignorance."

From the Ray Rice fiasco, I'd learned to trust my gut when talking to my audience. From the Ayesha Curry imbroglio, I learned to listen and grow.

I clearly had more growing to do—I'll always have more growing to do—and so while I was denounced and embarrassed by my latest foot-in-mouth mishap, I wasn't as defensive. I didn't resent anyone for attacking me for what I'd said.

Instead, I kept my eye on the ball: Have a positive impact, Stephen A.!

The guests that came on the show were needed not just to address me and my words, but to address the entire nation, or at least the sports world watching at that hour. I wasn't the only one who needed to be educated about Asian hate and what Asians and Asian Americans have had to endure.

If the price to help make things better was some public shaming on my part, so be it. It all might have happened the wrong way, for all the wrong reasons, but a lot of good came out of it. The end result is why I love sitting in the hot seat on *First Take* in the first place.

I walked away from the Ray Rice incident alternately embittered but more alert. I eventually walked away from the Ayesha Curry matter with my eyes opened, and grateful for it. After the Ohtani blowup?

I felt educated and fulfilled, as I hope many of my viewers did, because I shut my mouth and allowed those who needed to be heard to have the platform to speak their peace. It's exactly what Laura Gentile talked to me about over dinner.

I was better for it.

ESPN was better for it.

The Asian community was better, having had their collective voices heard. And maybe even America was a little better because of it, since more than five hundred thousand people saw it unfold that morning on TV, along with tens of millions more on YouTube and other digital and social media outlets.

Mind you, it doesn't mean I won't make mistakes again. That's the nature of the beast when you take chances by speaking what's in your mind and heart to people in a particular moment—especially on live television. But if the price to be paid is that a dialogue is started, which results in all of us becoming a bit more educated, a bit more tolerant, compassionate, and understanding of our fellow men and women, then it's all worth it.

CHAPTER 19

COME HELL OR HIGH WATER!

In July 2021, while the Milwaukee Bucks were beating the Phoenix Suns in the 2021 NBA Finals, it seemed like, at last, something was going to change. I felt that if the bosses decided they wanted to move me off *First Take*, it wouldn't be a bad thing.

Truth is, I never wanted to do *First Take* for this amount of time. When I first went to Kellerman in L.A. and told him that I'd move on in three to five years, it was absolutely my plan. I had my eyes on bigger prizes. As many viewers as *First Take* had attracted each weekday morning since my arrival in 2012, I always fantasized about being on in the afternoon or evening.

The Stephen A. Smith Show.

SportsCenter with Stephen A.!

Late Night with Stephen A.!

Anything that drew additional eyeballs, paid well, and allowed me to get up later in the day—which would enable me to stay up later at night—was ideal for me.

Frankly, I didn't give a damn concerning what choice they might make pertaining to keeping either myself or Kellerman on the show. My contract was guaranteed. Kellerman had a multi-year, multi-million-dollar contract, too. Neither of us were going to end up unemployed. This time, unlike what happened to me in 2009 and to Skip Bayless in 2016, no one was going to get screwed.

However, when I spoke to the honchos nearly a month after the NBA Finals ended, and there still hadn't been any decisions made, I was determined to make sure they knew exactly how I felt.

Come hell or high water.

I was exhausted. I was frustrated. And I was getting angrier by the week. I had no desire to sit around and watch *First Take* falter, listening to our audience tell us, "Y'all just ain't that show anymore."

I had to do something. So I let them know.

"I'm not asking you to take Max off *First Take*. I'm sick of folks walking around acting like this is personal. It is not. I have nothing against the man. We both are assets to this company.

"But we do not work on a debate show, and we never will. This is *First Take*. I know what I'm talking about here."

Then I added: "So, if you don't want to take Kellerman off the show, then take me off the show. I'll understand. I'm sure we can find something else for me to do here."

That was the end.

I went on vacation. The next thing I knew, about a week later, Roberts gave me a call to inform me change was coming: I would remain on *First Take* and Kellerman was moving on.

The need for change wasn't just about where we were. It was about where we were heading. In sports—which we cover for a living—we report and pontificate all the time about what individuals and teams need to do in order to maintain or achieve a higher level of success. Almost never in this business will you hear someone say an individual or a team needs to stand still and do nothing.

So why ignore it when it comes to our own professional lives?

I've repeatedly stated that it's nothing personal.

The Max-and-Stephen-A. combination just did not work for the purposes of a debate show. But Max Kellerman the man is someone I will always respect and appreciate.

The public brouhaha Kellerman's departure caused in headlines and on talk radio missed the fact that my feelings about our pairing were no secret to Kellerman. Though I imagine it was still a blow to be taken off a show he helped run for years, he wasn't caught by surprise.

The only conversation we've had since he moved off the show was cordial. When I returned to work in January 2022 after a month-long absence from a near-death experience with COVID, being the considerate individual he is, Kellerman came up to me and said, "I had no idea you were that bad, brother. I'm really sorry to hear that."

No other conversation between us has taken place since his departure from *First Take*.

I'm not surprised by that. I totally understand, and I'm okay with it.

When Kellerman departed *First Take*, he was more successful and richer than when he arrived. He got his own TV show, *This Just In*, each weekday afternoon, and joined Keyshawn Johnson and Jay Williams on ESPN Morning Radio. I was happy for him.

Kellerman didn't depart from a gig on ESPN to unemployment—as I was forced to endure back in 2009. He and I were just not working together anymore. That's all. Speaking strictly for myself, his departure didn't make us mortal enemies. We're still colleagues. If he ever needed me for anything, I'd happily be there to help out in any way that I could.

When I was gone from ESPN from 2009 to 2011, I reached the conclusion that you learn an awful lot more about life from being exiled than you do from leaving of your own volition. Regardless of the numerous mistakes I'd made, what vexed me to no end was that I had let my guard down. Reflecting on negotiations that had gone wrong, nothing irked me more than remembering how I had forgotten to protect myself!

I believed the bosses when they said I was still in their long-term plans!

I had done the unthinkable as a Black man in America: completely placing my trust in the bosses, totally convinced I was too valuable to be let go.

That trust ultimately left me blindsided, unemployed, devoid of options, and with my career in shambles. Worse, it left me on the verge of being one of the biggest laughing stocks in the industry's history; a Black man who'd lost it all due to acts of stupidity and immaturity an intern would know better than to commit.

Following Kellerman's removal from *First Take*, I was in position to know that was not going to happen again. I was under contract, and I was still going to be around for a while, no matter what. It provided me with some insulation.

Only a year earlier, ESPN had granted me a five-year extension. Having four years left on my deal provided some cushion. Courtesy of a conversation I had back in 2006 with then real estate mogul Donald Trump in the green room of my ESPN2 show *Quite Frankly*, I was also aware that it made ESPN vested in my continued success.

"When you go to a bank, you borrow $3 million dollars and you can't pay it back, you've got a problem," Trump began. "But when you go to a bank, you borrow $300 million dollars and you can't pay it back . . . *we've* got a problem.

"The moral of the story is . . . make sure someone invests as much in you as possible. Get as much as you can. Don't come cheap. Make sure you do that and there will always be someone else as committed to ensuring your success as you are. You won't be left standing alone."

First Take was making money. Which meant ESPN could afford to pay me money and did so on my contract extension. Which meant it was in no one's interest to mess things up.

ESPN and I were in this together, this time around!

On the other hand, as *First Take* moved beyond Max Kellerman, I still had worries. The bosses had made the decision, but what if they'd felt like their hands had been forced? If they felt that way, how would that leave them feeling about me? And if the producers weren't happy with Kellerman being gone, what kind of position was I going to be in, having to deal with the staff on a day-to-day basis? What about the fans who liked Kellerman? What about those who were simply looking for an excuse to hate me more than they already did? Whether they liked Kellerman or not, it didn't negate the fact that I'd provided ammunition for any and all to come after me in any way they could!

The "Black" element in Kellerman's departure didn't escape me, either.

Search high and low for any successful Black person and we'll tell you our belief is that most folks outside of our community, fair or not, are far more inclined to feel as if we're lucky to have achieved affluence. Rarely is it considered earned!

Hence, who the hell did I think I was, getting rid of Kellerman? How dare ESPN grant "Stephen A." that kind of power? With every headline, the danger intensified in my mind:

Stephen A. has Max Kellerman removed from First Take*!*

Did ESPN make a mistake removing Max Kellerman?

Does Stephen A. have too much power?

I was not paranoid at all, but I was not blind, either. Every word being uttered was a nugget placed out for public display by the media and blogosphere, intentionally, to irritate the bosses and set me up to be taken down.

The year 2021 might as well have been 1970 to me. Or earlier. As a former newspaper writer, familiar with the thinking that takes place inside a newsroom, I was firm in my belief that making life completely uncomfortable for the bosses was the objective of my critics. They'd contemplated the ripple effect it could ultimately cause.

Question whether the bosses made the right decision!

Question if they were smart to stick with me!

Rattle their cage, as it were, by questioning their judgment! Their willingness to cater to the prima donna, Stephen A.! Irritate Stephen A. into saying or doing something that would make ESPN say, "Yeah, we may have messed up here!"

To my way of looking at it, I had influence, and I wasn't about to apologize for that. All that really meant was I had the bosses' ears; they'd at least *listen* to what I had to say.

But that's entirely different than actually *doing* what I suggested.

On an annual basis, I hear "no" from the bosses at least 60 percent of the time, not bad considering the multitude of requests—taking *First Take* on the road, traveling on my own to different cities, games I'd like to attend, interviews I'd like to do, people I'd like to have hired on *First Take*, etc.—I throw in their direction. But the average Joe Public would not know such a thing. Nor would they care. Perception is what they knew the bosses would care about, and it was not on my side.

So, when we started the post–Max Kellerman era, on September 6, 2021, I knew what I was in for. But I arrived armed and ready. *First Take*'s Monday-through-Friday lineup—one that had to be okayed by Norby Williamson and Dave Roberts—consisted of rotating cohosts:

Mondays: Michael Irvin
Tuesdays: Keyshawn Johnson
Wednesdays: Marcus Spears
Thursdays: Dan Orlovsky
Fridays: Tim Tebow

Weekly contributors and analysts included Orlovsky (Mondays), Ryan Clark (Monday and Fridays), Mina Kimes and Jeff Saturday (Tuesdays), Kimberly Martin (Wednesdays), Kendrick Perkins, Louis Riddick, Bart Scott, Sam Acho, Monica McNutt, and others.

I spoke with every one of them before they came on, telling them exactly what was needed in order for *First Take* to be successful. The goal was simple: DEBATE! No matter what!

Be clear and stern in your opinions. Don't hesitate to come at me, if necessary. Give the people what they tune in for, debate, and have an absolute blast doing it.

Anytime change occurs, so do hiccups. That's precisely what happened the first couple of weeks without Max. But it didn't take long for us to hit our stride. Each contributor embraced what I'd asked for—then delivered with flying colors every single time they appeared on-air.

The show caught its rhythm and the audience responded quickly: viewership jumped nearly 25 percent the first year, remarkable for a show that was already a ratings leader. A decade old, *First Take* was fresh again!

Every single contributor on the show deserved credit. They were highly intelligent, eloquent, informed, passionate—and cared every bit as much as I did about giving the audience what they tune in to see. I love and appreciate every single one of them for what they did.

But our success was most owing to Molly Qerim.

As the host of *First Take*, Qerim was forced to endure so much friction, it's a miracle she didn't ask to leave the show.

I realized we had been holding her back.

Especially me!

As the star of the show and therefore most responsible for its success or failure, I spent so much time preoccupied with what Max and I were not doing as a team that I failed to give the necessary attention to making sure Qerim was left alone to be all she was capable of being. Extremely knowledgeable about football, and a clear expert on maneuvering through the terrain Max and I created, Qerim was forced to be so preoccupied with having to balance the tension between him and me that it compromised her ability to actually host, and contribute as much as she could.

I didn't see this until Kellerman was gone. Once that happened, and I encouraged Qerim to let loose, relax, and join in on debates as she saw fit, she was unleashed. Her questions were more pointed. Her personality shone.

Qerim laughed, she cried. She vacillated between being emotional and incredibly poised, telling jokes and responding to jokes, all while moving the show along with the fluidity of a seasoned veteran. She showcased a skill set we'd been waiting to see for years.

Molly Qerim was no longer just one of the hosts on *First Take*. She was the established matriarch keeping it all together. There is simply no way *First Take* would be successful without her.

And as for the contributors, they aren't just contributors anymore. They're stars in their own right. Once upon a time, I did them a favor by bringing them on. Now, the favors are provided by them, their willingness to come on *First Take*. There was no shortage of information and intel, but the show was also fun again. There was lots of laughter. No one was devoid of passion, perspective, or a willingness to put their opinions on the line. Every single one of them was overtly committed to making sure *First Take* worked. In turn, they made me want to come to work.

I wasn't just doing a job anymore. I was performing, and having a blast doing so.

I was ecstatic about coming to work every day, working with every single individual that came on the show each week. Not only did I fail to take time off, I didn't *want* any days off.

I was having the time of my life, and they were the reasons why. For the first time since 2016, I felt like I could do *First Take* for years to come.

CHAPTER 20

WHEN TAKING THINGS FOR GRANTED NEARLY KILLED ME

The shivering was what first alarmed me.

It started on December 16, 2021, while I was lying in my bed trying without success to watch a football game on TV. I'd been sweating profusely for an hour. Nine hours before that, I'd undergone an endoscopy—a procedure where a flexible tube with a camera on the tip was inserted down my throat so doctors could examine my digestive system. Their search was prompted by weeks of constant bloating, along with a burning sensation whenever I coughed, burped, or hiccupped.

The camera discovered the cause of my problems: an inflamed esophagus. Not great news, but at least I finally knew what the issue was. Doctors could treat it with steroids and antibiotics and I could move on. But now, instead of recovering comfortably in my bed at home while watching the Chiefs win a 34–28 overtime thriller over the Chargers on Thursday Night Football, I was drenched in sweat, suffering from a 102.7-degree fever—and questioning what the hell was happening to me.

What I didn't know at that moment was that I had COVID. But I'd heard enough horror stories and was familiar enough with the symptoms to know I might be in some trouble.

Fever. Consistent cough. Migraines. Extreme fatigue.

I had them all. There wasn't a single symptom I didn't experience within twenty-four hours after my endoscopy. I was tired and light-headed. I lost taste and smell. Any stamina I had was gone.

I immediately called my doctor and told him what I was experiencing. He referred me to a clinic a couple of miles away in midtown Manhattan for a COVID test. I rushed to get it because I was planning a pre-Christmas weekend with just me and my daughters.

Petrified of potentially infecting my daughters, I begged for instant results, but doctors told me that I wouldn't get definitive results until the following morning, when I was already scheduled to be with them.

They came over to bake Christmas cookies, but I kept my distance from them both and wore a mask. I refused to hug or kiss them.

My panicky feeling was validated in a matter of hours.

The clinic called and asked that I check my email before verbally confirming that I had tested positive for COVID. As it turns out, so did my sister Carmen, who had been with me the night before. My heart sank. I immediately arranged for the girls to go back to their moms.

Working in-studio? Canceled! Trip to L.A. to work on NBA Count-down for a slew of Christmas Day games? Canceled! Holiday festivities with the family? Canceled!

But all of that paled in comparison to what I was experiencing with my daughters. Seeing disappointment in your daughters' eyes is hard for any dad. But seeing fear? That causes an entirely different reaction. When I told Samantha and Nyla I had COVID, there was no teenage pout-ing or petulance. In fact, that would have been preferable to what I wit-nessed.

"What?!" Nyla said when I broke the news, her eyes wide and frightened as she sat on my couch staring at me. "Daddy, are you okay?"

When I answered that I was fine and attempted to reassure both her and her older sister, their voices lowered.

"Daddy, be honest," Samantha responded in a disbelieving tone that made it clear she wanted truth rather than reassurances. "Are you really okay?"

The truth: I had no idea and I was scared as hell.

The bigger truth: They both knew it, and that scared them even more.

Samantha and Nyla both had reason to doubt my claiming to be okay. I wasn't stuck in bed, but I was sweating. My strength and stamina were gone. I was light-headed, so I had difficulty focusing. Plus, they had both always been scared of my contracting the virus, getting on me constantly about the importance of wearing my mask and keeping my distance from folks. Nary a day had gone by for the last two years when my daughters didn't remind me, either, to wear my mask or cover my nose when wearing my mask. In supermarkets, on elevators, at restaurants, on airplanes, it was always:

"Daddy, covering your mouth isn't good enough. Stuff travels through the nose, too. You've got to do better."

They'd become tired of my dismissing the impact the virus would have on me, and my willingness to be around other folks, particularly in the workplace, with little or no fear at all.

My girls had harped on me about my nonchalance. Sometimes it got so annoying I had to shut them down by reminding them "I am the boss."

"Enough is enough," I'd bark. "Now y'all be quiet!"

They had a point, of course. The fact is, I watched the news religiously, listened to the cable and network shows report on a litany of hospitalizations and deaths, and but there were times when I just didn't care, when I grew tired of all the pandemic talk.

To be clear: I was not a COVID hypocrite. I'd gotten my Pfizer vaccine shots in March 2021, announcing it on *First Take* the morning before I did it. I wore a mask religiously. I visited indoor facilities infrequently, avoiding the office, arenas, and airplanes as much as possible. You name it. I followed whatever rules that public or private businesses mandated, no questions asked.

I used my platforms on television and social media to encourage others to do the same. I also made sure both of my daughters were vaccinated as soon as it was permitted for those between the ages of twelve and eighteen.

I felt compelled, as if something was pulling me toward serving a higher cause, a higher purpose.

But to me, it also seemed that nobody was on the same page. From doctor to doctor, one infectious disease after another, different stories appeared on different networks, causing more confusion than anything else, in my view.

One minute the vaccine was a cure-all, the next minute it didn't prevent COVID at all. Wearing a mask was pivotal one minute, the next minute you didn't need to wear one as long as you were vaccinated.

Keep six feet apart. Keep three feet apart. Don't get together in a room with more than ten people. Don't get together in a room with more than fifty people. Quarantine for ten days. Quarantine for five days.

There seemed to be something new every damn day.

Like many folks, I became frustrated and sometimes even dismissive. At one point, I actually said to someone: "To hell with this. Just let me get the damn virus over with. They've got me to a point where I think I'm going to die if someone yells 'hello' from across the room." I was that annoyed.

Now here I was shortly after the girls left, the weekend before Christmas, almost down for the count in my own bed, with COVID. And fading fast!

I still felt the need to tackle a few obligations, a move that nearly cost me dearly.

ESPN had a slate of five NBA games scheduled for Christmas Day. I couldn't appear in-studio, but I could appear via satellite from my home.

The bosses insisted that I take the time off and rest, but I wouldn't listen.

"I'm in my home and I'm not going anywhere anyway," I said. "I'll be just fine."

So on Christmas morning, I broke out my suit and tie and went to work.

I went on *NBA Countdown* from 10 to noon. By the time the show was over, I'd collapsed in my bed; my fever had reached 102.5 degrees. I had pushed myself to exhaustion.

But I still followed that up with another appearance on the show at 2 p.m. on ABC, feeling even weaker after that. By the time I showed up again nearly five hours later for another half hour show, my fever was closing in on 103 degrees.

"Dad, what are you doing?" Samantha asked via FaceTime, checking in on me after watching me on that final show. "Why are you doing this? You're going to make yourself worse!"

She was right. The fever got worse and the coughs got more violent. My head throbbed relentlessly. I woke in the wee hours of the night drenched. It stayed that way for two weeks, as if I had jumped into a pool fully clothed every single night. I'd shiver on my way to the shower to wash away the COVID-induced sweat that covered me.

In my exhaustion and sickness, I thought back to some of the things Samantha and Nyla said to me over the last few years, before the pandemic, that addressed a much bigger picture:

"Why do you work so much, Dad? Do you really have to work that many jobs? All those hours? Can't you take a vacation? Did you really have to go to that game? I mean, we appreciate and love you and know you work so hard to take care of us. But it's kind of better for us if you're around for the long haul, ya know?"

In hindsight, I'd paid little attention to those concerns. My mentality was that the work and the sacrifices were all for their benefit. The very things that enabled me to provide for them in the present would also serve to secure their future in the event that one day I wasn't around. I harbored no guilt about it whatsoever.

I didn't forget how much love matters. Expressing that love every day to both of my girls is something I've always deemed important. But equally important was providing for them and protecting them with all the means available to me. And that's exactly what I did—unapologetically.

I was not going to replicate my father. I would be a better dad—so help me God!

The long haul is what I thought I was always thinking about. The marathon was always on my mind, not the sprint. So, when I worked extra hours, took extra business trips, skipped vacations, missed family functions—all to solidify a career that would secure my family's future—I honestly didn't think I was taking anything for granted.

But once I got COVID, my outlook changed. I was solemn thinking of the vacations and family gatherings I'd missed. I can't get those moments back. Now, with my fever and shortness of breath, I became convinced I'd run out of chances to experience even a second chance, let alone a third or a fourth.

My regrets grew as my health still failed to improve fourteen days after my diagnosis. By this time, just before New Year's, I'd sent my daughters away on vacation with their moms. When they called every day, it marked the only time in their lives their Daddy ever lied to them.

I kept telling them I was okay

Then New Year's Eve arrived, and things took a turn for the worse. My breathing was more labored. My fevers were lasting longer. And my nightly delusions were getting worse and worse. Ultimately, I just couldn't take it anymore, so I went to an emergency room, on New Year's Eve, about ninety minutes before midnight.

At this point my fever was at 102.5, and just taking a deep breath was difficult.

As I sat in the emergency room approximately thirty minutes before the ball dropped to bring in 2022, one particular doctor sensed the urgency of the moment and insisted upon X-rays. Dr. Booth was her name, and she didn't believe my symptoms were due only to COVID. After taking the X-rays, she discovered my liver was inflamed. Pneumonia had filled both lungs.

Dr. Booth then echoed the seriousness of the moment, confirming that had I not been vaccinated, I could have been gone.

Yet even vaccinated, I was still in some trouble.

The doctor insisted I get treated with steroids and antibiotics. I was told if it worked, I'd know within three hours. If not, I would really be in trouble.

It worked. I was let out of the hospital about three a.m., in the first hours of the new year.

When I got home I couldn't sleep, but it was for a different reason this time.

Feeling stronger by the minute, believing the worse had passed, I was finally free to focus on how perilous things had been. I was ecstatic I had an estate plan, that my daughters would be taken care of, but I still found myself reflecting on what might have happened. And what the lives of my loved ones would have been like had I truly perished from this earth.

The weeks away from work and the seriousness of my illness had provided an opportunity to reflect on all I had ignored.

Why didn't I spend more time with the girls? I wondered. Sure, I had taken them to Disney World myself, along with other places. I sent them on vacations with their moms several times each year. But what about the quality time they wanted with Daddy? Just hanging out and doing nothing except being with one another?

And what about time with my four older sisters? My fifteen nieces and nephews? My boys from childhood and college? All the loved ones whom I trusted, who make me smile and laugh, whose joy refuels me and allows me to tackle each day with the fervor I need to be successful? What happened to enjoying life?

I hadn't asked myself those questions in years. I was asking them now.

Success breeds a lot of things. But what it often breeds most is an insatiable appetite to keep succeeding.

In my case, that meant a hunger to keep the ratings up. Keep advertisers and sponsors happy. Keep making money for the bosses so I could get more of it for myself.

Keep building the brand. Keep pursuing the dream of breaking out of sports and becoming host of a late-night show, one that would make me the next Johnny Carson, David Letterman, Jay Leno, or Jimmy Kimmel.

In COVID's aftermath, none of that mattered nearly as much as it had before. I realized that I was an employee doing far more for my employer than I was doing for myself, rather than an entrepreneur evolving to solidify a happier future for myself and my family.

I was deteriorating, because I wasn't truly looking out for me. I was just working, working, working.

I discovered that wasn't something to be proud of any longer.

I've never taken work for granted. I was a Black man who'd tasted unemployment. I knew what it was like to think you have it all and then feel like you've lost everything. Yet, no matter what my professional achievements might be, I now realized that satisfaction was never a part of the equation. Despite the money, acclaim, and success I'd already achieved, I was not satisfied. In fact, none of it would end up mattering unless I changed my mind-set.

I had been satisfied years earlier, of course. But that was when I had nothing and was trying to build something. Now, after building the *First Take* brand for ESPN, I found myself asking: What am I truly doing for myself? What could I sustain?

I'd won before. But what was I winning now?

Something had to give. My definition of "winning" had to change.

My epiphany boiled down to this: When you spend too much time doing things you don't want to do instead of the things that make you happy, you die a slow death. Life begins to feel monotonous and mundane. You question how you spend your time, what you're doing with it, and whom you're spending it with. Ultimately, you ask yourself if you have a life worth living at all.

COVID was a life-altering experience. It pushed me to a place of reflection, forced me to ask myself if I was truly happy and, if I wasn't, what was I willing to do about it.

The questions I asked myself were brutal to confront: Did I still want to do *First Take*? Was being in front of a camera more important than creating and producing shows through my production company? I found the answer to these questions was still an emphatic *yes*.

I just wanted the freedom to do my own thing rather than just what my employer wanted me to do.

As much as I love working for ESPN, I'd finally arrived at a point where I was thinking beyond the "World-Wide Leader." Was I tapping into my full potential? Producing, acting, brand representation, and podcasting? Did I need to exercise more control over my destiny and prioritize my personal life in a way that would benefit my loved ones and myself, too?

I didn't have answers to any of those questions. I just knew that after contracting COVID and suffering immeasurably from it, I needed to think more about moving forward, and less about those who benefitted from my efforts, outside of my baby girls.

I had to change. Throughout my adult life, I'd committed the cardinal sin for anyone who believes in a higher power: I assumed that tomorrow was guaranteed.

COVID taught me to never do that again. Every day was a blessing, and for the first time in my life, those words weren't just a cliché.

I knew that every time I took a deep breath now.

Because just weeks earlier, I could hardly take a breath at all.

CHAPTER 21

YOU AIN'T SEEN NOTHING YET

I did a lot more than breathe on my first day back in-studio after recovering from COVID.

It was a Monday morning. January 17, 2022: exactly thirty-one days from the last time I was on the set of ESPN's *First Take*. I wasn't just breathing. I was hollering. I was howling and bantering back and forth, feeling more energized and enthusiastic than I had felt in years.

But it wasn't only because I was alive, having survived COVID.

The Dallas Cowboys had just lost 23–17 to the San Francisco 49ers the day before in the wild card playoff game. To know me is to know there's very little in the world of sports that makes me happier than a Cowboys loss.

As the sports world knows, I have no love for the Cowboys. Though it's really not because of the Cowboys at all.

I love owner Jerry Jones and his family; I think they're great ambassadors for the National Football League. AT&T Stadium, the home of the Cowboys, is unquestionably one of the greatest stadiums ever built in this nation's history. They've had Super Bowl champions, Hall of Famers, and cheerleaders who mesmerize onlookers on Sunday afternoons.

My issue is that I believe they have the most disgusting, nauseating fan base in the annals of sports. The misery a Cowboys loss evokes in that fan base is greater than almost any positive feeling I could get elsewhere in sports. It just thrills me; I know of no other way to put it. Dallas Cowboys' fans get on my last damn nerve. As I've religiously stated, they can go 1–15 on a season. Their last game could end on January 5 at 7 p.m.—and by 7:15 p.m. they'll come out of everywhere saying, "You know we're going to win the Super Bowl next year, right?"

They never take a second to smell their stench. They walk around every day of every year like they're champions, despite having failed to win a title since 1995. They have no humility about themselves. They don't engage in reality checks. Just because they play in a billion-dollar arena, have their cheerleaders, and are clearly the number one brand in sports, they think that makes them a champion.

As I've often quibbled, a nuclear bomb could drop on us all and you can rest assured the three things will survive and ascend from the rubble: rats, roaches, and a Cowboys fan.

Once I was notified that I'd tested negative for COVID, on Thursday, January 13, I started planning my return. Anticipating that the Cowboys would lose their game that Sunday, I was full of ideas.

I probed as to whether *First Take* could get a bunch of Cowboys cheerleader uniforms, wondering if I could mark my return by sliding into the studio and dancing with some ladies wearing them. I asked if it was possible to rent a horse, so I could be filmed riding on it while donning a cowboy hat and cigar. I considered making a bet with Michael Irvin and Marcus "Swagu" Spears—both former Cowboys players who now appear on *First Take*—that would have allowed me to create a song for the Cowboys after a loss, with them as my background singers.

Cowboys fans everywhere feared the possibility of a loss. They knew I was coming back to the show Monday, and that after a month-long hiatus I'd roast them with all I had. I understood this. I stoked those flames. I tortured them with my bravado and prognostications, further elevating their nightmarish expectations—and I loved every minute of it.

This wasn't pure cruelty; it was done with a purpose. I wanted a huge audience to tune in to *First Take* for my return, just to see what I had in store. It was marketing.

When my predictions came true and they lost, I was gleeful. The team failed to get off a snap in the final fourteen seconds of the game. Tears streamed down the faces of Cowboys fans everywhere. I laughed. Hysterically.

As I'm writing these pages, I'm still laughing. Yes! Seven months later.

In the end, I didn't laugh all the way to the bank; just to the ratings. They were as monstrous as I'd hoped.

First Take customarily averages approximately 450,000 viewers every weekday morning.

That morning, the number was 986,000—an all-time record for the show. And that didn't count the millions of views on YouTube and beyond.

In truth, there was some backstory to my all-out effort to market my return. Dave Roberts had given me a call a week before I came back, telling me that *First Take*'s ratings had remained good in my absence. He thanked me for building the show to a place where that was possible, and that's mostly how I took it. I was proud, not surprised, and had very little concern about my status or my future on the show.

But still, I wasn't dumb enough to ignore the other interpretation of Roberts's statement. *Perhaps* First Take *can go on without me.*

If ever there was validation of my significance to *First Take*, it arrived that day of my return. The world was reminded that I was the number one sports media talent in the industry, that my light hadn't dimmed just yet, and that I had no intention of its dimming for a very long time.

"You are the man, Stephen A.," Roberts called to say after getting the ratings. "My God, you are something special."

*   *   *

It was nice to hear. It meant a lot to me. But in that moment, I also could feel how something had changed. The Stephen A. that Roberts had known wasn't the same Stephen A. anymore.

My return was more about enjoying myself than having something to prove. *First Take* can and will eventually go on without me. I've known this for years. After contracting COVID, I was more accepting of that fact.

I consider the folks who appear regularly on *First Take* during the football season to be nothing short of sensational: Molly Qerim, Michael Irvin, Keyshawn Johnson, Swagu Spears, Dan Orlovsky, Tim Tebow, Ryan Clark, Kimberly Martin, Mina Kimes, Jeff Saturday, Paul Finebaum, Domonique Foxworth, Chris "Mad Dog" Russo, and Bart Scott. They are always excellent, and they stepped up even more in my absence.

ESPN is still incredibly important *to* me, but it's no longer more important *than* me. The work gets done. The results matter. The money matters. But not at the cost of sacrificing my health.

Getting COVID had given me time for introspection—something I'd done when reaching the biggest crossroads throughout my life.

I engaged in introspection when I got left back in school. I did it as a young man when I reflected on my relationship with my father. I did it when I contemplated what I needed to do to relieve my mother. I looked inward when I failed to make the high school basketball team.

I pondered what my future would be when I left Winston-Salem State to rehab my knee. I had to look deep within myself to find the humility to regain trust with Coach Gaines and Theodore Hindsman, the financial aid adviser. I did the same many times in my journalism career at the New York *Daily News* and then the *Philadelphia Inquirer*, and when I was fired by ESPN. So I damn sure wasn't going to be afraid to do it when I got sick.

Life easily overwhelms those who remain stagnant, rife with excuses for their willingness to stand still, their refusal to adapt and change.

"Do it anyway," I can hear my mother telling me, forever the pragmatist. "You're grown. Move forward!"

"Always have a plan and move forward," Philadelphia's favorite son, Sonny Hill, once told me. "You're winning even when you don't know it. Because you're striving to make things happen."

I've never learned from the past by ignoring it. I've elevated because I recall details of how and why I fell, and what obstacles I faced while trying to resurrect myself. I've scratched and clawed until I've achieved, doing so beyond my wildest dreams.

Eventually, I became the face of ESPN, *The Worldwide Leader in Sports.*

To say that I love ESPN is an understatement. Sometimes intentionally, sometimes not, the people there have helped me become a better professional, a better man, a better human being. I have a blast appearing on the air.

I've gained riches financially, and in terms of relationships. Stars I've idolized—Magic Johnson, Michael Jordan, Isaiah Thomas, Shaquille O'Neal, Charles Barkley, Denzel Washington, Jamie Foxx, Snoop Dogg, Kevin Hart, Ice Cube, Omari Hardwick, Omar Epps, Michael Ealy, soap opera stars Maurice Benard and Eric Braeden, and many others—have become genuine friends over the years, espousing words of wisdom that have helped me greatly, both professionally and personally.

But despite achievements that lifted me from being a poverty-stricken kid from Hollis, Queens, to a millionaire, I still wake up hungry every morning. I'm still scared, too.

Fear can be healthy at times.

In the past, that fear has pushed me only to work harder. But the fear of dying with COVID expedited something that should have taken place years earlier: the tempering of my insatiable need to exert myself, to prove I can do so much more than I'm doing.

Spending time with my daughters is now priority number one. But building something they can latch on to and springboard from is definitely a very close second. As much as I love appearing on television and debating, as much as I hope to be on ESPN for the rest of my career, I've realized *First Take* is not the commodity that's going to get me where I want to go. I want more. I need more. And I'll need to expand my horizons to get it.

Owning my own production company? Now that's another matter entirely.

Mr. SAS Productions is the name of the company I've started. Both my daughters own a piece of it. My intent is to produce scripted and non-scripted series and films, podcasts, write books, and do whatever else comes my way that interests me and makes an impact. I believe I can be the next Tyler Perry, Will Packer, or Spike Lee someday. Motivational speaking is very important to me, too. For the kid from Hollis who got left back, so is creating a foundation focusing on literacy.

No limitations!

I used to fantasize about producing content for the company that owns ESPN: Walt Disney.

Now, I envision it! ESPN is under the Disney umbrella. That means I'm in-house; I am a part of the family. A family with Mickey Mouse as its logo, known for making dreams come true.

Make no mistake, that's exactly what I'm aiming to do.

As noted rap artist 50 Cent once said in his remix of "I Get Money":

"Man, they tryna buy some Gucci, I'm tryna buy the mall. / I ain't come to get a little bit, I'm tryna get it all."

None of it will be possible without TEAM, and I now have that team in place.

I stopped being so pig-headed about being a solo act and brought

Rushion McDonald into my life as my business manager. He's always in my corner. "You need a team, my brother," Rushion has echoed at every turn. "You've done amazing on your own. Now it's time to go to the next level."

I recruited my friend Mark Shapiro of William Morris Endeavor to be the face of my representation. I knew he'd ultimately select stellar agents like Jon Rosen and Josh Pyatt to run my day-to-day.

"You've been masterful in what you've done thus far," Shapiro explained in front of a room full of agents when we started planning out the future agenda for Team Stephen A. "You've been amazing in build ing your brand on your own all of these years. But your true brilliance is in assembling this team, in bringing all of us together.

"It's rare that folks in your position realize you can't get to the next level by yourself. You're trusting us to do that for you. Now it's our job to take you to that next level. To capitalize on what you've done, and what you'll continue to do."

I got to the position of number one sports-media personality in America, if not the world, by trusting ESPN executives Jimmy Pitaro, Norby Williamson, George Bodenheimer, Steve Anderson, Ed Erhardt, and Dave Roberts, and my manager Rushion McDonald among many others. And I know that turning to my team will get me to the next chapter. True winners in this business have a team they are willing to trust, because they'll spot the bumps in the road before you hit 'em.

A quality team saves you from yourself. It doesn't inhibit you, something Rushion preached about long enough. Eventually, I listened. And I've benefitted ever since.

I finally feel like I have every base covered. I'm surrounded by brilliance on a personal and professional level. My pastor, A. R. Bernard, keeps me somewhat contained whenever I'm threatening to veer too far out of bounds. My four sisters and fifteen nieces and nephews love their uncle Steve. I have two beautiful daughters who are extremely territorial because they love their daddy—and laugh at how much their daddy loves them back. My family and friends keep me balanced, displaying no interest in Stephen A.! To them I'm just Steve.

I've got buddies from childhood, college, and a slew of others I've cultivated in and out of the business world over the years—along with a true brotherhood, courtesy of Omega Psi Phi fraternity.

I encounter hardly any issues or problems that prove to be too difficult for me to resolve, most times with a mere phone call. When you know people, you know you're covered. Networking has its privileges, particularly when you come to love the people who support you.

Thanks to the generosity and belief of Disney CEO Bob Chapek, former chairman of Disney General Entertainment Content Peter Rice, and chairman of the Media and Entertainment Distribution division Kareem Daniel, I was allowed to show my lighter, jovial side and scratch something off my bucket list by guest-hosting *Late Night with Jimmy Kimmel.* There's no way it would have happened had it not been presented to them and pushed by Chapek's predecessor, Bob Iger.

Iger, known as "the Mastermind" in the entertainment industry because of the true visionary that he is, is simply the greatest executive I've ever known; the Michael Jordan of executives, dare I say. And I mean it.

To know Iger is one thing. To have someone like him in my corner, providing constant support and guidance—voluntarily—has taken my mind-set to another stratosphere.

Iger's presence in my life elevated my focus toward the big picture, and toward what it takes to achieve big things. You want something? Well then, what's your plan? What does the execution look like? Who stands to benefit, aside from yourself? Who are you willing to help uplift along the way?

You may *think* you're contemplating all those elements, but it's nothing compared to the laser-like focus you have on those questions after a conversation with Iger—the man who propelled Disney to astronomical heights in his sixteen years at the helm as CEO. If you want to build a team, you've got to be the first one willing to be a part of a team.

As President Obama once said: "It ain't about, 'Yes he *will!*' It's about, 'Yes we *can!*'"

It doesn't matter that President Obama was talking politics when he uttered those words at the Democratic National Convention in Philadelphia back in 2016. Those words are applicable to any walk of life, for anyone in search of success.

You've got to have a team. You can't do it alone.

As arguably the largest distributor of content in the world, Disney allows me to pursue my dreams without feeling like they're pipe dreams, to explore pushing beyond the boundaries of the sports world to display my skills in a multitude of other platforms. And why not?

"A lion raised in captivity has never been in the wild," Bishop T. D. Jakes once explained to Oprah's audience. "All of his experiences have been in the cage. If all of his experiences have been in the cage and that would be his natural habitat to him, then why do they lock the cage?

"They lock the cage because, even though his experiences do not validate it, his instincts tell him, 'There's something else out there!' And the reason why so many of us are frustrated today is that we are pacing around in the cage of a job, or a life, or a situation that has limited us. We may not have the background for it. We may not have the training for it. But our instincts tell us, 'I belong out there.'"

Finally, I've learned: I belong out there. Out there betting on myself. Taking chances on myself. Fearlessly pursuing my goals and wherever it takes me, knowing in my heart the worst thing I could do to myself is *not* try. Especially now, since I know that there's nowhere I should go alone.

In my mind, God can stop me. Self-inflicted mistakes can stop me. Stupidity and immaturity can stop me. But fear isn't a part of the equation any longer.

Looking in the mirror can be painful, as my mother once proved to me. But grown-ups can take it, because they know it'll make them better. Looking in the mirror provided me the opportunity to reflect, then realize that the same skepticism and cynicism I've been accused of expressing on-air for years is exactly what stymied me.

I spoke doubt into existence. That's exactly what I did, until I learned better and surrounded myself with a support base who wouldn't allow me to do so any longer.

I am not alone any longer. I have an army of support now. Enough to allow Mommy to finally rest in peace, knowing her baby boy is going to be okay.

If I can pull all the things off that I'm dreaming of, I'd love for it to occur while I'm still on television. But if that part of my career has to fade into the twilight to make the rest happen, then that's the price I'm willing to pay.

As I've stated on numerous occasions, no one will ever hear me speak against ESPN. They are my family.

Is it perfect? Hell no! They get on my damn nerves a lot.

But it's been an honor to work for them, to build such close relationships.

When you have relationships like those I've been lucky enough to have, you don't sully them with pettiness and negativity. You listen, learn, and articulate what your vision is, then lean on them to guide you.

I've done that. I've excelled because of it, and I'll be eternally grateful to everyone who has helped me along the way.

Above all else, however, I'm grateful for the greatest mother God could have ever given me.

I don't always measure up to it, but I live every single day to make her proud.

* * *

Okay, I know I said "above all else," but as Snoop Dogg once said, "Most of all . . . I want to thank ME."

For the hard work, the dedication, the sacrifice, and never-say-die commitment.

That's what has gotten me to this point.

Folks will say, "Smell the roses, bro! You've done it."

My answer is: "I'm not finished at all. I'm just getting started."

Good Luck trying to stop me now!

Some folks are going to need to move over.

Because Here The Hell I Come!!!

ACKNOWLEDGMENTS

The first order of business is to give thanks to God.

None of what I've accomplished in life would have been possible without him. Although I've known this for quite some time, it helps to have a spiritual father like Pastor A. R. Bernard, a great man of God, a born leader, and a stellar citizen of the human race. I love you, Pastor.

Despite the bombastic and demonstrative tendencies that I've been known to display, I've always been grounded. Humility is a mandate—not a choice—when you're blessed with a great mom. Everything I am that's good, everything I aspire to be, is because of her. She is my personal angel, hovering over me at all times. I've lived my whole life aspiring to make her proud; falling short more often that she'd have ever preferred, but rarely for a lack of effort. This book was written because of her—as acknowledgment for all that she means to me and how worthy she is of the eternal praise that she will receive.

Of course, I also have four older sisters, plus friends and loved ones, to thank. Folks who care more about who I am than what I do.

My sisters—Linda, Arlyne, Abigail, and Carmen—define my humanity. I can't forget Carmen's fiancé, my future brother-in-law Darren Ottey, and my cousin Derrick Dawson. Both are truly like big brothers to me—my ultimate protectors. When I lost Basil, as painful as it was, you two filled that role to the hilt, guiding and inspiring me and keeping me balanced. Love y'all, forever. Thank you.

To my childhood buddies: Poolie, Kardell, Ben, Bobby, Mark and Marshall, thank you for always reminding me no matter how high I climb, I'm not worth a damn if I forget home, and my homeboys. They don't know who Stephen A. is; I'm just Steve. We're friends for life. That's the best way I can say it. Love y'all.

To my college buddies: Marc Turner, Kevin "Skeet" Edwards, Boris Battle, Monte Ross, Gary "Spank" Stephens, and Phil Hayes, thank you for living up to the old mantra about "the friends you make in college are friends for a lifetime." It's so true. Y'all will be my boys FOREVER. Don't ever forget that.

The same can be said for my brothers from the Omega Psi Phi Fraternity, who never fail to remind me what a real brotherhood truly is, especially my bruh, Evan Murray. Love you, my man. A special thank you is reserved for Mr. Mark Stevens, whose presence in my life can only be explained this way: The greatest friendship I've ever made in my adult life is meeting "Money Mark." A brother to the core. A ride-or-die if there ever was one. Absolutely hilarious. And one of the best human beings I've ever known. Mark has proven to me you can truly learn to love a friend later in life as deeply as the friends you've known all your life. Love you, bro. Of all the great things in life my Big-Lil' Bro, Shaq, has done for me over the years, nothing compares to him introducing you, Mark, into my life.

A special thanks to my Thomas A. Edison High School buddy Jeff Brown. We lost touch when he went in the Navy, but reconnected in 2000, nearly fifteen years after we graduated. We have been inseparable ever since—courtesy of his lovely wife, Nina, and their two beautiful children, Nicole and Nicholas—who host me for Sunday dinners every time I'm in L.A., and who I absolutely love being around. The Browns are my second family. My love for them, my trust in them, knows no limits.

To Sumatra Hawkins, my personal executive assistant: there's a reason you've been in my life for more than fifteen years. Your loyalty and devotion have made you, arguably, my most trusted confidant. As I rise, so will you. Thank you for being that person in my life.

To my bodyguard, Juan "Juvi" Santiago: Thank you for safeguarding me all these years. And for being my trusted brother. Love you, bro.

To my former WSSU professor Marilyn Roseboro, whom I affectionately call "Momma Roseboro," perhaps the greatest compliment I could ever extend to a woman goes to her: she was an extension of my mother, Janet Smith. She loved. She cared. She extolled. She demanded. She held me accountable. She nurtured me. She turned me into a man.

Professor Marilyn Roseboro's love, affection and devotion were served on behalf of my mother when Janet Smith was in New York, and I was at school at Winston-Salem State. If Big House Gaines was my father figure, she certainly was the momma figure. And she still is today.

I love you, Momma Roseboro. Forever and always.

To Mr. Robert DeVaughn, who mentored me into adulthood. A true father figure who elevated my confidence, implored me to be all I could be because he believed I could be as great as I wanted to be, and who passed away in 2008 from cancer: you are with me always, "Mr. D." I think of you every day, and I smile when I do so. No one in this world understands what you still mean to me, even though you're gone, as much as your son, Robert Jr., and my dear friend Ms. Audrey Irvine, who both loved you every bit as much as I did, possibly more.

Along the way, there's the inordinate number of friendships I've been blessed to have with colleagues at ESPN, as well as people who don't work at ESPN: Snoop Dogg; Jamie Foxx; Charlie Mack; Michael Ealy; Charles Barkley; Shaq; Kenny Smith; Chris Rock; Isaiah Thomas; Ice Cube; Michael Jordan; Will Packer; Earvin "Magic" Johnson; Steve Harvey, and a host of others who've espoused their words of wisdom over the years, making me a better person. A better man. My gratitude to them is endless—especially to Kobe Bryant, who certainly never needed to embrace me, but did so anyway. To the Black Mamba: You are missed every single day. Your greatness, your commitment to excellence, your tireless devotion to helping others maximize their potential. Your spirit lives on, my brother. Always.

To Angela Barnes, we've got more than twenty years in one another's lives. Thanks for your love, your pragmatism, and your guidance, and for elevating my level of compassion and empathy. You've helped make me better at everything I've done. I'm grateful to have you in my life.

To Kendra Lee, you've been on me for thirty years to write this book. It took me long enough, with some intervention, but I finally got there. Thank you for pushing me and believing in me.

To Garry Howard, how could I possibly forget about you? You believed in me when I was covering high school sports for the *NY Daily News*. You told me I'd be a star in sports journalism one day. You're the one who got me hired at the *Philadelphia Inquirer*. You are the only human being alive who calls me "Stevie A.!" You are my brother in every sense of the word, and my friend. I love you, bro.

To Mr. Mike Bruton. It's been years since we've seen one another, but you're with me every day. Because of you and the late, great Acel Moore, I excelled in Philadelphia, which prepared me for what followed. You will always be a mentor and big brother to me. I love you.

To Robert Rosenthal, Butch Ward and Phil Dixon—the top editors who ran the *Philadelphia Inquirer* in my formative years there—along with Rob King and Dan McGrath, former Deputy Sports Editors in Philly. I can't forget you either. And I never will. Thank you so much for all you did for me. And Rob King, thank you for still taking care of me as a top executive at ESPN.

The most special of places is reserved for JJ Smith—aka the Green Smoothie Queen. Long before she was setting the world ablaze with her nutritional and motivational tips, she was someone I met when I was unemployed. Feeling lost and eviscerated, my career and life in absolute shambles, she believed in me anyway. She stood by my side. She pushed, she prodded, she demanded, all because her belief in me was greater than all the naysayers combined.

I'm not only grateful to her, I owe her for blazing the trail (she is a bestselling author, after all), continuously reminding me not only of who I am but what I could be. She's also responsible for the incredible friendship I've had the pleasure of developing with her business partner, the phenomenal "Millionaire Mentor" himself, Todd Johnson. I'll love them both for life.

To my former boss, John Wildhack: Thank you for getting to know me, for displaying faith in me and nurturing me through some tough times. I value your guidance and our relationship. Always.

To my present boss, ESPN President, Jimmy Pitaro: I don't hear "Yes" all the time, but it's because of you that I don't mind. Your integrity and core decency, along with your compassion and leadership, remind me every single day that there are far worse jobs to have. So long as I'm working for you, I have no doubt that I'll continue to be that way.

To Norby Williamson, we've been through a lot of ups and downs over the years. But we're on top now. From the leadership you provided hovering over *First Take* over the years, to the wisdom and insight you've provided as to why and how decisions are made, thank you for helping to elevate me from just a talent to a full-fledge adult in this industry.

Ditto to Nick Khan, my former agent and present co-CEO of World Wrestling Entertainment. You are one of the brilliant ones, my brother. To know you is to learn something substantive and valuable every single day. Thank you for making me better. You'll always have a friend in me.

To the great Bob Iger: Thank you for the counsel you've offered and the guidance you've espoused. It's not every day a Black kid from the streets of New York can call a former CEO, as influential and brilliant as you, a mentor. That I've been lucky enough to have you volunteer to play that role in my life is truly one of the greatest blessings I've ever received. I'm honored and humbled to have you as someone I get to bounce things off of, Mr. Iger. I march forward every day in my career striving to validate your belief in me and to make you proud. My sincere hope is that I never disappoint you.

The same goes to Mr. Dave Roberts. Your tenacity and commitment to excellence can't be usurped. But neither can your guidance. Words can't begin to express the appreciation I feel towards you for teaching me the business, what goes into it, and what's truly required to gain the level of excellence I continuously aspire to achieve. Thank you so much, Dave. For being a fantastic boss, mentor, and big brother to me. I'll never forget what you've done for me. Never.

Of course, a special thanks goes out to the late Clarence "Big House" Gaines, the iconic coach who never hesitated to educate and inspire. The same can be said of Hall of Fame coaches John Chaney and John Thompson. I knew them all. I've learned from them all. May God bless their souls. I'd also be remiss to neglect including Coach Larry Brown in that equation, and the great Sonny Hill, who mirrored their efforts and then some with their guidance and tutelage.

Thank you to Pat Croce, forever enthused and excited, who taught me to feel that way when it came to whatever I wanted to do in life, along with my former agent, Steve Mountain. I'm a much better man today than I was when both of you guys met me. You had something to do with that.

Of course, there are too many people to count within the National Basketball Association, but I'll try.

Allen Iverson must be mentioned. He never had reason to trust anyone, but he trusted me. No matter what anyone saw from him on the court, he's a much better person with a much bigger heart off the court, not appreciated nearly as much as he should be. People who truly know Iverson know this. He is the little brother I never had, plain and simple. I love you, lil' bro. You know this.

There is always my ace Tonya Fox, whom I've loved and adored for nearly 40 years. You've loved me. You've watched my back. Once I departed from New York, every place I've moved into was a place you literally discovered yourself. No matter how much I've gotten on your nerves, you've always been there for me — no matter how many times I didn't deserve it. I'll love you always. Thank you.

To Arnelle Martin, thank you for your love and friendship — and being there for me in the worst of times. The meals, the conversation, the trust. You were there for me when I had nothing. I'll never fail to return the favor.

To Angela Barnes. I'm not about to repeat the conversations involving our history, but your love and counsel were pivotal in me overcoming a lot of hurdles. I'll always be grateful to you. And Sierra, who's like a daughter to me.

To Maurice Bernard and Eric Braedon—the two biggest soap opera stars in American history: I am no actor, but thank you both for making me feel like one anyway. Most of all, thank you for being the big brother figures that you are, constantly edifying me with your wisdom, passion, and empathy. I'm lucky to have met you both, but even more fortunate to call you both my friends.

Frank Valentini, the same goes for you. As executive producer of *General Hospital*, I'm grateful for all the guidance you've given me throughout the years regarding the business of entertainment. Few know, perhaps not even you, how valuable you have become to me regarding my career aspirations, teaching me about what it takes to continue to ascend, and the time and interest you've accorded me out of the sheer kindness of your heart. Thank you.

To my business manager, Rushion McDonald: Thank you for being the brilliant creative mind, the tireless worker, the brother and friend you've been in my life for nearly the past twenty years. Without you, I don't know where I'd be right now. I certainly would not have adopted the entrepreneurial spirit with such fervor in the way that I have. Thank you for being that spark plug. Big things are ahead in the future. I can say that because of you, sir.

To Mark Shapiro, Jon Rosen, and Josh Pyatt, I don't plan on going anywhere without you guys, either. Thank you for the friendship and stellar representation. I'm looking forward to seeing what we can create in the future, together.

Let me not forget the great editors and minds at 13A/Simon & Schuster. From the phenomenal Aimée Bell to my brother Charles Suitt. From Jennifer Bergstrom, Max Meltzer, Sally Marvin, and Jennifer Robinson to Bianca Salvant and Jonathan Karp, I can't put into words how exceptional you all are. I've thanked the good Lord every moment I've spent writing this book that I picked you guys to help produce my memoir. It's one of the greatest decisions I've ever made. Thank you all for being so exceptional. No wonder Simon & Schuster is number one.

To Drew Jubera for the early jump start.

To my nephew Josh—the son I never had. All I can say is: Uncle Steve loves you. You make me smile just thinking about you. The same to my nephew TJ. You both mean the world to me. To all of my nieces— Danielle (NeNe), Keturah, Carmella, Tamiya, Shanelle, Candice, Shanna, and Janet—Uncle Steve loves you to pieces.

To Katawna: You know what you mean to me and you know why. Thank you for brightening my day in ways that only you can and being there for me as much as you have, in ways few will ever know. You're incredibly valuable and precious to me and I will never forget all you've done to help me through my worst of times. You've had my back always and I love you for it.

Thank you, Stacy Robinson, the true epitome of loyalty and friendship, who also happens to be an expert at helping me save and preserve my money as my financial adviser. I've lost count of the amount of times you've looked out for me in my darkest hours and saved me, propelling me to this point in my life. Thank you.

You too, Charles Holmes, the best accountant going. Thank you for the guidance. Thank you for looking out for me. Trust is everything when it comes to such matters, and you've honored that time and again. Same to you, Ed Hovatter, thank you, as well.

To colleagues like Galen Gordon, Rob Parker, Kevin Frazier, Chris Broussard, John Mitchell, Mike Wilbon and all my boys at ESPN (y'all know who y'all are), you are not just friends, but brothers. I'll always be there for y'all.

Thank you to Charlie Grantham, who literally taught me collective bargaining in 1995, and continues to monitor minefields one day after another for me to this day. Eddie Tapscott, I haven't forgotten you either. Your incomparable wisdom saved me on more occasions than I count. Thank you.

To Kerry Chandler, Karen Hunter, Leah Wilcox, I know I already said it in earlier pages, but y'all are like sisters to me. I love y'all that much. So I'm saying it again, damnit! Not everyone is blessed to have such tremendously accomplished women in their lives whom they can trust completely. I have that in all of you and I absolutely know it. Thank you so much.

The same applies to my attorney, Johnine Barnes. You've not only been my lawyer throughout the years, but one of my best friends. Our relationship spans a quarter century. Your love and guidance have never gone unnoticed. You are a rock in my life. I'm proud to be your friend and the godfather to your wonderful son, Jonathan. I love you both so much, along with your husband—my Omega brother—Eric. He's family to me, just as you are.

Most of all, to Angela and Stephanie—the mothers of my two daughters. No matter how much my daughters adore me, and I them, the true heroes in their lives are the two of you. Teaching, nurturing, and loving them the way you have has made them into sensational young ladies whom, I believe, will help change the world for the better sooner rather than later. I thank God every day I have my daughters, knowing I'm far more blessed than I deserve to have them. You two have everything to do with that. My gratitude to you for them is endless. I will be here for you both, forever and always.

And finally, saving the best for last, to my baby girls: Samantha and Nyla.

Thank you for allowing Daddy to know that no matter what I may endure, I will smile every single day. Thank you for your compassion and thoughtfulness, your focus on being a bright light, a good person, and someone who aims to make Daddy so proud. Thank you for tolerating Daddy's diatribes and discipline. Thank you for sharpening my debate skills with your intellect. Thank you for constantly reminding Daddy there's a world out here that extends beyond my occasional narrow-mindedness. I know I won't miss much with you two around. Thank you for making me so proud.

I wake up every single day knowing that every sacrifice, every day of hard work and dedication, has a light at the end of the tunnel. That light is the both of you. My everything!

Daddy loves you so much. And there's so much waiting for me in my future all because of you two: the greatest joys of my life.

You really are.

So help me God!